FORECLOSED

In *Foreclosed*, Chris Odinet gives voice to the stories of homeowners who have been neglected, particularly those facing foreclosure and deep financial distress. The book reveals the powerful and often invisible mortgage servicing industry, the tremendous discretionary power it wields over the housing lives of most Americans, and the servicing problems that still persist today. In doing so, it unveils a quiet and dangerous market shift in mortgage servicing – namely, an ongoing move toward a shadow banking sector where regulation is weak – that threatens the stability of our housing finance system. Ultimately, the book demonstrates how the law does not afford homeowners the protection most think and how regulation of these mortgage middlemen remains weak. *Foreclosed* should be read by anyone concerned with the state of housing and homeownership in the United States.

Christopher K. Odinet is an associate professor of law and an affiliate associate professor in entrepreneurship at the University of Oklahoma. Professor Odinet is a national expert on real estate transactions finance law, and consumer protection.

Foreclosed

MORTGAGE SERVICING AND THE HIDDEN ARCHITECTURE OF HOMEOWNERSHIP IN AMERICA

CHRISTOPHER K. ODINET
University of Oklahoma (Norman, Oklahoma)

CAMBRIDGE
UNIVERSITY PRESS

University Printing House, Cambridge CB2 8BS, United Kingdom

One Liberty Plaza, 20th Floor, New York, NY 10006, USA

477 Williamstown Road, Port Melbourne, VIC 3207, Australia

314–321, 3rd Floor, Plot 3, Splendor Forum, Jasola District Centre, New Delhi –110025, India

79 Anson Road, #06–04/06, Singapore 079906

Cambridge University Press is part of the University of Cambridge.

It furthers the University's mission by disseminating knowledge in the pursuit of education, learning, and research at the highest international levels of excellence.

www.cambridge.org
Information on this title: www.cambridge.org/9781108418706
DOI: 10.1017/9781108290906

© Christopher K. Odinet 2019

This publication is in copyright. Subject to statutory exception and to the provisions of relevant collective licensing agreements, no reproduction of any part may take place without the written permission of Cambridge University Press.

First published 2019

A catalogue record for this publication is available from the British Library.

Library of Congress Cataloging-in-Publication Data
NAMES: Odinet, Christopher K., author.
TITLE: Foreclosed : mortgage servicing and the hidden architecture of homeownership in America / Christopher K. Odinet, University of Oklahoma (Norman, Oklahoma).
DESCRIPTION: Cambridge, United Kingdom ; New York, NY : Cambridge University Press, [2019] | Includes bibliographical references and index.
IDENTIFIERS: LCCN 2018034107 | ISBN 9781108418706
SUBJECTS: LCSH: Foreclosure – United States. | Mortgage loans – Law and legislation – United States. | Mortgage loan servicing – United States. | Home ownership – United States.
CLASSIFICATION: LCC KF697.F6 O35 2019 | DCC 346.7304/364–dc23
LC record available at https://lccn.loc.gov/2018034107

ISBN 978-1-108-41870-6 Hardback
ISBN 978-1-108-40635-2 Paperback

Cambridge University Press has no responsibility for the persistence or accuracy of URLs for external or third-party internet websites referred to in this publication and does not guarantee that any content on such websites is, or will remain, accurate or appropriate.

*To my husband Dub, without whom nothing worthwhile
was ever accomplished.*
—CKO

Contents

Preface		*page* ix
	Introduction	1
	PART I THE HOUSING CRISIS, ITS ARCHITECTS, AND ITS VICTIMS	13
1	The Lead-Up to the Crisis	15
2	The Crisis Hits	32
3	At Your (Mortgage) Service	40
	PART II FORECLOSURES, MIDDLEMEN, AND HOMEOWNERS IN CRISIS	63
4	The Most Important Document You've Never Read	65
5	Lost and Sign on the Dotted Line	78
6	Break-In Foreclosures	93
	PART III SOLUTIONS AND MOVING FORWARD	107
7	Regulating Mortgage Servicing	109
8	Reforming Mortgage Law and Practice	132
	Conclusion	152
Notes		160
Index		213

Preface

I was in law school at the time of the financial crisis. Although I had little understanding of financial markets and the law that buttressed them, I knew that what was happening outside the walls of my classroom was significant. More importantly, I knew that real estate was at its center. There was something about property – about the home – that made all this happen. And perhaps it was this simplistic view that led me to be a real estate lawyer. During my time at the law firm, I learned about the complex structuring of real estate transactions – everything from structured finance and credit underwriting to foreclosure and bankruptcy. My practice, however, was mostly focused on commercial real estate transactions, and I knew that it was on the residential side that the crisis originated. So, I began to spend time learning more about how residential closings worked and how money moved around in the home loan market. I was particularly interested in people's stories. I was fascinated (and often horrified) by the struggles of American homeowners in the aftermath of the crisis. About this time, it was hard to scroll through Facebook or turn on the television without reading headlines about people losing their homes or about whole neighborhoods turning to blight as a result of foreclosure. I often wondered: "How was this happening?" "Why isn't someone doing something to help these people?" "Are they to blame or is there more to it?"

It wasn't until my first year on the faculty in the fall of 2013 that I zeroed in on the subject of this book. I was teaching a seminar on housing and community development at the Southern University Law Center (SULC) as a first-year assistant professor. We focused a great deal on the 2008 crisis and its aftermath because these topics were still so timely. Every week, I would have students bring news stories to share with the class. Midway through the semester, one student shared a story published in the *New York Times* that chronicled the use of bank contractors in kicking homeowners out of their homes prior to foreclosure. Many of the tales were deeply disturbing, including individuals having their doors broken down and their children's belongings thrown out on the street. Another student shared the tale of a distressed, elderly couple seeking a loan modification from their bank so they could stay in their home, only to be given the endless runaround and ultimately forced to start again at square one. As the class collectively dug deeper into these stories, we became interested in the all-important industry that occupies the space between homeowners and the ultimate owners of their home loan. These are the mortgage servicers – the middlemen. My fascination with mortgage servicers began a multiyear project of coming to more deeply understand these firms and the key position they occupy in American housing finance. And, through a series of events, my captivation with these hidden players led me to write this book.

As this is the first book I've ever written, I quickly learned that the process would be more difficult than I had originally thought. Needless to say, in any such monumental endeavor one acquires many debts – and acquire them I most certainly did. I acknowledge them completely and am confident that I could never accurately name and duly thank the many individuals who have played such an enormous part in this effort. I have been blessed with many wonderful friends and mentors in the legal academy who have provided extensive comments and critiques, either in conversation or in writing, to various chapters of this project. These include Wilson Freyermuth, Adam Levitin, Kathleen Engel, Tanya Marsh, Timothy Mulvaney, Pamela Foohey, Kellen Zale, Gregory Stein, Andrea Boyack, Sean Sullivan, Andy Grewal, Anya Prince, Ann Lipton, Gregory Shill, David Fagundes, Tara Twomey, Peter Carrozzo, Christopher Bradley, Stephen McJohn, Kate Sablosky Elengold, Judith Fox, Matthew Lambert, and Jeff Sovern.

Several other people, however, merit particular acknowledgment. First, I give special thanks to my mentor and friend Joseph William Singer of the Harvard Law School, who gave me the confidence and support early on when the idea for this book was just a draft law review article. I join the many property law professors in the United States and abroad who found their voice in the legal academy under his guiding hand. In figuring out how to write a legal academic book, I also thank Ronald Krotoszynski of the University of Alabama School of Law for his sage advice, candor, and good counsel. I give thanks to Thomas Cox, a skillful banking attorney turned consumer rights lawyer who single-handedly discovered the robo-signing foreclosure scandal in 2010 and who so graciously gave me expert comments on numerous chapters of this book. The superb staff of the National Consumer Law Center, with whom I have had the pleasure of working with over these past few years, are also due acknowledgment – particularly Tara Twomey and Lauren Saunders.

I am especially indebted to SULC and Chancellors John K. Pierre and Freddie Pitcher Jr., both of whom provided me with generous research support and funding throughout the process. I give similar thanks to the University of Iowa College of Law and Dean Gail Agrawal who provided me with research support during my time as a visiting faculty member in the fall of 2017. And of course, I thank Joseph Harroz, the dean here at the University of Oklahoma College of Law (OU), for his support of my project. Relatedly, so much of the heavy lifting related to this endeavor is due to the hard work, patience, and talents of Michael Waters, editorial advisor for the OU law journals, Elaine Bradshaw, assistant director at the OU Law Library, and Leslee Roybal, OU faculty support legal assistant. I also thank my wonderful current and former colleagues at SULC, Iowa, and OU for helping me sharpen my arguments and better define the project's goals.

I presented portions of this book and had the benefit of helpful feedback at the University of Cambridge; Texas A&M University School of Law; the Harvard University Law School; the University of Montana School of Law; the Washburn University School of Law; the Southeastern Association of Law Schools Conference; the American Association of Law Schools Annual Meeting; the American Bar Association's Real Property, Trust, and Estate Law Spring Symposium; and the Association of Law, Property, and Society Conference, among other gatherings. I received exceptional suggestions and comments at these various venues from Lisa T. Alexander, Thomas W. Mitchell, Christopher Serkin, Bethany Berger, Nestor Davidson, Sarah Schindler, David Dana, Patricia McCoy, Rashmi Dyal-Chand, Nadav Shoked, Audrey McFarlane, Marc Roark, Jim Kelly, Tim Iglesias, John Lovett, Erin Ryan, Julie Patterson Forrester, Kristen Barnes, Steve Clowney, Asmara Tekle, Sally Richardson, Jamila Jefferson-Jones, Julie Hill, Matthew Bruckner, Melissa Lonegrass, Blake Hudson, Donald Kochan, Drew Dawson, Kara Bruce, Shelby Green, Monika Ehrman, Katheleen Guzman, Melissa Mortazavi, Rebekah Taylor, Donald Bogan, Jonathan Forman, Karen Lynch-Shally, Peter Byrne, Juanita Roche, and Gregory Alexander.

As with all projects, not everyone who is thanked in these pages agreed with my ideas or views. I endeavored to seek the advice of individuals with varying ideologies and points of views, all of which helped enrich the project and forced me to rethink some of my own beliefs about the financial crisis and mortgage regulation generally. To that point, all views and errors in this book belong to me alone.

I also thank my bright and hardworking research assistants, Robert Davidson (Iowa Class of 2018), Glenn Kats (Iowa Class of 2019), and Zachary Harrison (SULC Class of 2019). They provided invaluable assistance and attention to detail at every step of the way. At Cambridge University Press, I am thankful to Matt Galloway, who championed this project and helped shepherd the work (and me) through the publication process. I further had the benefit of comments from several anonymous peer reviewers in the fields of property, commercial and consumer transactions, and law and finance. Kathleen Engel and Patricia McCoy's tremendous work on the subprime mortgage crisis, Tara Twomey and Adam Levitin's research on the economics of mortgage servicing, and Matthew Desmond's illuminating book on poverty and the American landlord–tenant system all served as inspiration for this project, although I could never hope to match the significance of their contributions.

And last but not least, I thank my husband, McHenry "Dub" Lee. This book is for you. Thank you for always being there for me. And for cooking me dinner every night.

Introduction

There is an entire world behind how homeownership works in America, one completely hidden from view and governed by rules that hardly anyone knows and even fewer understand. At its center is an industry – a group of middlemen – that you've probably never heard of and the significance of which you most likely don't appreciate. But fear not – you aren't alone. Unbeknownst to the American public at large, the mortgage middlemen – known as *mortgage servicers* – are some of the most (if not *the* most) essential players in the story of modern homeownership. But, despite the immensely important role that servicers play in propping up the American housing finance structure, they have been given little attention by policy makers, the media, academics, or anyone else.[1] This book is about these mortgage middlemen and why it is time that we all start paying attention to them.

As of this book's date of publication, it will have been roughly a decade since the financial crisis of 2008 – the massive downturn in the global economy in which institutions failed, taxpayers bailed out banks and Wall Street firms, and several companies were taken over by the federal government. As the country faced the most significant financial challenge since the Great Depression, these enormous interventions in the private sector were heralded as the only way to save the U.S. economy.

The financial crisis revealed not only the complex and multifaceted architecture behind homeownership in America but also that this same complicated edifice was systemically defective and would easily crumble when just a little pressure was applied to it. As the walls started to fall, everyday-Americans began to get a glimpse of the massive machine behind their mortgage loan, previously hidden from view and seemingly inscrutable to most. While an individual who purchases a home typically does so through a loan procured from an area lender or broker, that transaction is only the beginning of a much more protracted process. Most loans are quickly sold, packaged, and repackaged several times before finally being turned into an investment product that is purchased by parties far removed from the homeowner. This process is known as *securitization*.

The securitization scaffolding, which holds together the entire American housing finance system, is administered by the mortgage servicers.[2] These entities – which I refer to in the preceding text and often throughout this book as the *mortgage middlemen* – have become important players in American homeownership. Despite not being chosen or even understood by the homeowner, servicers enjoy an outsized role in the housing economy. First, they are the sole point of contact between homeowners and their most important creditors – the ones that own their mortgage loans. Second, servicers are vested with extraordinary powers over the lives of homeowners, including not only the mechanics of making payments but also sometimes having physical authority over the home, even before a foreclosure takes place. When homeowners have questions or encounter problems, they go to the servicer to obtain a resolution. And importantly, servicers have been given or vested with the unilateral power to alter the obligations of the homeowner, all the while enjoying significant legal and practical power over the home. Servicers are the ferrymen of American homeownership. They can shepherd you across the waters of paying off your loan and ultimately becoming debt free. But, when those waters get rough, they can also throw you overboard.

Homeowners, for their part, are often completely unaware of the role played by the servicer. Most Americans believe they are paying their lender,[3] or at least some party that their original lender sold the loan to after it was made. This simplistic belief could not be further from the truth. In fact, the servicer generally owns no part of the loan.[4] Rather, the servicer acts on behalf of the owner of the loan and deals with the homeowner only in a representative capacity.

Yet, mortgage middlemen are far more than mere agents for the finance companies for which they work. Rather than servants that simply carry out the orders of their masters, servicers have enormous independent authority to deal with homeowners. More concerning, servicers have little to no direction to guide them in how best to deal with the homeowner or the mortgaged property in times of distress. Instead, the structural features that govern the relationship between the investors who own the loans and the middlemen who manage them leave remarkable discretion in the hands of servicers.

Servicers have often deployed this discretion in haphazard and abusive ways. Take, for example, the case of a Florida woman named Trish and her mother with a disability.[5] Prior to the financial crisis, Trish's mother bought a modest home with her husband and never missed a monthly payment. The elderly couple's mortgage payments were auto-debited from their bank account each month. But in August 2011, it was discovered that the installment amount suddenly included an extra $300. Trish helped her mother contact the servicer to find out what happened because the change was made without notifying or asking the permission of the homeowners. As it turns out, in 2011 the servicing of her mother's loan was transferred to a new company. The new servicer – using an obscure provision in the standard mortgage contract dealing with "force-placed insurance" – took out additional property insurance on the home and included the new premium amount in the August payment (without anyone's direct permission). Trish and her mother explained that the property had been insured continuously for years, but the new servicer declared that it had determined that the insurance was insufficient. And, unknown to Trish and her mother (and indeed, most homeowners), the servicer has the unilateral right to not only select additional insurance at will but also to tack on the resulting extra premiums to the monthly mortgage obligation. When Trish and her mother tried to dispute the additional insurance, the servicer advised them that they had better pay up or else a foreclosure was coming.

A servicer's power, however, is not merely limited to matters involving property insurance. Servicers can also physically enter a person's home, even prior to a foreclosure and even when the owner is not present. Barry Tatum learned this the hard way.[6] Barry had fallen behind on his mortgage payments to his loan servicer, Bank of America. One day in December 2012, Barry returned home to find that the front and back doors to his house had been ripped from the hinges, leaving the contents exposed to the cold Chicago winter. But, this was not a street crime. Rather, a letter revealed that his servicer had hired a property management company, Safeguard Properties, to go out to the home and, further, that this contractor had determined that the home was abandoned. Despite calling Bank of America and Safeguard Properties multiple times over a series of months to tell them that he was still living in (and indeed, still owned) the property, Barry received twelve more abandonment notices pinned to his door.

The constant transferring of loan servicing rights can cause significant problems for homeowners. In 2003, Ceith and Louise Sinclair purchased their home in Altadena, California with a mortgage loan.[7] The couple, who lived in the house with their four children, never missed a payment. In 2012, when so many homeowners fell on hard times and after home values had plummeted, the Sinclairs applied for and received a loan modification from their servicer. Then, in June 2013, the Sinclairs's monthly mortgage payment was unexpectedly returned. Evidently, the servicing rights to Ceith and Louise's loan were transferred to a new company, Nationstar, that refused to honor the prior loan modification, claiming that one page of the application had not been notarized. The servicer then foreclosed on their property and sold the home to an investment firm. The Sinclairs, however, stated that they only found out about the sale when a representative of the buyer came to their door one day and told the couple that they had two weeks to get out. Calls to Nationstar, according to Louise, were met with runarounds and frequent requests to "call back in two days." The family would have been kicked out on the street but for a local news station picking up the story – and all despite the fact that they had never missed a single mortgage payment.[8] In the end, the Sinclairs retained a lawyer and were able to remain in their home. As it turned out, the page in the loan application had been notarized.

Mortgage servicers are the curators of the securitization system. Leading up to the crisis, they were the firms that managed the flow of funds from vulnerable, subprime borrowers to Wall Street investors, all the while taking a cut of the mortgage payments for themselves.⁹ Many servicers were subsidiaries or affiliates of the very lenders that targeted and made risky loans to unsuspecting borrowers in the first place.¹⁰

What was (and what remains) one of the most interesting features about mortgage middlemen and the financial crisis is that although they occupied positions of colossal power and discretion when it came to the mortgage finance system, servicers were completely ill-equipped for the job assigned to them. They were frequently under-resourced and under-staffed, with little training on how to deal with homeowners in such dire straits or how best to handle distressed loans. In the aftermath of the crisis, servicing companies sent homeowners mixed signals, often by moving forward with foreclosures despite having promised that a workout was possible and then suddenly transferring the servicing rights to a different company on the eve of completing a workout with the homeowner.¹¹

Even when the federal government attempted to implement programs to give homeowners relief from foreclosure,¹² servicers often failed to qualify individuals or act on applications for assistance. Jeremy Fletcher of Northridge, California owned a successful swimming-pool construction business before the financial crisis, but, like so many others, he saw his business tank in 2008 as his sales dropped significantly.¹³ Facing a monthly home mortgage payment that he could no longer afford, he applied for assistance from an Obama administration program. This program was aimed at incentivizing servicers to help troubled Americans stay in their homes and avoid foreclosure by furnishing them a loan modification. Jeremy called his servicer, CitiMortgage, and tried to apply but was told that because he had not yet missed a loan payment he was not eligible. A few months later, when Jeremy was getting ready to try to sell his home, he got a call out of the blue from CitiMortgage telling him that his modification was approved for a trial run. Jeremy was told that his monthly payment would be dramatically cut for a period of five years. He readily agreed and immediately made a payment over the phone in the new amount. The CitiMortgage employee said that if Jeremy made all his payments on time for a period of ninety days and filled out additional paperwork, then his modification would become permanent. Everything sounded great.

After Jeremy sent in all the required documentation and made timely payments for the full ninety days, his inquiries about making the modification permanent were met with statements by CitiMortgage that the servicer was "backed up but everything was fine" and that he should "continue to make trial payments." This holding pattern kept up for an entire year with different employees at CitiMortgage variously assuring Jeremy that everything was "fine" and that approval of his permanent modification was just a matter of time. Then, in June 2010, Jeremy got a call from CitiMortgage's collections department telling him that he was one year late on his loan and that he owed $12,000. After being transferred around on the phone from person to person, he was finally told that he had been dropped from the modification program. If he did not pay the necessary amount within the next month, CitiMortgage told Jeremy that he would lose his home. Jeremy struggled for weeks to get someone to help him and, only after he had retained a lawyer, was he able to get a mortgage specialist at CitiMortgage on the phone. The CitiMortgage specialist told him that it appeared his application had been dropped in error – it "got lost in the cracks."[14] Jeremy had to redocument the application but was otherwise told that everything would be fixed. Things seemed to come together until two days later when Jeremy received notification that CitiMortgage had just sold the rights to service his loan to a different company, Saxon Mortgage. After a year of painstaking good-faith efforts, Jeremy was back to square one.

The story was even worse for Alisa and her seventy-year-old parents living in Mississippi. Alisa's parents had always remained current on their mortgage payments and had a good deal of equity built up in their home.[15] One year after the crisis hit, her parents received a letter offering a loan modification from their servicer, Houston-based Litton Loan Servicing. Because Alisa's parents were retired, the drop in their monthly mortgage payments to $600 was extremely attractive. Although the arduous process involved the submission of numerous pieces of paper whereby Alisa's parents were often told by the servicer that the documents were either incomplete or never received, eventually Litton granted approval. Then, a year into the modification, Alisa reported that her parents received a letter stating that their modification was not approved and that they now owed more than $10,000 in late mortgage payments. Litton threatened foreclosure if payment was not made immediately.

The elderly couple living on retirement income did not have sufficient cash to make the overdue payment, and so they were forced into bankruptcy – something they never would have envisioned. In the end, the bankruptcy was not as successful as hoped, and the bank was said to have received $15,000. Now out of bankruptcy and still seeking a modification, the homeowners discovered that the servicing rights to their loan were suddenly transferred to a new company. Alisa's parents immediately received a default letter threatening foreclosure. The new servicer also issued a new demand that the couple start making monthly payments into an escrow account to cover end-of-the-year insurance and property tax expenses. About the same time, Alisa's mother was diagnosed with cancer. Despite her mother's illness, Alisa and her father were finally able to get a loan modification offer from the servicer, but not without having to pay a steep price. According to Alisa, the agreement required, among other things, that her parents sign away their right to dispute any past inaccuracies with how payments on their loan were processed or accounted for and that more than $19,000 would be added into the principal loan amount with little explanation.

Sharing these heartbreaking stories was not the only reason that inspired me to write this book. I also embarked on this journey because, as a law professor who writes and teaches in the areas of property law and finance with a particular interest in mortgage lending and consumer protection, it is my job to try and make the complex and arcane seem understandable and even interesting to everyday people. I have chosen this goal not merely because I think Americans should know something about the people who manage their loans and with whom they have to contend in the event the ups and downs of life threaten them with the loss of their home. Understanding mortgage servicing is also important because it helps us be better advocates for ourselves in the political process – the arena where the rules that govern the mortgage middlemen (and thus homeownership) are made and enforced.

But my goal is not only to put the spotlight on mortgage servicing. I also want to pull apart and explain how the industry operates. I endeavor in the pages that follow to show not only how it works, but also how it has changed over time and how it should be better regulated in the future. Mortgage servicing is necessary. We will never return to the *It's a Wonderful Life* version of banking, where George Bailey runs a small community bank that makes portfolio-held mortgage loans to the good folks of Bedford Falls.[16] Securitization and the secondary mortgage market are here to stay, and, truth be told, homeownership in the United States would likely look very different today (probably for the worse) without both. So, because mortgage securitization and mortgage servicing go hand in hand, the middlemen are here for the long haul as well.

Admittedly, not all servicers are bad. Many servicers were simply ill-equipped to deal with the flood of defaults and foreclosures that overwhelmed the housing market after the 2008 crash. But there certainly were some bad actors who, in coordination with fraudulent originators, were guilty of some of the worst abuses. Later chapters will share some of these harrowing stories with you. Because of this, some generalizations will be made throughout the book, recognizing that the mortgage middleman industry is not without its bright lights.

Yet, it is not enough merely to understand mortgage servicing and the very important position it occupies in the lives of American homeowners. We also need to understand how it should be properly regulated, particularly as this important function moves more aggressively into the so-called shadow banking sector. We need to ensure that the foreclosure and servicing abuses of the past ten years – like those experienced by Barry, the Sinclairs, Jeremy, Alisa's parents, and countless others – do not occur again. We also need to guard against future breakdowns in the mortgage servicing system similar to those we saw during and after 2008.

In truth, meaningful mortgage servicing regulation has been lacking for a long time. That is not to say that that this industry has been unregulated – at least not in theory. The mortgage middlemen have been subject to some regulation, but it has not always been very effective or well coordinated. Rather than having clear and deliberate rules and standards to govern its proper operation (particularly as it relates to protecting the interests of homeowners), the industry has both benefited from and been burdened by a complex patchwork of rules and oversight requirements that stretch from the offices of state-level banking regulators to the halls of regulatory agencies in Washington, D.C. Even for those servicing firms that have only the best intentions, complying with the crisscrossing array of rules and overlapping governmental authorities invites mistakes and inadvertent consumer harm.

In this book, I show not only how this byzantine regulatory structure left homeowners with little protection from abusive servicing practices but also how servicers would have benefited (and still can) from rules on how best to prepare for and handle the extreme stresses of the foreclosure process and borrower delinquencies. I also suggest how a better regulatory system – one that draws on federalism principles to create a state/federal partnership for the licensing and prudential regulation of mortgage servicing – should be designed.

Some progress has already been made in the servicing arena. In response to the financial crisis, Congress passed comprehensive legislation in 2010 known as the Dodd-Frank Wall Street Reform and Consumer Protection Act (Dodd-Frank).[17] This act, among other things, amended a host of federal lending and banking statutes and established a new federal agency, the Consumer Financial Protection Bureau (CFPB), to protect consumers in all forms of financial transactions going forward. Part of this legislation involved creating new rules to govern many of the consumer-facing aspects of mortgage servicing. Also, in 2012 a number of the country's biggest servicers entered into a massive settlement with federal agencies and state attorneys general from across the United States regarding their shoddy foreclosure and lending practices.

While that may sound promising, there is yet work to be done. The mortgage servicing industry is still deeply troubled. Despite the fact that so many years have passed since the crisis occurred, enforcement actions by the CFPB and state-level regulators and attorneys general for foreclosure-related abuses continue against these firms.[18] Additionally, the market for the mortgage middlemen has gone through some significant changes (and challenges) since 2008. For instance, the value of mortgage servicing as a bank asset fell 33 percent at the end of 2008 – the period when the financial crisis was at its worst.[19] In the earlier part of 2008, bank-related mortgage servicing was valued at $78 billion. Between 2011 and 2012, that number dropped to somewhere between $30 and $40 billion.

What is the story behind these numbers? It is that banks – the ones that hold our money, issue our debit cards, and are insured by the federal government – are getting out of the mortgage servicing business in a big way. Into this gap have stepped nonbank servicing companies. Nonbanks are those financial institutions that, despite not being regulated like banks, are generally viewed as having many of the same attributes as banks. This corner of the financial sector is often known as "shadow banking."[20] As the name ominously suggests, shadow banks are those financial institutions that operate outside the general banking regulatory regime.[21] These firms do not take deposits or issue checks and debits cards like the banks around the corner, but they do play a significant role in the banking and broader financial economy. Shadow banks include hedge funds, payday lenders, private equity funds, investment banks, mortgage lenders, and insurance companies, and they often provide incredibly important services to the American economy and the world.

Shadow banks came into prominence in the aftermath of the crisis because they, in large part, contributed the disaster.[22] A prime example is the notorious fall of Lehman Brothers – a well-known shadow bank.[23] This firm, which played an enormous role in subprime mortgage lending and securitization, held as much as $600 billion in assets a year prior to its bankruptcy.[24] Other shadow banks that became central figures in the tale of the 2008 crisis include Goldman Sachs, Morgan Stanley, New Century Financial, Countrywide Financial, Ameriquest, and AIG – the list goes on.

Since the crisis, shadow banking firms have been purchasing sizable amounts of mortgage servicing rights from banks.[25] For instance, in early 2017 Citigroup – the subsidiaries of which have been fined up to $29 million by the CFPB for foreclosure-related abuses[26] – announced that it was selling off billions worth of mortgage servicing rights to the nonbank firm New Residential Mortgage LLC.[27] In 2012, Bank of America sold $10.4 billion worth of its mortgage servicing assets to nonbank Nationstar Mortgage.[28] All this buying has added up. Whereas in 2012 the percentage of mortgage loans serviced by shadow banks was only 6.8 percent, that number rose to at least 24.2 percent in 2015, with some estimates being as high as 31 percent.[29]

So, why does it matter that shadow banking institutions have taken such an interest in mortgage servicing? First, shadow banks operate outside the traditional banking regulatory system, which reduces oversight of their activities. Also, as a general matter shadow banks tend to be very active in minority communities and with at-risk borrowers.[30] They also originate and service a huge portion of Federal Housing Administration (FHA) loans and a sizable portion of loans sold to Fannie Mae and Freddie Mac.[31] Between 2013 and 2016, the servicing of FHA-backed mortgage loans by nonbanks increased from 35 percent to more than 70 percent. This market share growth is important because the FHA loan program and Fannie and Freddie are major drivers of homeownership for families of modest means.[32] The result is that the mortgage servicing activities of shadow banks have a great deal to say about how low- to moderate-income Americans and homeowners of color manage their mortgage debt (and thus keep their homes during financial downturns). From this perspective, mortgage servicing is changing in fundamental ways and is becoming dominated by firms that, although subject to some federal and state laws, are not regulated in the same way as banks and traditional financial institutions. And for an industry that is already relatively hidden from view and little understood even by those who have glimpsed at the structure of America's mortgage finance system, the ascendancy of shadow banks in the area of mortgage servicing carries much importance and significant potential danger.[33]

Americans, for the most part, do not have sufficient understanding of the servicing industry to form their own views about how best to regulate it or to look with a critical eye at what other people – such as industry advocates or politicians – have to say about it. Though most homeowners remain in the dark, mortgage firms (including mortgage servicers) and their lobbyists pour long strings of acronyms, economics catchphrases, and generally confusing financial services jargon over the heads of members of Congress, regulators, state legislators, and the media. Because most people lack the basic background knowledge of the architecture of mortgage finance, they do not challenge the industry. A central goal of this book is to change that when it comes to mortgage servicing.

Many who work in or lobby on behalf of the financial services and banking industry argue that any kind of serious financial reform effort would have an adverse impact on the ability of individuals to access credit[34] and that it would hobble a financial firm's ability to grow the economy.[35] This argument is frequently made through the lens of mortgage lending specifically: regulation of mortgage markets – including servicing – will drive up the cost of credit and thereby shut out many homeowners from the American dream. They argue that if we want credit to flow and homeownership to flourish, we need to tread lightly and keep regulation at a minimum. Wall Street executives declare that lessons have been learned, that points of breakdown have been identified, and that controls have been put into place to make sure a disaster does not happen again. Trust us, they say, this stuff is complex: We understand it better than anyone else. For example, in April 2017 Jamie Dimon (the CEO of JPMorgan Chase, which has a substantial mortgage servicing business,[36] and the de facto voice of Wall Street) attacked postcrisis mortgage regulatory efforts, stating that they hurt "lower income buyers, first-time homebuyers, the self-employed[,] and individuals with prior defaults who deserve another chance."[37] He argued that the post–Dodd-Frank regulation of mortgage lending is too complex and creates too much risk for lenders to operate effectively.

Dimon is not alone in his "industry knows best" attitude to the regulation of mortgage finance. Financial industry advocates, invoking appealing catchphrases rather than sound arguments, state that the government should end its "failed experiment with top-down government control of housing, and let markets once again do the job they do best."[38] If we fail to do so, they assert, then "we may soon face a housing-related financial crisis worse than the last one." Also, Dodd-Frank is "driving consolidation" and may result, most ominously, in making "lending markets less able to serve core economic demand."[39] The way banks are regulated is "anti-American"[40] and "the housing collapse ... was largely the result of government interference in the mortgage market."[41] Rather than regulating the types of loans that are offered to borrowers and how those loans are managed, "[b]orrowers and lenders should be free to negotiate the terms of mortgage agreements."[42] Financial regulations, including mortgage regulations, "limit mortgage options and access to credit – and further erode Americans' freedoms."[43] And, Dodd-Frank and the regulations that flow from it should either be repealed[44] or greatly curtailed.[45]

The truth is that lobbyists and financial executives do not know what is best, and although mortgage lending and servicing are multifaceted, the basics are not that difficult to understand. They are at least not as complex as some would have us believe. True, the labyrinth of securitization takes some time to navigate, but a mastery of the topic is not necessary to gain the foundational knowledge necessary to see mortgage servicing and how it constitutes an integral part of the scaffolding of housing finance. Understanding a few terms and their definitions, accompanied by some explanation of process and a few concrete hypotheticals, is all that is needed to get up to speed. And with that process behind us, we can begin to see why servicers are so important and to also better appreciate how crucial they become when a homeowner hits rough waters.

Mortgage finance lobbyists have incentives to keep the curtains in place because the more people understand how the hidden financial architecture behind their home loan works, the less likely they will be to accept, unchallenged, assertions that any new rule or new requirement would overly burden the lending industry and create adverse consequences for consumers. And unfortunately, even in the aftermath of the financial crisis – when the hearts and minds of our elected leaders were as receptive as they ever would be to looking out for the rights of consumers and fighting back against Wall Street risk-taking – the flawed narratives and rickety arguments made by financial sector lobbyists often won the day in Congress and with federal regulators. Legislative proposals were steered in a particular direction and suggestions from consumer groups were frequently sidelined. It is no surprise that, considering the wealth and power of banking lobbyists and lending trade groups, most of the comments and critiques submitted to governmental agencies relative to financial regulatory rule-making efforts come from them.[46] Reports from 2013, a few short years after the Dodd-Frank Act was passed, revealed that numerous bills passed by the Republican-controlled House of Representatives and aimed at rolling back many of the act's provisions contained almost the exact same language (word-for-word) as proposals submitted by banking lobbyists.[47] In one bill, seventy of the eighty-five lines contained in the legislation were copied verbatim from a Citigroup document.[48]

Knowledge is power in all spaces, and mortgage finance is no different. Those who understand the system have the ability to shape and steer it. This means that lobbyists and the industry, armed with the best information and having created the perception of impenetrability, can ensure that regulations are weak and enforcement is ineffectual. Americans need to better understand the world of mortgage servicing and the reality that it exists around them rather than in some far-off glass building on Wall Street. Armed with that knowledge, homeowners will be better equipped to participate in the political process and make their voices heard by elected officials when housing finance reform finally does come up again in Congress (something that the Obama administration was not eager to undertake and that remains uncertain in the Trump era). And lastly, I hope that even just a little bit of knowledge about the servicing process will help homeowners better deal with their own middlemen.

It's an interesting time to write about the mortgage lending industry because the pendulum is swinging back toward the interests of the financial sector. After the crisis there was such outcry – such outrage – regarding the greed and fraud that permeated the financial sector that Congress and consumer advocates were able to pass significant legislation in the form of the Dodd-Frank Act, which resulted in the creation of the CFPB. Without the crisis, these legislative and policy feats would not have been possible. But now, with the election of Donald Trump and the dominance of a deregulatory agenda in the U.S. Congress, the recent focus on consumer rights appears to be over – or at least on pause.[49]

But it does not have to be that way. Protecting American consumers (particularly homeowners) and providing for an effective and appropriate regulatory system to achieve that goal is not a partisan issue. A stable financial system that allows for competition, provides credit where appropriate, promotes safe innovation, and guards against fraud, information asymmetry, and predatory practices is in the interest of everyone. And an understanding of the hidden architecture behind homeownership in America can help everyday people become armed with the basic knowledge they need to challenge the conventional wisdom of Wall Street lobbyists and bank executives when the big policy questions related to consumers and mortgage finance come before our elected leaders. With this project, I hope to do my part in pulling back the curtain so that, eventually, we will not only be more collectively aware of the fragility of this architecture but also that we may strengthen it.

PART I

The Housing Crisis, Its Architects, and Its Victims

1

The Lead-Up to the Crisis

Understanding the problems faced by homeowners in dealing with mortgage middlemen is impossible without first understanding how homeowners found themselves facing the loss of their homes in the first place. It is the foreclosure process – the point at which the borrower stops making payments on the loan and the lender proceeds to enforce its rights against the home – where the vulnerability of homeowners and the abuses of the mortgage middlemen come into focus. Foreclosures played a huge role in the troubles that spread across the country in the aftermath of the 2008 crisis. At the height of this period – between 2007 and 2012 – nearly one in every twenty individuals in the United States lost their home in foreclosure or a similar proceeding (that's more than ten million Americans).[1]

So, how did this enormous problem come about? The causes range in everything from adjustable interest rates resetting, predatory lending practices, overindebtedness, housing speculation, too much supply, the proliferation of financial products that masked their inherently risky nature, inadequate governmental oversight and regulation, and poor federal housing policies. A full exploration of these issues is not the focus of this work, and, frankly, matters very little when it comes to the hurt and distress felt by countless American homeowners – those who found themselves facing the greatest financial crisis since the Great Depression. Nevertheless, it is important to have some background for understanding how homeowners found themselves confronting the mortgage middlemen. Such a simple understanding is the goal I undertake here.

HOUSING BUBBLES AND BAD POLICY MAKING

Broadly speaking, the beginning of the crisis can be traced back to the point at which the U.S. housing bubble finally burst (the period between 2005 and 2006).[2] The effect of the bubble on home pricing can hardly be understated. The national average rise in home prices between 2000 and 2003 was 9.8 percent per year, but some markets proved particularly heated up. For instance, between 1995 and 2000 home prices jumped 4.1 percent each year and then began rising to an incredible 11.1 percent between 2000 and 2003.³ The rise in California was even more striking: consider that a California home purchased in 1995 for $200,000 would, nine years later, be worth more than $450,000.⁴ The average, annual home pricing jump in California from 1995 to 2000 was 6.1 percent and from 2000 to 2003 it was a stunning 13.6 percent. For a longer-range perspective, from the period between about 1997 and 2006 the average price of a home in the United States increased 124 percent.⁵

The rapid rise in housing prices produced yet another (albeit superficial) effect on the American economy: It increased household wealth. Families suddenly found that their homes were quickly rising in value, thereby increasing their net worth – "household wealth rose to nearly six times income."⁶ More homeowners began using the equity in their homes (the number achieved by subtracting the amount of mortgage debt that is secured by that home from the actual value of the home) as credit cards, refinancing their loans for a larger amount than what was owed and then using the extra cash to make various purchases or to pay other bills. In 2013, the mortgage market saw about one in every four mortgage loans get refinanced – a truly shocking number.⁷ Between 2001 and 2003, homeowners pulled out $427 billion in cash from the equity in their homes using refinancing and another $430 billion in cash using home equity lines of credit, which were second loans secured by a junior mortgage on the property.⁸

So how did homeowners use this borrowed money from the equity in their homes you might ask? In a 2004 Federal Reserve survey, about 45 percent of participating homeowners reported using these funds to cover taxes, medical expenses, electronics, and trips, while another 31 percent used the money to make improvements to their homes.⁹ The final 24 percent used the money to make investments or acquire more real property, as well as purchase consumer goods like clothing or jewelry. What this meant was that consumer spending was high during the run-up to the 2008 crash. People were saving less cash and were spending (borrowed) money faster than what their incomes would allow. Personal savings rates between 1998 and 2005 dropped from 5.2 percent to 4.1 percent, while consumer spending as a share of the gross domestic product (GDP) was anywhere from 67 percent to 168 percent in a given year during that period.¹⁰

This all meant that buying a home seemed like an excellent investment, and indeed there was a huge effort by the government to encourage homeownership. In the middle of the 1990s President Clinton released his National Homeownership Strategy and, in doing so, set a national goal for the country to reach an all-time high homeownership rate by 2000.¹¹ His efforts also included permitting Fannie Mae and Freddie Mac (called the *government-sponsored entities*, or GSEs) to spread affordable-housing credit by "buying subprime securities that included loans to low-income borrowers."¹² But the push to expand homeownership cut across party lines. President George W. Bush, who came into office in 2001, launched his own policy initiative – the Ownership Society.¹³ In March 2004, he stated that "[n]ot enough minorities own their own homes .... One thing I've done is I've called on private sector mortgage banks and banks to be more aggressive about lending to first-time home buyers."[14] Part of his plan involved setting ambitious lending goals for Fannie Mae and Freddie Mac, particularly in the way of providing increased access to credit for black and Hispanic borrowers, as well as rolling out a number of affordable housing tax incentives.

The Federal Reserve (sometimes called the "Fed") also played a part in this story. In 2001 the U.S. economy began to slow its growth. To help give the economy a shot in the arm, the Fed, through its Open Market Committee's control over the short-term interest rate, lowered the federal funds rate by half a percent.[15] The Fed would continue to cut the rate 11 times throughout the year, which would ultimately leave the rate at 1.75 percent (a 40-year low). The lowering of the interest rate did more, however, than just help boost the economy – it had a massive impact on the housing market. Construction work took off in 2002, with states like Florida seeing a 14 percent net job growth in that industry and California gaining more than 21,000 new construction jobs.[16] "From 2002 to 2005, residential construction contributed three times more to the economy than it had contributed on average since 1990."[17] In turn, would-be homeowners with healthy credit profiles in 2003 could obtain a home loan at an interest rate that was three whole percentage points lower than what they could have gotten in 2000. This allowed (and, indeed, encouraged) individuals to purchase more expensive homes because their monthly note payments would be lessened by the favorable interest rates. It allowed a homeowner to pay the same monthly note amount in 2003, as in 2000, but afford a $245,000 home rather than a $180,000 home.[18]

All these various policy initiatives worked their magic, for good and for bad. In 2005, shortly before the crisis, homeownership in America was up to nearly 70 percent – an all-time high.[19]

THE RISE OF DANGEROUS FINANCIAL PRODUCTS AND THE DECLINE OF UNDERWRITING

The bubble bursting had such a devastating effect on homeowners because in or around the early 1990s individuals who lacked the ability to qualify for credit under customary underwriting standards were nevertheless granted mortgage loans by many banks and financial institutions across the country.[20] While, at the time, most traditional lending institutions were unwilling to offer credit to these borrowers (often because they had no credit history, they were marked by indicators of financial distress, and the loans were not eligible for sale to Fannie or Freddie), a growing number of new financial firms decided there was money to be made in lending to such individuals.[21]

These subprime borrowers were enticed to take out loans based on favorable repayment terms. However, the favorable terms were deceiving; in fact, these subprime loans had a number of features that made them all the more likely to end up in default.[22] For instance, a borrower would take out a loan where the interest rate would be fixed for a number of years in the beginning of the loan's term (called a *teaser rate*), but after that period had expired (often two or three years), the interest rate would spike, causing the monthly payments to increase dramatically – often doubling.[23] This was known as a hybrid adjustable rate mortgage because the rate would initially be fixed but would convert to a rate that adjusted according to a set formula tied to a margin and then readjust periodically throughout the remaining term of the loan.[24] By one account, interest rates would start around 18 percent but then jump after a period up to nearly 30 percent.[25] But other borrowers – particularly those who only intended to be in their homes for a set period – were given loans that allowed for low, interest-only payments for the first few years with a large balloon payment of all outstanding interest and principle due shortly thereafter.[26]

Other subprime loans provided for pay-option terms, whereby the individual could choose each month to pay either the full principal and interest due for that month's installment, to pay only interest on that installment, or to pay only some stipulated, nominal amount of interest. The third option would result in any unpaid interest due for that period being added to the principal, thereby ballooning the principal amount of the loan significantly. Pay-option loans (sometimes called "Pick-A-Pay" loans) were particularly dangerous for borrowers and particularly lucrative for mortgage lenders.[27] This is because the commission or fees earned by lenders or brokers for making these loans were double that available for regular mortgage loans.[28] These pay-option loans, from the originator's standpoint, had the lowest loss rate in the entire mortgage lending industry. They were basically a "sure fire thing" for originators. As a result, some mortgage brokers reported that their bosses instructed them to aim for making sure that half of all the loans they made were "Pick-A-Pay."[29]

To ease a borrower's fears, a lender would often assure the individual that he or she could simply refinance the loan prior to the time the interest rate changed. Because home prices continued to rise, it seemed logical for a borrower to feel comfort in the prospect of such a deal. With so much equity in the property, refinancing a home loan seemed like a great idea.

Extraordinarily high fees typified subprime loans. According to one account, one individual was given a subprime loan that, after multiple refinancings, totaled $45,000 in principal, $19,000 of which was purely fees to the lender/broker.[30] One former mortgage broker for Countrywide shares another fairly typical story. If a borrower took out a loan for $1 million that included an adjustable interest rate under a pay-option setup, that individual would be given a brief period (about a year) in which he or she would only be required to make miniscule interest payments (almost nothing compared to the true interest on the debt). No principal payments would be due at all during this period. Further, if the loan included a provision that prohibited the borrower from making any prepayments (i.e., refinance) or else be forced to pay six months' worth of interest at the much higher adjusted rate (usually 3 percent higher than the normal market interest rate), then Countrywide would pay that mortgage broker a commission of $30,000.[31] Thus, when things started to get rough for the borrower, Countrywide would cash in by collecting the prepayment penalty should the borrower try to refinance the loan. Prepayment penalties produced big money – Countrywide collected $268 million in such fees during 2006 alone. With such a lucrative product, it's no wonder lenders like Countrywide financially incentivized their brokers to make these kinds of loans. More broadly, subprime loans almost always garnered higher commission fees for mortgage brokers – subprime mortgages typically earned .50 percent of the value of the loan while more quality mortgage products only brought with them a .20 percent fee.

High interest rates were a hallmark of subprime loans. Initial rates on these loans (typically falling under the adjustment rate structure) would be low for a period, and then double once the rate reset (often reseting multiple times). For instance, in 1999 Jose Pomales purchased a modest home in the Hyde Park neighborhood of Boston for himself and his young family.[32] He subsequently refinanced his home loan with New Century (a lender that since closed its doors due to making too many bad loans), and the new loan used an adjustable interest rate. Initially the monthly payments were about $2,100. When the interest rate reset, the monthly payments went up to $2,400. Further resets were built into the loan that would result in the monthly mortgage payments hitting more than $2,800. Pomales said he had no idea how the adjustable interest rate worked or how he was going to continue to afford to pay for his home. In another story, Jennie Haliburton, a widow in her late seventies and living in Philadelphia, refinanced her home loan to a subprime mortgage with an adjustable interest rate.[33] Although payments were low at first, the rate later spiked and caused her payments to grow from $800 to $1,100. At the time of her story, it was estimated that when her rate reset again in May 2008 the monthly payment would go up to $1,700 (taking up 95 percent of her Social Security benefits).

Subprime lenders also started waiving requirements that borrowers put down money on the home purchase prior to receiving the loan (a practice that at one time required a customary 20 percent down payment). By 2005 the average down payment amount was a meager 2 percent, and more than 40 percent of home buyers were excused from putting down any money at all.[34] Subprime borrowers were encouraged not only to take out subprime loans to purchase homes but also to use their homes as piggy banks to pull out money that was gained through rising equity in the home. Individuals, particularly those who had already paid off their mortgage loans, were offered the option of putting a new mortgage on their home and using the proceeds from that new loan to pay off or consolidate consumer debt, such as that arising from credit cards, auto loans, student loans, or healthcare costs.

While this seemed like a clever idea at first, in reality the borrower had converted unsecured debt, which might have been able to be modified in bankruptcy, into secured debt on their homes – something for which bankruptcy protections could offer little help. Lenders would even pad the application of some borrowers to make it look like they could afford loans – even bad loans – when they clearly could not.[35] This included manipulating the real estate appraisal process to make the property being used as collateral appear to be valued at more than what it really was, thereby meriting a larger loan amount. If an appraisal for a home being purchased for $230,000 came back as being valued at only $200,000, then either the seller would have to lower the purchase price or else the buyer couldn't get the loan at that amount. The deal was dead, and no home purchase would take place. Because of this, mortgage lenders started to put pressure on appraisers not to tank deals with their valuations. Appraisers, in turn, feared losing business and around 2003 reported being "pressured to ignore missing kitchens, damaged walls, and inoperable mechanical systems" all so that the bank and the borrower could get the value they needed.[36] Even after a series of reforms in 2005, mortgage originators continued to handpick their appraisers based on who would give them the most favorable valuation reports or who would change their reports if the appraisal came in too low.

Lenders also manufactured pay stubs, employment data, and income information to form the basis of these subprime loans.[37] One account of this comes from Long Beach Mortgage (a subsidiary of Washington Mutual, which eventually went out of business).[38] Mortgage brokers would regularly find subprime borrowers and send accompanying loan applications, riddled with fraudulent information, along to Long Beach Mortgage to originate the loan. Long Beach Mortgage required little documentation, often accepting letters of credit from landlords, fake tax returns, or suspicious-looking pay stubs in lieu of verified statements of income. One former employee, speaking on condition of anonymity, said that higher-ups at the company would frequently offer gifts to the loan reviewers in exchange for looking the other way on questionable loan applications. Antoinette Hendryx, a former loan reviewer for Long Beach Mortgage, said: "They'd offer kickbacks of money" or said things like "'I'll buy you a bottle of Dom Perignon.' It was just crazy."[39] And some online companies assisted mortgage lenders in perpetuating this underwriting fraud. For instance, some firms would offer potential borrowers a pay stub from a fake company or the opportunity to "rent" a cash-laden bank account to facilitate the loan application.[40] One company in particular, RaiseCreditScoreNow.com, offered consumers "four separate $20,000 credit lines with ten years of 'perfect payments' for $4,000 (although they did not have access to the actual credit line)."[41] By doing this, the company advertised that the consumer's credit score would increase by as much as 200 points in a mere 90 days – something that can result in making the difference between purchasing a home or not. Another company, SeasonedCreditLines.com, offered to potential mortgage borrowers favorable credit card account histories going back to the 1970s, featuring the slogan on their website: "How would your life be different with a 700+ credit score?"[42]

And sometimes loans were made using only the borrower's "stated income" on the loan application without the lender conducting any independent verification or requiring documentation. This was often called "low-doc" or "no-doc" loans because hardly any documentation about the borrower was needed to advance credit. In certain instances, the borrower could put down any numbers he or she wanted, and the lender would nevertheless make the loan, relying solely on the ever-rising value of the real estate subject to the mortgage.

It was not long before mainstream Wall Street financial institutions wanted in on the action – ones whose names had been long associated with the stability and security of the American financial market. In 2000, Citigroup purchased Associates First, which was the country's second-largest subprime lender and known for its high fees, prepayment penalties, and shoddy loan documents that targeted borrowers who were least able to understand the terms of the deal. Lehman Brothers (one of the largest investment banks) began purchasing subprime lenders to serve as subsidiaries. Bear Stearns, another giant of Wall Street, purchased three subprime mortgage lenders between 1998 and 2004. Merrill Lynch, Morgan Stanley, and Goldman Sachs also acquired their own set of subprime loan machines. Mortgage lending companies like New Century, Countrywide, and Ameriquest became increasingly aggressive. Volume was the name of the game, and Ameriquest "paid its account executives less per mortgage than the competition, but it encouraged them to make up the difference by underwriting more loans."[43]

PREDATORY AND FRAUDULENT LENDING PRACTICES

Many of these subprime loans were specifically marketed to borrowers in low-income and minority neighborhoods. The 1990s saw the start of a robust campaign to focus subprime lending in communities of color, where credit was often scarce, but people wanted access to borrowed money. As a result of litigation in 2001, it was revealed that Wells Fargo had created a special unit in the mid-Atlantic area to aggressively seek to refinance loans with black borrowers.[44] One loan officer in that unit stated: "They referred to subprime loans made in minority communities as ghetto loans and minority customers as 'those people have bad credit', 'those people don't pay their bills' and 'mud people.'"[45]

Some subprime lenders used biblical references in their names and focused their marketing on gospel and other traditionally African American media outlets.[46] Some mortgage lenders would hold special events at black churches and have black employees of the lender make the high-cost loan pitch. One way to entice church members was to offer a "rebate" whereby the lender would donate a certain amount of money to the entity of the borrower's choice (typically the church) as part of taking out the loan.[47] Other efforts involved hosting workshops and seminars at black places of worship, masked as altruistic events aimed at helping the church goers find ways to build wealth and economic strength, all the while serving as a sales pitch for various forms of subprime credit.[48]

The focus on black borrowers was dramatic. Subprime loans to black borrowers went from an overall of 2 percent in 1993 to 18 percent in 2000.[49] By the time the crisis hit, 50 percent of all mortgage loans made to African American individuals were subprime.[50] In one study of 2006 mortgage loan data, black borrowers were found to be 2.8 times more likely to be denied credit when compared to similarly situated white borrowers.[51] When black borrowers were extended credit, they were 2.4 times more likely to be given a subprime loan than comparable white borrowers. African American women, according to a study by the Consumer Federation of America, were five times as likely to receive a subprime mortgage loan than upper-income white men, even when credit worthiness was otherwise equal.[52]

Additional predatory practices persisted, as lenders would often engage in a bait and switch with subprime borrowers, telling borrowers the fees and charges were one thing while the actual loan documents told a different story. When the borrower would try to ask questions or request more time to read the documents (which were often only available to the borrower at the time of the closing), the lender or broker would waive off any concerns and pressure the individual to continue quickly with the process. Lenders would also direct otherwise credit-worthy individuals toward subprime loan products. In this way, certain institutions made high-cost loans to individuals who clearly qualified for cheaper credit with lower interest rates and less fees. Indeed, this practice became so pervasive that the *Wall Street Journal* reported in 2005 individuals with very healthy credit profiles made up a little more than 50 percent of all subprime loans.[53]

The aim of these lenders was obviously not to make big money from the loan. Indeed, it was almost guaranteed that the borrower would default. Rather, it was through the collection of fees that mortgage lenders made their money. Each time a loan was originated the lender collected a fee (whether an origination fee for a mortgage originator or a commission for a mortgage broker). And, as mentioned previously, sometimes that fee could be substantial because they were based on a certain percentage of the total loan amount. That meant the bigger the loan, the bigger the commission. This incentivized lenders to encourage borrowers to borrow as much money as possible and thereby maximize the lender's profit. Likewise, when adjustable rate mortgages hit the trigger date and the interest rate went up, or if the borrower wanted to use his or her equity in the home as a credit card, borrowers would need to refinance. The refinance would, in turn, produce even more fees for the lender.

GOVERNMENT'S FAILURE TO ACT

One might question where the government was amid all this corruption and bad behavior. For a long time, financial regulators showed little interest in policing real estate lending practices. Some even argued that the government's role in the financial sector shouldn't involve looking into the underlying lending practices of lenders. For instance, in the early 1980s when the U.S. Office of the Comptroller of the Currency (OCC) was confronted with the possibility of creating rules to govern the underwriting of mortgage loans by national banks, the agency opined that "factors such as market forces and management philosophies are the real determinants of banks' real estate lending practices."[54] As such, this major federal regulator declared that "[d]ecisions concerning the forms and terms of national bank lending are properly the responsibility of each bank's directorate and management" and not a space to be occupied by the government. Courts were no better, as judges generally declined to impose upon lenders a common law duty to determine whether their borrowers possessed the ability to repay when advanced mortgage credit.[55]

Things worsened in the 1990s as state and federal regulators started to notice the highly questionable and even outright predatory practices of many subprime lenders. But many government leaders argued that they lacked the resources and sometimes also the power to deal with the growing problem. When it came to mortgage lending by state-chartered banks, the Federal Reserve, the Federal Deposit Insurance Corporation (FDIC), and state banking supervisors had regulatory authority. When it came to nationally chartered banks, the Comptroller of the Currency was in charge of supervision. Thrifts (which are financial institutions that have a primary focus on taking deposits and originating home mortgages and generally have access to more low-cost funding than large commercial banks) were, at the time, governed by the Office of Thrift Supervision or state banking supervisors. Lastly, mortgage brokers came under the purview of state banking regulators. As for mortgage lending broadly, the power to promulgate rules under the Truth in Lending Act belonged to the Federal Reserve Board, but enforcement of those rules was scattered to a patchwork of various government entities. The Federal Reserve also had the power to regulate those subprime lenders that were not banks, but rather were owned by bank or financial holding companies. Many of the largest and most well-known banks in the country had subprime lending subsidiaries.[56] By the height of the housing bubble in 2006, 14 of the country's most systemically important financial institutions (including JPMorgan Chase, Wells Fargo, Bank of America, and Citigroup) were responsible for originating one in every three higher-priced mortgages.[57] But regulators were slow (if not inactive) about regulating nonbank entities like subprime lenders.[58] The Federal Trade Commission (FTC) stated that they lacked the budget or staff to effectively supervise these companies. The Federal Reserve, however, felt that although they technically had the authority, it would be an agency overreach to exert its authority without a more express authorization from Congress. In 1998, when the Federal Reserve and the U.S. Department of Housing and Urban Development (HUD) issued a joint report making recommendations on mortgage reform, particularly when it came to predatory lending, Congress refused to enact any of the agencies' recommendations. The same resulted from a spring 2000 effort by HUD and the U.S. Treasury to identify and make recommendations in response to the growing predatory and abusive practices flourishing in the American residential mortgage market.[59] Again, Congress (and the agencies) took no action. As one senior government official stated, "There wasn't much appetite or mood to take these recommendations."[60]

In early 2000 and 2001 former FDIC chairperson and then Treasury official Sheila Bair took notice of the immense subprime lending by the shadow banking (nonbank) sector and the ways in which a borrower's ability to repay the loan played almost no part in the underwriting process. Shadow banks grew tremendously in the lead up to the crisis, overshadowing the activities of conventional banking institutions. From the period between the financial crisis and October 2016, the shadow banking sector grew 25 percent.[61] Bair felt that mandatory regulations might not be possible, but that perhaps best practices guidelines for underwriting would be acceptable to the industry. Her efforts, however, came to nothing. She tried to engage the Federal Reserve, which had authority over bank and financial holding companies and their nonbank subsidiaries but was told that "Greenspan was not interested in increased regulation."[62] In fact, in 2004, Alan Greenspan stated that prohibiting subprime credit products, even with their unfavorable terms, would be most undesirable. He noted that when given to individuals "meeting appropriate, underwriting standards" these loans were perfectly safe, and they "facilitated the national policy of making home-ownership more broadly available."[63] Greenspan did think that fraud and egregious abuse of consumers deserved government attention, but that it should come in the form of prosecution, rather than prudential supervision – but even that only went so far. From 2000 all the way to the end of Greenspan's tenure as Federal Reserve chairman in 2006, the Federal Reserve only referred three mortgage lenders to the U.S. Department of Justice on account of discriminatory lending violations.

One reason the Federal Reserve refused to act was due to its obsession with not reacting to anecdote. If it cannot be empirically shown to be a broad-based problem, then the Federal Reserve will not act, noted Federal Reserve advisor and law professor Patricia McCoy.[64] No matter how many stories were reported about predatory practices, the steering of subprime loans to even prime borrowers, or to the outright rejection of any underwriting whatsoever, the Federal Reserve governors would not use their authority to police this dangerous market behavior among the mortgage industry.

Attempts by state banking supervisors proved no more fruitful. A number of state financial regulators did indeed try to curb predatory mortgage practices, particularly when it came to the amount of fees that a lender could charge to a borrower when making a mortgage loan and the ability to continuously refinance one's home mortgage debt. It did not take long, however, for the federal government to step in and thwart these efforts. Before long, the Comptroller of the Currency (in 2004) and the Office of Thrift Supervision (in 1996) asserted that thrifts and banks established under federal law were exempted from complying with state-level laws of this kind. This preemption approach greatly crippled the ability of well-intentioned state regulators to make a dent in the subprime mortgage problem. The federal regulators argued that without a single set of rules, lenders could not operate effectively on a cross-country basis.

While government attempts (feeble and halfhearted as they may have been) failed again and again, the subprime market roared onward.[65] Subprime loan originations continued to grow into the early 2000s. In 1999 subprime loans made up three of every four first lien home mortgages, with more than 80 percent of those being used to refinance existing debt, rather than for new purchases.[66] More than half of these were piggy bank refinancings as homeowners continued to chip away at their ever-dwindling home equity. In 2006, nearly 24 percent of all mortgage loan originations were subprime.[67] By March 2007, the value of subprime mortgage loans was pegged at $1.3 trillion and comprised one-fifth of all home loan financing in the United States.[68]

THE BIRTH AND GROWTH OF THE SECURITIZATION MACHINE

Because so many of these subprime loans were likely to go bad, one may wonder why lenders engaged in these transactions. Surely, even with the collection of fees and commissions from originations and refinancings, the overall effect of these transactions eventually failing should have been a deterrent. That would have been true, except for the rise of securitization. In the olden days a lender was a one-stop shop. It would not only take the borrower's application, review it for underwriting purposes, and advance the funds, but it would also collect the monthly payments from the borrower over the course of the loan, answer any borrower questions as they arose, and would either facilitate the retirement of the debt when the borrower paid off the loan or else deal with the borrower if there was a default (through, for instance, foreclosure proceedings). During this period (generally in the 1980s and the early 1990s) lenders would use old-fashioned indicators to decide the creditworthiness of an individual. Sometimes these factors were known as "the four Cs" – which stood for credit, capital, capacity, and collateral.[69] The lender would look to how the borrower handled his or her existing debt obligations and what amount those obligations totaled. The borrower's stated income and the stability of that income would also play a part, in addition to the amount of savings and other liquid funds the individual had at his or her disposal. And last, but certainly not least, the value and condition of any real property that the borrower might offer to secure the loan. The decision on whether to lend funds and in what amounts was made carefully on a case-by-case, borrower-by-borrower basis. All that changed with the advent of securitization, or as it is sometimes (ironically) known: structured finance.

The securitization process involved a labyrinthine scheme of buying, selling, swapping, and insuring intricate legal instruments that comprised a host of mortgage and credit rights through various nominees of the true parties. This system started with the lending institution that initially made the loan to the borrower: This could be either a banking institution or a nonbank mortgage lender or broker, which is a person who merely arranges the loan. In either case, this party is called the *mortgage originator*. The originator would, nominally at least, review the credit history, employment status, and other financial indicators of the borrower and assess whether the prospective borrower had the ability to repay the loan. It was at this stage of the transaction that subprime borrowers – those who, by all accounts, could not repay the loan – were nevertheless approved for subprime credit (loans with high fees, deceptive terms, and surprise interest rates). The borrower would receive the purchase funds in the form of loan proceeds and would contemporaneously sign a promissory note and a mortgage on the property.

The next step is where things diverged from the traditional model. Although the securitization structure can vary, depending on the type of entity handling the process, the overall framework is fairly the same.[70] Almost immediately after making the loan, the mortgage originator would sell the mortgage and the note to a third party called a *sponsor* or *arranger*. These sponsors would purchase hundreds and thousands of mortgage notes from various mortgage originators from across the country. The sponsor would then transfer the loans to a subsidiary company (called a *depositor*) that had no other assets or liabilities. By making the transfer in this way, the loans were removed from the balance sheet of the sponsor. Next, the depositor would sell or otherwise transfer the loans to a special purpose entity (like a trust). Finally, the trust would then create a form of security (like stock or a bond) called a *mortgage-backed security* (MBS) that was backed by the pool of mortgage loans. These securities could then be bought, sold, or traded on the open market to third-party investors. Sometimes the depositor would receive the securities in payment for transferring the loans to the trust, and then the depositor would sell the securities to investors. But other times the trust would sell the securities directly to investors. Often an underwriter was involved who could go out into the market and attract investors.

These securities/MBSs, often called *pass-through certificates*, entitled their holders to the monthly payments made by the homeowners. In this way, the payments were "passed through" to the MBS-holders. While it is the trust (or, rather, the trustee) that owns the mortgage loans, the investors have a beneficial interest because it is to them that the payments flow. From this point, although nothing had changed in terms of the borrower's position, the mortgage payments no longer were directed at the originator. Rather, the third-party investors who purchased interests in the securitized pool of mortgages rely upon yet another third party – the mortgage-servicing agent, the middleman – to handle the monthly collection of note payments and to otherwise deal directly with the borrower. The fragmentation is really quite astounding. Many hundreds of individuals can have some (even if only minimal) interest in the payment stream from a single mortgage loan, yet the homeowner will have practically no connection to them.[71] Indeed, the homeowner almost never has

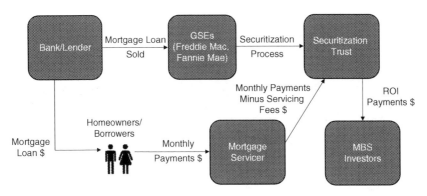

FIGURE 1 Residential mortgage securitization

the ability to interact with the trustee who manages the special purpose entity that holds the mortgage loan. Rather, the mortgage middleman – the servicer – is the sole point of contact between the homeowner and the various investors that practically own the loan. Figure 1 displays the structure.

Where did these third-party investors come from, one might ask? The answer is everywhere. Domestically, there were a host of cash-heavy firms that were ready and willing to put their money into a long-term investment – and what could be a better investment than the strong and ever-growing American residential housing market? Foreign investors were also quick to the table. Oil-producing countries and fast-growing Asian economies quickly began purchasing MBSs. Also, interest rates were incredibly low during this period, which both made access to credit cheap and had many firms seeking higher yields. Subprime loans came to represent a growing portion of mortgage securitizations. In 1994, only about 4.5 percent of all mortgage securitizations (about $35 billion) were comprised of subprime loans. That number went up to 9 percent in 2003 (a tenfold jump to $332 billion), and they reached 21 percent in 2005.[72]

Naturally, the mortgage lender's ability to offload its risk to third parties almost immediately on making the risky loan removed a major protection for borrowers.[73] Under historical lending practices, the bank assumed the risk that a default might occur if the borrower was unable to pay. Due to this risk, lenders were very concerned about the creditworthiness of their borrowers because a failure to adequately assess a borrower's financial position or advancing credit under dangerous terms could result in a direct hit to the lender. But securitization allowed mortgage lenders to be relieved of that worry.[74]

Once it arrived on the scene, securitization took off with a vengeance. In 1990 U.S. debt hovered around $13.8 trillion with only 11 percent of that amount consisting of securitized mortgage debt. That number would eventually jump to 18 percent of all U.S. debt (an amount even greater than U.S. Treasury bonds). The 1990s saw a rapid expansion of the securitization of debt (mostly subprime) with Wall Street giants like Merrill Lynch and Salomon Brothers (called the *private-label market*[75]) churning out new securities for hungry banks and other financial institution investors.[76] Fannie Mae and Freddie Mac (and Ginnie Mae[77]) were involved heavily in securitizations, although only the securitization of "conforming" mortgage loans that had stricter underwriting criteria. The guarantee provided by Ginnie Mae for mortgage-backed securities is backed by the full faith and credit of the federal government (meaning the federal government will make sure that payment is made to someone invested in a security that is backed by Ginnie Mae). Fannie and Freddie don't technically have a government-backed guarantee, but they do promise timely payment to their investors. But because Fannie and Freddie were, at one time, government-owned corporations like Ginnie, a general feeling long persisted among investors and the broader marketplace that the government implicitly guarantees GSE securities.

While securitization is a big part of the activities of the GSEs and Ginnie Mae, what really caused the hurt were subprime securitized loans. It is certainly safe to say that subprime mortgage loan originations and the securitization process were intertwined. Subprime mortgage loan originations jumped from $70 billion in 1996 up to $100 billion in 2000. Of that amount, at the end of the 1990s about 56 percent of all subprime loans were securitized. By 2009, the year after the crisis, roughly 90 percent of all first-lien residential mortgage loans in the United States were securitized.[78]

The goal of securitization was, in part, to create and then tune financial products to the risk tolerance of the investor. Risk-averse investors might purchase mortgage-backed securities issued by Fannie or Freddie because their loans were conforming and therefore met certain creditworthiness requirements. More risk-loving investors (such as those seeking higher yield) would prefer securitizations issued by Wall Street (the private-label securitizations) that consisted of many subprime loans. The two government-sponsored entities (Fannie and Freddie) maintained a stronghold when it came to prime loan securitization, but in the year leading up to the crash the private-label market was securitizing one-third more loans than what were being securitized by Fannie and Freddie and 71 percent of those loans were subprime.[79] Fannie and Freddie's market share continued to diminish and that of the private-label market only grew. In 2003, the nationwide share of mortgages purchased by Fannie and Freddie was about 57 percent, but that number dropped to 37 percent in 2006. The private-label market hungered for new mortgage loans. Countrywide Financial was the biggest and most successful originator of mortgages leading up to the crash, declaring a goal of capturing 30 percent of the market for mortgage originations. Other lenders such as Ameriquest, Washington Mutual, and many others started mass marketing an ever-growing number of risky and dangerous loan products to customers. As one commentator to the Financial Crisis Inquiry

Commission noted: "The definition of a good loan changed from 'one that pays' to 'one that could be sold.'"[80]

The complexity of securitization can hardly be understated – take for instance the following private-label securitization example described in the Financial Crisis Inquiry Commission's report.[81] In 2006, a subprime lender named New Century Financial made roughly 4,500 subprime mortgage loans and then sold them to Citigroup. Citigroup then created a separate entity that collected investments from various third parties and, using those funds, "purchased" the loans from Citigroup. The purpose of putting these loans into the new entity was to remove them from the books of Citigroup and thereby insulate the investors from any financial trouble that Citigroup might later face. The separate Citigroup entity then issued securities that entitled their holders to the payments that were made by the borrowers of the 4,500 subprime loans. However, these securities were not all of the same type but rather were divided into different sets called *tranches* (19 in total). Which tranche an investor had dictated when that investor would get paid and at what interest rate they could expect as a return on its investment. At the top of the priority ladder were the senior tranches of mortgage-backed securities, which entitled their holders to being paid first from the flow of monthly payments coming from the invisible homeowners. Right after the senior securities were the 11 middle or "mezzanine" tranches. The holders of these securities would only get paid after the senior debt holders, but the benefit was that the interest rate paid on these securities was higher than those at the senior level. Finally, the lowest of the tranches was known as the "equity" or junior level. These holders were paid from whatever money was left after the senior and mezzanine tranches were paid. If there were any defaults on the loans in the pool backing the securities, the holders of the junior tranched MBSs would take the hit. Of course, in return for this risk these investors were entitled to the highest rate of return. Sometimes the MBS tranches were not set up to have all payments flow through the payment waterfall equally. Rather, sometimes a certain series of investors would have a senior claim to the principal payments, or the interest payments, or even any penalties before another group of investors.[82] The slicing and dicing was practically limitless.

In this particular securitization transaction, Citigroup, as well as a number of hedge funds, were the investors of about half of the entire junior tranche (thereby taking on the most risk and also the potential for the most reward in the deal).

It was quite common for the financial institution that was sponsoring the securitization to, like Citigroup did as previously mentioned, retain a large portion of the equity tranche for themselves. The reason for keeping these was not just to have them, but rather to create yet another securitization. The new product that resulted was called a *collateralized debt obligation* (or a CDO). Essentially, a bank like Citigroup would take all of its equity-tranched MBSs and put them into a new pool and then issue securities (CDOs) backed by (that's right) the MBSs. The CDOs would then be put into tranches just like in the original preceding example so that some were senior to others.

To help investors gauge the level of risk they were undertaking when they purchased nonconforming mortgage-backed securities, national ratings agencies like Moody's and Standard & Poor's began scoring these investment instruments. Because most investors, even sophisticated ones, lacked the ability or will to unravel these complex products to understand the quality (or lack thereof) of the mortgage loans in the pool, the opinion of ratings agencies became more important. Using the previously mentioned Citigroup transaction, the agency Standard & Poor's scored securities as AAA if they were the safest and least risky investments, AA for those that were a bit less safe, followed by A, BBB, and BB (with accompanying pluses and minuses added thereto) down the line. A product that was rated below BBB- was considered to have a junk rating and thereby quite risky. Moody's used a similar system. The ratings agencies gave the senior tranches in the Citigroup deal a rating of AAA. Of the 11 mezzanine tranches, three were given a score of AA, three were given only an A, three more were rated BBB, and the remaining two were accorded junk status. The final junior/equity tranches were, in fact, viewed so poorly that they were not rated at all.

In some transactions, however, even the junk bonds could be polished up for investors to feel better about (or be tricked into) buying. This typically happened through the purchase of bond insurance. Surely, it was common for even the holders of senior tranche MBSs to purchase bond insurance that would guarantee their payment. But purchase by the equity tranche folks was also quite common. MBSs that were backed by subprime, hybrid-adjustable interest rates would nonetheless be given AAA ratings by the credit agencies due to the fact that a credit enhancement like bond insurance was attached to the asset. This proved to be a particularly useful tool for pension and insurance funds who were restricted in the types of assets they could purchase to only those with fairly high ratings scores. These credit enhancement tools allowed for what would otherwise be junk bonds to be magically transformed into highly rated investments. Indeed, pension funds in Norway were among the large number of institutions that collapsed as a result of investing in the subprime market.[83]

These ratings agencies would also rate the CDOs. The senior tranche of the CDOs would shockingly receive an AAA rating because the top tranche would be entitled to payment first. Now, of course it is clear from being able to see the entire transaction that these top tranche CDOs could not possibly be that safe because they (all of them) were the riskiest part of the original securitization. Indeed, in the end they all failed. Such was the game played by the ratings agencies – assigning scores to products that they either did not understand (at best) or purposefully misrepresented (at worst). By the time the crisis hit, deference to the scores of ratings agencies became the primary means by which investors and the money managers decided whether and which mortgage-backed securities or CDOs to purchase.

If that was not complex enough, there is just a bit more financial engineering that needs to be added to this mix. Many investors who purchased these creative financial products wanted some insurance to hedge against the possibility that the assets would fail to perform. In other words, if the various homeowners – whose monthly mortgage loan payments provided the stream of cash used to pay the holders of the MBSs and the CDOs – ended up defaulting, then the investors would be hit. To guard against this, investors would purchase yet another product called a *credit default swap* – which is a form of derivative contract because it is derived with reference to another asset. Insurance companies and special derivative companies were in the business of selling these products – one of the biggest and most notorious was the giant American Insurance Group, or AIG.

Last, but certainly not least (and probably the most divorced from the idea of value conjured up in the heads of most hard-working Americans), was the synthetic CDO. This financial product was basically nothing more than a gambling contract. It allowed financial institutions to make bets on how a certain CDO or series of CDOs would perform – but there was no requirement that the betting party have an interest in the CDO. In essence, the entity could make a bet (using a synthetic CDO) on how someone else's product (a real CDO) would perform. What resulted from all of this was that speculative investment started to outsize investment in real assets (the securities that were backed by mortgages). Instead, a whole sector of the financial economy was comprised of money spent on bets – like (as the former FDIC chair Sheila Bair called it) an enormous fantasy football game.[84]

With the ability to sell a loan immediately after making it, the most fundamental borrower protection that was originally built into the system of lending (self-interest), was completely eviscerated. A bank need not worry about the quality of the borrower because a subsequent default would be someone else's problem.[85] This was especially true because in the early years of hybrid adjustable rate subprime loans the borrower was indeed able to make the monthly payments. It would not be until about two to three years into the loan, when the originating lender had long since sold the loan to a third party, that the rate would reset and cause the loan to become too expensive for the borrower to manage. In the run-up to 2007 and 2008, the hunger of the financial sector for subprime mortgage-backed securities was insatiable, and securitization seemed to provide an endless source of new investment products for Wall Street investors to gobble up.

2

The Crisis Hits

This defective mortgage finance system, underpinned by deception and buttressed by artificially inflated home prices, finally came crashing down beginning in 2006 when the bubble burst and home prices sunk.[1] In spring 2006, shortly after home prices hit historical highs, the rate of sales began to slow, and the number of months needed to sell a home reached a ten-year high.[2] At the time, Ben Bernanke, the chairperson of the Board of Governors of the Federal Reserve System, opined that a housing market correction would be beneficial, provided it did not impact the rest of the economy. His predictions were shortly proven wrong. In October 2006, a chief economist at Moody's warned that:

> With over 100 metro areas representing nearly one-half of the nation's housing stock experiencing or about to experience price declines, national house prices are also set to decline. Indeed, odds are high that national house prices will decline in 2007.[3]

By the time September of 2008 rolled around, home prices fell 20 percent from their mid-2006 peak.[4] This decline in value resulted in many homeowners finding themselves "underwater" – a term used to describe a situation in which the amount due on a loan secured by a mortgage on real estate was more than what the real estate was valued. By March 2008 almost nine million American homeowners (which amounted to almost 11 percent of all homeowners nationwide) were underwater, and by September 2010 that number had risen to 23 percent.[5]

As property values decreased, subprime borrowers, who up until now believed they could refinance their debt before the adjustable interest rates reset, found themselves unable to do so.[6] Because they could not continue to enjoy their relatively low monthly payments, and because they could not sustain these now adjusted and much higher payment obligations, many homeowners defaulted en masse.[7] Indeed, the ripple of early payment mortgage defaults (typically meaning that the borrower is 60 days or more behind in his or her payments during the first year of the loan) across the country was one of the first indications that the storm had arrived.[8] By the summer of 2006, 1.5 percent of loans made within the prior 365 days were in default. That number went up to 2.5 percent in 2007.

Moreover, mortgage loans that were in default for 90 days or more or those that were in foreclosure (sometimes called *serious delinquencies*) reached nearly 10 percent by the end of 2009. The areas of the United States with the highest housing prices experienced the highest rates of default. Serious delinquencies in states like Arizona, California, Florida, and Nevada reached 15 percent by the end of 2009. The type of loan also dictated the seriousness of the default. In 2007 the default rate for subprime mortgage loans with adjustable rates rose to 20 percent and then up to 40 percent in 2009. In mid-2006, 2.75 percent of all subprime securitized mortgage loans were in default within a mere six months of having been issued. Although to a lesser extent, prime loans with fixed-interest rates (considered by many to the safest) also began to see an uptick in rates of delinquency.

To make things worse, by the time the crisis hit, most Americans had very little savings to help them ride out the hard years ahead. In 2000 household debt was pegged at $7.4 million and rose rapidly to $14.5 trillion by the time the crisis hit in 2008 (representing about 134 percent of most American's personal disposable income).[9]

In turn, banks – through their agents, the mortgage servicers – began to foreclose on these defaulted properties across the United States in massive numbers. However, because these properties were underwater, foreclosure sales failed to bring in an amount sufficient for the banks to recover their losses.[10] As a result, lenders were forced to purchase the mortgaged property themselves (called *real-estate owned*, or REO), which thereby created a situation in which lending institutions became the owners of a massive number of foreclosed properties – a role for which they were entirely unfit and unprepared.

ECONOMIC CONTAGION AND THE HOUSING CRASH

Because many borrowers were no longer making loan payments, the market for and the value of many mortgage-backed securities that were now in the hands of various financial institutions, pension funds, and other investors came crashing down. One major goal of securitization (or so it was said) was to spread risk efficiently across the market. This proved, in some way, to be all too true. At the time of the crash, toxic MBSs were mostly held by major financial institutions, the health of which was intimately tied to that of the national and global economy.[11] Major financial institutions not only in the United States but also across the globe had invested heavily in the MBS market. As mortgage defaults spread like wildfire, these firms began reporting massive losses. And because these financial institutions were deeply intertwined with parts of the economy, the meltdown reached far beyond just the housing market. Essentially, these mortgage-backed securities that had come to permeate the entire U.S. economy and reach into every sector became almost valueless. As one noted commentator stated, this set off "a disastrous chain of events affecting the secondary mortgage markets, the broader financial sector, and the entire United States – and global – economy.'"[12]

The middle of 2007 saw an almost complete stop to all new mortgage securitizations. Already down from previous periods, in the second quarter of 2007 about $75 billion in subprime residential mortgage securitizations were issued.[13] That number dropped to a mere $27 billion in the following quarter and again down to $12 billion in the fourth quarter of that year. In 2008, the number of new securitizations went to $4 billion and then they dropped to almost zero. Former powerhouses like IndyMac saw a 21 percent drop in loan originations due to the fact that it stopped making subprime loans and Washington Mutual (which was the largest savings bank in the country at the time) stopped all subprime lending.[14]

Casualties were inevitable. First, the global investment bank Bear Stearns began to fail: The firm had become heavily involved with subprime mortgage securitizations. As the crisis hit, the bank started experiencing major losses. In spring 2008, the Federal Reserve Bank of New York tried to stop the panic by making a $25 billion loan to the firm to help it avoid going under. That effort, however, proved unsuccessful because its losses were too great even to be reversed by a capital infusion of that magnitude. In March 2008, Bear Stearns was acquired by JPMorgan Chase – with major assistance from the Federal Reserve – for a mere $10 per share (against a high of $172 per share in January of the prior year).[15] Commercial banks and thrifts that held toxic assets on their books started to see downgrades by banking supervisors. Institutions like Citigroup, Washington Mutual, and Wachovia went on a hunt to raise new capital to ward off disaster – with little success. Unfortunately, downgrades, oversight, and enforcement actions came too late.

The GSE giants Fannie and Freddie were next. As the crisis unfolded the housing finance market started to crumble. Home values were taking a major hit, homeowners were defaulting, and MBSs were turning into worthless pieces of paper. One of the major problems with the GSEs was that they had almost no capital cushion (in other words, no money in their savings accounts) to rely upon. Instead, Fannie and Freddie – unable to securitize subprime loans themselves – had acquired massive amounts of toxic mortgage–backed securities from the private-label market.[16] These toxic assets were causing the company to report billions of dollars in losses toward the middle of 2007. In fact, in 2005 Fannie and Freddie had together purchased one-third of all the outstanding mortgage-backed securities in the United States.[17]

The Treasury Secretary at the time, Henry Paulson, believed strongly that the housing market would only survive if Fannie and Freddie did as well – specifically by purchasing toxic mortgage–backed securities from various financial institutions whose balance sheets were crippled by these assets. The GSEs' federal housing regulator began loosening its restrictions on what Fannie and Freddie could purchase, thereby giving them the leeway to take on many of the failing assets out in the marketplace. This, of course, caused both Fannie and Freddie to become even more financially unhealthy as their own balance sheets filled with worthless, subprime mortgage-backed securities. In the winter of 2007 both entities reported losses in the billions. Then, in December of that year, Fannie Mae stated that "it had $44 billion in capital to absorb potential losses on $879 billion in assets and $2.2 trillion of guarantees on mortgage-backed securities."[18] It concluded that if the company's losses went higher than 1.45 percent "it would be insolvent."[19]

After further losses and major liquidity concerns, in October 2008 Congress passed the Housing and Economic Recovery Act (HERA). HERA put the GSEs into conservatorship, placing them under the control of a new oversight agency created within HUD – the Federal Housing Finance Agency (FHFA). Further, the Department of the Treasury was authorized to spend up to $100 billion dollars in taxpayer money to purchase an ownership stake (i.e., equity) in Fannie Mae and Freddie Mac, as well as to also purchase toxic mortgage–backed securities from the GSEs so that the two entities could remove these nonperforming assets from their books. Without the bailout, both entities would have gone under. The GSEs had engaged in a number of dangerous practices in their efforts to increase market share and in their purchase of toxic MBSs, which further crippled these already troubled institutions. To this day, Fannie Mae and Freddie Mac remain under the conservatorship of the FHFA and are subject to mandatory fund sweeps, meaning that all their net earnings are handed over to the U.S. Treasury – making Fannie and Freddie so weak that they cannot even withstand a slight economic fluctuation, much less another crisis.

Next on the chopping block came Lehman Brothers. The investment bank was nearly 150 years old and had a storied history on Wall Street. It was also one of the first entities of its kind to become aggressively involved in mortgage securitization. Prior to the crash, Lehman reported assets of significant value, but most Wall Street and banking regulators knew that these assets were overvalued by as much as $60 to $70 billion according to the former president of Bank of America.[20] In June 2008, for the first time since it became a publicly traded company in the mid-1990s, Lehman Brothers reported a $2.8 billion quarterly loss – its stock price dropped to $30 in response. Later that fall, a $3.9 billion loss in the third quarter would be announced. But this time the federal government decided that it would not spend a penny. In other words, there would be no bailout for Lehman Brothers.[21] Treasury Secretary Henry Paulson and others in the federal government believed that it would be politically impossible for the government to bailout the financial giant when so many homeowners were still hurting. With no other options and no American (or foreign) banks willing to step in as a white horse, on September 15, 2008, the company filed for bankruptcy. It was and remains the largest bankruptcy in the history of the United States. This titan of Wall Street had fallen, and all due to its risky trading, overleveraged position, and the lack of adequate government oversight into its investments. Unlike Bear Stearns (which was quite a relatively small operation that lived at the periphery of Wall Street) and the GSEs, however, the government decided not to bail out Lehman Brothers.

Next, came the collapse and subsequent rescue of AIG. As noted in the preceding text, AIG was heavily involved in the credit default swap (CDS) market. So, when the tsunami of MBS defaults started to occur AIG found itself owing astronomical premiums dictated by the unfavorable terms it had granted to its CDS counterparties. It stood to lose everything. By September 2008, AIG had already been called upon to pay $7.6 billion to Goldman Sachs. AIG also faced downgrades by the credit rating agencies, which would in turn trigger further payment obligations. However, even at this point the negligence of federal regulators was still on high display. AIG's federal supervisor, the Office of Thrift Supervision, noted in August 2008 that it was "generally comfortable with [the] firm's liquidity" position.[22] As more homeowners went into default, more mortgage-backed securities failed and that triggered more payment calls to AIG by various credit default swap counter parties. AIG was hemorrhaging money, and fast.

A major problem in the minds of federal officials was that almost every bank and financial institution in the country had some form of exposure to AIG. Unlike with Lehman Brothers, the failure of the company would have wrecked the entire American economy. To prevent this, the Federal Reserve and the Treasury together plowed $182 billion into AIG to keep it afloat, and in exchange the federal government took a controlling stake in the failing company.

Last, but not least, came a major infusion of public funds into the major investment bank Citigroup, which had massive exposure to failing collateralized debt obligation instruments. In the third quarter of 2008, the company announced a $2.8 billion loss (mostly due to losses on subprime MBSs), followed by a 17 percent drop in stock value.[23] By November, Citigroup traded for a mere $3.77. The FDIC worried that the failure of Citigroup would undermine the American financial system, both for businesses and households. By winter 2008 the entity was insolvent and in need of capital – again the federal government came to the rescue. The bailout package included $25 billion from the Troubled Asset Relief Program (TARP), almost $69 billion in debt issuance from the FDIC, and $88 billion in liquidity support from the Federal Reserve.[24] In turn, the federal government took shares in the company requiring an 8 percent dividend payment.[25]

Other disasters and failures followed. Bank of America bought (for far too much money[26]) the failing Merrill Lynch around the time of the AIG bailout. In June 2008, the subprime mortgage giant Washington Mutual (the sixth-largest bank in the United States at the time) experienced a nine-day bank run (losing more than $16 billion in deposits), went into receivership with the FDIC, and its parent company subsequently filed for bankruptcy. It became the largest insured-bank failure in American history, and Washington Mutual was thereafter purchased by JPMorgan Chase for $1.9 billion. The major bank holding company Wachovia (which had previously purchased the notorious "Pick-a-Pay" mortgage lender Golden West) also experienced a major liquidity problem as more funders pulled out. It was eventually forced by the government into a sale to Wells Fargo in December 2008 to avoid a collapse. Other firms lived on, but only with substantial capital infusions. Morgan Stanley only survived with a $9 billion investment from Mitsubishi Bank in Japan, and Goldman Sachs had to rely upon a $5 billion investment by Warren Buffett to calm market fears about its future.

JOB LOSSES, WEALTH DEPLETION, AND ECONOMIC DISASTER

These bailouts and various government interventions are mentioned not because they are particularly important to understanding the facts on the ground for homeowners facing foreclosure or for understanding the way mortgage middlemen played into that process. Rather, they are described to show what great lengths the federal government went to ensure the survival (and some might say comfort) of the financial services industry – of Wall Street. Nor did the firms seem to acknowledge the massive role they played in the crisis or how fortunate they were for the corporate welfare doled out by the federal government. On the contrary, now that it had been saved from the brink of ruin by the American taxpayer, in spring 2009 AIG announced that it was paying $165 million in bonuses to its executive management. Yet even in the face of these events, government leaders did little for everyday Americans facing the loss of their home.[27]

The fall of the financial giants and the drying up of credit for large and small businesses each had major effects for the economy and its workforce. An untold number of individuals lost their jobs and, although previously financially capable of making their monthly mortgage payments, defaulted on their home loans. This resulted in yet more foreclosures and more bank-owned properties. By one estimate, these otherwise prime borrowers comprised 60 percent of all mortgage defaults in 2006 alone.[28] Nearly $17 trillion in household wealth vanished in a mere 21 months and by October 2009 the unemployment rate hit 10 percent. Wealth in the form of retirement accounts also took massive hits. In 2008, the S&P 500 (the United States' major stock market index tied to 500 of the country's largest, publicly traded companies) dropped by a third – a fall this dramatic had not occurred since 1974. Between 2007 and 2008, Americans' 401(k) accounts lost a third of their value, signifying a $2.8 trillion loss.[29]

The hit to the economy hurt, but it hurt some more than others. In the period between 2007 and 2010, the average white American family saw an 11 percent drop in their household wealth,[30] but it was even worse for communities of color. During that same period black families saw their household wealth decline by 31 percent and Hispanic families saw a stunning 44 percent drop.[31]

And even the fortunate individuals who were able to avoid a loan default and foreclosure often became anchored to their mortgage loans because they were unable to sell their homes. The cheap and easy credit of the precrash period disappeared quickly. Financial institutions immediately stopped making loans – not just mortgage loans but also business loans. This caused further layoffs and downsizing as American industry was no longer able to access credit markets for working capital purposes. The ripple effects of the mortgage crisis were thus felt in parts of the economy unrelated to housing.[32] In 2008, the American economy saw the loss of 3.6 million jobs and by the end of 2009 a further 4.7 million jobs disappeared. Needless to say, there were no more new homes being built. The once bustling construction industry had ground to a halt.

As more homes went into foreclosure or were abandoned by distressed homeowners, property values sunk even further (although unfortunately for America's tenants, rents remained high).[33] Whole neighborhoods across the country – particularly in the sand states[34] – became ghost towns. In cities such as Detroit, Baltimore, Philadelphia, Cleveland, Cincinnati, and Buffalo, local government officials ordered whole residential blocks of abandoned homes bulldozed.[35] Those who remained in their homes found their communities slowly becoming blighted – havens for crime and public health hazards.[36] With lower property, sales, and income taxes to fund government, state and local governments saw their school systems buckling, state budgets diminished, and everything from basic to essential services cut.

FORECLOSURES AND THE NUMBERS

The number of homes lost in the crisis was unprecedented by orders of magnitude. Between 2006 and 2014, more than 9.3 million Americans either lost their homes to foreclosure or else gave up their homes to the bank outright.[37] Typically foreclosures hovered nationally at less than 1 percent, but in 2009 – shortly after the crash – it had climbed to 2.2 percent. Certain states saw more foreclosures than others. For instance, Nevada's foreclosure rate in 2010 was five times higher than the average in the nation.[38] The number of underwater homes was similarly staggering. This state of affairs, called *negative equity*, hit hardest in places like Arizona, California, Florida, Michigan, and Nevada, where the housing market had been hottest. The increase in the volume of foreclosures was also shocking. In 2008 the national number of homes undergoing foreclosure was 2.3 million, an increase of 81 percent from 2007 and 225 percent from 2006.[39] "One in every fifty-four homes had received a foreclosure filing."[40]

Having spent literally billions of dollars to save the same financial giants that had caused the crisis, the federal government attempted to help people stay in their homes, but their efforts proved both belated and ineffective. One of the ideas behind the TARP funds was to use some of the money not to merely bail out banks but to help individuals stay in their homes through loan modifications.[41] However, instead of using the funds in this way (as many in Congress had intended) the Treasury (now in between the outgoing Bush and the incoming Obama administrations) took the approach of making capital contributions to banks in exchange for their agreement to modify the loans of their distressed borrowers. Unfortunately, the government never attempted to find a way to make sure the banks lived up to their side of the bargain. Of the $700 billion in TARP funds appropriated by Congress, only $28 million was used to directly help distressed homeowners get loan modifications.[42]

The Home Affordable Mortgage Program (HAMP) is perhaps the most famous failure of the Obama administration's efforts to directly help homeowners. Passed in February 2009, this overly complex and cumbersome program, along with ancillary initiatives, was geared toward helping individuals stay in their homes through loan modifications when the loans had become too expensive or when home equity had gone into the negative. Hardly any borrowers were able to benefit from the program, mostly because it required homeowners to produce overly burdensome documentation as to their financial situation. As one commentator put it, it was like the program essentially required a borrower, with a mortgage that they already could not afford and with seriously distressed finances in the wake of crisis, to qualify for a whole new loan.[43] What was worse is that the program allowed some borrowers, prior to getting final approval for a modification, to go through a trial phase where they would receive a preliminary modification. These borrowers would then proceed to pay – timely and in full – the new monthly loan amount, only to then not be able to meet the stringent documentation requirements for final approval, and ultimately still wind up in foreclosure. It was not just a few applicants that were unable to produce the necessary paperwork. About 70 percent of all homeowners who applied for the HAMP program were denied.[44]

So how many homeowners did HAMP help? The Obama administration predicted that the program would help four million Americans keep their homes. "It will give millions of families resigned to financial ruin a chance to rebuild," President Obama declared at the program's launch event in Phoenix, Arizona.[45] "By bringing down the foreclosure rate, it will help shore up housing prices for everyone." By the time the program ended in December 2016, only 1.6 million homeowners saw their mortgage loans modified to something they could afford. Of that amount, one-third eventually defaulted again. Then again, with such a complex program and with so little money allocated to it, what could one expect?

In the end, the housing crisis wrecked the lives of countless individuals. It destroyed household wealth, caused working families to lose their jobs, destroyed the fabric of a number of cities and communities, and resulted in the loss of the homes of as many as ten million Americans. But when it came to helping these individuals – these everyday people and their families struggling to make ends meet, facing the loss of their homes, those whose lives were entirely divorced from the mahogany conference tables and steel and glass buildings of Wall Street and D.C., where billions of dollars are passed from hand to hand with the stroke of a pen – little was done. These people would have to make do and try to pick up the pieces themselves – no bailouts for the American homeowner.

3

At Your (Mortgage) Service

When it comes to the housing crisis, there was more than enough blame to go around: The creation of this massive financial collapse had many participants. It takes a village[1] to take down an entire economy. But, when it came to the actual plight of homeowners in distress – those facing the loss of their homes – there were few groups as front and center as mortgage servicers.

HOW SERVICERS WORK AND WHAT THEY DO

When one thinks of homeownership, what comes to mind is generally the beginning and the end of the process – getting the loan and buying the home, and then paying off the loan or (in some cases) losing the home in foreclosure. Indeed, that's where most of the law and policy action takes places as well: how to make homeownership more affordable, protect homeowners against discrimination in obtaining the loan, and provide efficient processes for creditors when a foreclosure becomes necessary. But in fact, there's an incredible amount of importance when it comes to the often-neglected in-between period – the process of managing the loan.

Mortgage servicers traditionally played a rather mundane role in the housing finance relationship, albeit an important one. In fact, back in the old days when banks kept the loans they made on their own books, the bank likely served as its own servicer – keeping track of payments and handling borrower issues.[2] The first major separation of loan funding from loan servicing occurred in the early 1990s as a result of the savings and loan crisis.[3] During this period, a little more than 1,043 of the total of rough 3,234 savings and loan associations failed in the United States (about 32 percent).[4] As a result, the government-created the Resolution Trust Corporation (RTC) which took over and sold off the assets of these failed institutions to investors and other financial institutions. Rather than just selling the loans of the troubled companies, the RTC also separately sold the right to service these mortgage loans – this became the first iteration of thinking of servicing rights as an asset that could be purchased.[5] Yet, it was truly securitization that drove the massive shift to third-party servicing. All securitized loans are serviced by these third-party mortgage middlemen, and as securitization exploded in the 1990s so did the servicing industry.

Recall the labyrinthine system of securitization described in prior chapters. The pool of mortgages was held in a special purpose trust and the securities (mortgage-backed securities, that is) issued in connection with this pool were sold to investors (pension funds, hedge funds, insurance companies, and, most prominently, Fannie Mae and Freddie Mac). However, it was the homeowners' monthly mortgage payments that served to pay the holders of the securities a return on their investment, and someone had to be responsible for collecting those monthly amounts. This became the job of the mortgage middlemen. The giant institutional investors of the MBSs were not equipped or interested in performing that task and neither were the trustees who technically owned the pool of mortgages. Instead, a special kind of firm known as a mortgage servicer handled that job.

The servicer accepts and processes the homeowner's monthly payments and then turns over a portion of the funds to the trustee of the pool of mortgages. The trustee is then responsible for passing along the payments to the holders of the mortgage-backed securities. The servicer also handles the escrowing of certain monies (like property taxes and insurance) and deals with any communications with the homeowners. Often, the servicer will disburse certain amounts related to the loan to third parties – such as paying the taxing authority for yearly property assessments, the homeowners association for its periodic dues, and the property insurance company its annual premium.

Sometimes there is more than one servicer for a given pool of mortgage loans. Driven by the fragmentation that securitization breeds, servicers can come in many varieties.[6] A primary servicer might be responsible for dealing with the borrower and collecting and distributing funds, while a master servicer might be employed to supervise one or more primary servicers. Then, if there is a failure on the part of either type of middleman, a backup servicer might be waiting in the wings. And finally, a default can result in a specialty servicer coming in to handle troubled loans. Thus, while one company may be the servicer of record, other firms (subservicers) are often engaged to perform various other duties.[7] Indeed, consumer advocates and attorneys note that servicers are increasingly farming out a number of functions – ranging from insurance, loss mitigation, and even mailing services – to third parties.

So, who are these mortgage middlemen?[8] Well, they come in many forms. Sometimes they are subsidiaries of banks, thrifts, credit unions, and nonbank financial institutions. Indeed, often the servicer will be an affiliate of the institution that originated some of the loans in the pool or sponsored the securitization.[9] Some of the names look familiar because they belong to the country's financial giants – like CitiMortgage, Wells Fargo, JPMorgan Chase, and Bank of America – while others seem more obscure to most Americans – like Carrington Mortgage, Nationstar Mortgage, Litton Loan Servicing, and Ocwen Loan Servicing.

From an aspiring homeowner's perspective, although he or she gets to pick the lender there is no choice when it comes to picking the servicer. This lack of choice ends up being significant because the lender who originates the loan may never communicate with the homeowner again. Indeed, that lender will not have any reason to because the loan will be sold and packaged shortly after being made and then turned into a mortgage-backed security that will be sold to some distant, faceless institutional investor. Who owns your loan? Many people is likely the answer because it has been pooled together with other loans and beneficial ownership has been splintered into numerous pieces and distributed to groups of investors.[10]

But ownership of the loan matters little because it is the servicer that the borrower is ultimately going to deal with – for everything from answering loan questions, making sure the escrow amounts are correct, handling interest rate modifications on adjustable rate loans, reporting to national credit bureaus, and (as discussed further in the following text) working to avoid foreclosure if something goes wrong. The homeowner, however, has no choice in who services his or her loan – whether it be a reputable and cooperative institution or one that is unresponsive or even malfeasant. Homeowners get what they get.

Mortgage servicers often specialize in dealing with certain types of loans.[11] For instance, some servicers have expertise in dealing with loans securitized by one of the GSEs or guaranteed by Ginnie Mae. Other middleman companies prefer to deal with private-label market securitizations. And lastly, some cross over and handle all or any number of these product types. And as noted previously, sometimes the job of servicer is divided between multiple middlemen, each with different rules for how they manage or service loans.

From a mechanics perspective, the mortgage servicer will enter into a very long and complex contract with the special purpose entity (the trust) that holds legal title to all the mortgage loans. This contract is called the "pooling and servicing agreement" or sometimes just the "servicing agreement" – and it is incredibly important.[12] All the servicer's duties and responsibilities are set forth in this contract with the trustee of the special purpose trust (and thus, indirectly, with the investors of the MBSs). One of the servicer's primary responsibilities is to achieve the greatest benefit possible for the holders of the MBSs.[13] For delinquent loans, much of this is achieved by the use of a special analysis (discussed further in the following text) called a *net present value calculation*.[14] If the investors feel they are not having their interests looked after, the pooling and servicing agreement typically allows the trustee (acting on behalf of the investors) to end the relationship – an event that almost never happens.[15] As one might surmise, the contract provides no obligation for these middlemen to look out for the interests of the homeowner.

WHEN A BORROWER DEFAULTS

When the homeowner is making his or her payments timely, the middleman does not cause much of a problem, but when a homeowner gets into financial trouble and becomes delinquent or is in default, things can (and often did during the financial crisis) go south quickly.[16] First, the servicer must contact the individual and try to work out a solution to the problem.[17] The servicer must also determine whether the home has been abandoned by the defaulting homeowner and therefore needs to be secured and protected from any damage or deterioration.

What is probably most striking is that despite the many lengthy terms and provisions found in a typical private-label securities pooling and servicing agreement, there are few actual instructions on how to deal with a borrower in the case of a loan default.[18] This became a huge problem in the wake of the financial crisis when mortgage defaults were going through the roof. No longer could a servicer rely upon the simple routine of processing payments. Now, homeowners needed real help and guidance as to whether they could stay in their homes and how their loans could be reworked.

Servicing employees, which were (and may still be) notoriously underpaid and undertrained, were not equipped at all to deal with this situation and the structure under which they operated was both faulty and corrupt.[19] Servicing employees held the power in their hands to decide whether a loan modification could be achieved or whether a foreclosure was necessary – and they had almost no guidance in how to make that determination.[20] Albeit with some limitations, it was almost entirely up to their discretion, but because of a fear of exercising too much discretion (and thereby violating their ill-defined duty to maximize the benefits to the investors), servicers were extremely hesitant to engage in any kind of innovative techniques to keep borrowers in their homes.

When a homeowner defaults the middleman has two choices – to help the borrower stay in his or her home through a process known as "loss mitigation" or to move to foreclose on the property (which the middleman industry obliquely calls "default management").[21] Foreclosure may seem like the quickest and easiest way to recover for an investor, but in reality, that's not quite true. It certainly allows the investor to put the borrower's personal ability to pay to the side and go directly after the value of the real estate subject to the mortgage, but that's only true in theory. In reality there is a great cost associated with initiating a foreclosure – so many costs that it might result in very little cash making its way to the investors. Some states allow for the lender to have the property seized and sold without having to deal with a judge or other public official (called a *nonjudicial foreclosure*). But even this system requires time and money in attorneys' fees, and the furnishing of adequate notice to the homeowner. Also, the property must be put to auction and typically the sale never brings in the exact fair market value of the property.[22] If the lender has to go to court to foreclose (because the process is taking place in a state that requires a judicial foreclosure), then the costs and delays can be even greater. Couple these factors with the declining value of many homes as millions of Americans went underwater on their mortgages after 2008, one can begin to see why moving directly to foreclosure would not necessarily be an obvious win for the investors. In fact, a 1995 study found that, on average, the total cost of a foreclosure (including legal fees and other property-related costs) was a little more than $7,000 per home.[23]

The other option is loss mitigation, which is a strategy that has been slow coming in the residential mortgage servicing world.[24] Loss mitigation generally comes in two types and both are aimed at (as the name would suggest) diminishing the amount of loss that the investors must absorb on the performance of the loan. First, there are what are known as "loan workouts," which are specifically about keeping the individual in the property and maintaining the relationship with the servicer going forward. The servicer may agree to a forbearance accompanied by a repayment plan. This is where the homeowner is allowed to temporarily pay a lower monthly amount but will then later pay a higher monthly amount to catch up with past missed payments (notably the total debt owed is not reduced, just delayed). Another process (and one that some in the federal government, like the FDIC, highly favored in the wake of the crisis) is a pure loan modification.[25] This is where the underlying economics of the loan are changed so that the period for payment is extended or the principal or the interest rate on the loan is reduced or written down (this typically results in the actual total debt being reduced).[26]

But if a loan workout is not in the cards, then the servicer can try for a different loss mitigation option known as liquidation.[27] In this case, the borrower might agree to voluntarily convey the property to the servicer in exchange for the servicer forgiving the debt. This is sometimes called a "deed in lieu of foreclosure" because the lender takes title to the property instead of going through a full-blown foreclosure proceeding.[28] Yet another type of liquidation is a short sale – where the servicer consents to allowing the property to be sold for less than the amount of the outstanding secured debt due on the home, even though the creditor will take a loss.[29] So, if the property sells for $120,000, even though the homeowner still owes $190,000 on the home, the servicer will nevertheless take the smaller amount and accept the hit.[30] This is, of course, done on the theory that something is better than nothing.

A foreclosure is costly, time intensive, and can often result in the investors taking a loss on the investment. In a declining real estate market like the one that existed after the crisis, the loss to the lender on a foreclosed loan can be anywhere for 30 percent to 60 percent of the outstanding balance due by the homeowner, indicating that it is better for both the homeowner and the MBS investors that a foreclosure be avoided.[31] All this would suggest that seeking some sort of loss mitigation, particularly a workout, would be in the best interest of the investors. If that is the case, then why were so many loss mitigation efforts a failure in the wake of the crisis? Part of that answer relates to the investors – let's go back to the tranches.

Recall that, particularly in the private-label world, not all MBS investors were created equal.[32] Some purchased MBSs from the senior tranche, some from the mezzanine tranche, and some from the junior/equity tranche. This created different economic motivations among the investors when it came to choosing between a foreclosure and loss mitigation.[33]

An explanation here is helpful: In the normal course of things the payments made by homeowners flowed to the private-label investors in accordance with their tranche (senior holders got paid first, then mezzanine, and then the juniors).[34] So, if a number of homeowners in the pool defaulted, the senior tranche wouldn't feel a thing. They would get paid first from whatever money came from the servicer to the trustee. It would only be those lower tranches that would feel the pain. Indeed, the senior tranche wouldn't suffer any losses unless between 20 percent and 30 percent of the entire pool of mortgage defaulted.[35] But, here's the important part: If there was a loan modification (where the actual principal amount or interest rate on the loan was reduced), then all the MBS tranches would see diminished returns on their investments (senior tranche included). So, if the servicer agreed to a 20 percent reduction in the principal amount owed by all the homeowners in the pool, then all of the MBS investors would take a 20 percent decline in their payments. But again, if the servicer foreclosed on the property (even if it did not result in the property being sold for its fair market value), the proceeds from the sale would go to the senior tranche first and then would then flow down the waterfall to the others. For tranches where payment rights are split between investors who get principal payments and those who get interest payments, there were also issues of how interest rate reductions versus principal write-downs affected different classes of investors. As one can see, complications abounded.

The interinvestor conflict is obvious. The senior MBSs investors preferred for the servicer to foreclose on delinquent homeowners because it would get them paid first. The MBSs investors in the lower tranches, however, preferred a loan modification because that was probably their best chance of continuing to see a return (or any return at all depending on how bad things had gotten with home prices). To make matters worse, it was frequently difficult for even the investors to obtain information about the nature of a loan modification and how it would impact loan performance. Loan-level information and modification information more broadly was generally not available.[36]

Yet, there in the middle sat the servicer. Recall that the mortgage middleman's main obligation under the pooling and servicing agreement is to maximize the benefits to investors. But what happens when the investors have different views on what is in their benefit? Middlemen and their surrogates often told stories of how sometimes senior tranche investors would even threaten them with lawsuits if they tried to engage in loan modifications, under the theory that doing so would be against their interests.[37] However, as one scholar notes, "Of all the lawsuits filed by investors in 2008, not a single one questioned the right of a servicer to make a loan modification."[38] In 2009, Boston Federal Reserve Bank research found that the various interests between MBS tranche investors produced no real difference in overall modification rates.[39] Indeed, some federal programs established in the aftermath of the crisis that where aimed at encouraging loan modifications shielded servicers from investor lawsuits that might result from amending a homeowner's obligations.[40]

In some rare cases, the pooling and servicing agreements put handcuffs on how far the middlemen could go in conducting workouts with homeowners. In a report by Credit Suisse that analyzed 31 separate pooling and servicing agreements, the investigators found that a small number of agreements practically prohibited loan modifications.[41] Another 12 in the dataset stipulated other restrictions, such as a ceiling on the number of loans that could be modified or a floor for how low a modified interest rate on a loan could be reduced.[42] Another common feature in pooling and servicing agreements provided a general limit for modifications at no more than 5 percent of the loans in the pool in a given 12-month period.[43] As the foreclosure pile mounted in the wake of the crisis (and political pressure built up as well), sometimes parties were successful in getting the investors or the trustee to amend the agreement to remove the caps – but not often.

In one interesting 2011 report provided by a number of Federal Reserve researchers, a mortgage servicer for a private-label pool of subprime mortgages chronicled the loss mitigation guidance provided in 500 different pooling and servicing agreements.[44] The servicer said that a little less than half of the contracts in the set contained no limitations on the discretion of the servicer other than the general rule that the investors' interests should be maximized at all times using a net present value (NPV) analysis. Another 26 percent of the agreements merely required prior approval by the securitization trustee before the servicer could modify a loan. About 18 percent gave free rein to the servicer to make loan modifications, provided however that none could result in an extension of the term of repayment beyond the period of the MBS pool's maturity date.

Shockingly, right under 5 percent of the agreements prohibited any kind of loan modification at all, and 3 percent provided the same restriction but carved out modifications that would result in the terms of the loan being reset to require a large balloon payment at the end of the period (a feature that would likely shock most borrowers who were accustomed to paying fully amortized loans). It is worth noting that in those cases in which the trustee's permission was required, such consent was not routinely forthcoming. This was mostly due to the fact that trustees desired not to be caught in any decision-making web with the servicer that might ultimately spark investor litigation. Trustees would often point the servicer back to the pooling and servicing agreement's vague language and tell them to make the determination on their own.

And lastly, it was often unfeasible to obtain the agreement of a majority of the MBS investors in a securitization, as there are frequently hundreds of them in a given mortgage pool, all having varying views of what is best.[45] The prevailing industry belief was that servicers are "less likely to be questioned by investors" if they go with a foreclosure.[46]

THE PROCESS (AND PROBLEM) OF DUAL-TRACKING

Servicers faced with the fork in the road would typically try to do both a loss mitigation and a foreclosure at the same time. This became what is known as "dual-tracking."[47]

Dual-tracking became a huge issue in the aftermath of the housing crisis.[48] Homeowners who often thought they were on the eve of achieving a loan modification or other workout would suddenly be shocked to discover that foreclosure proceedings had been commenced against them and a sale was forthcoming.[49] While this may seem like servicers were playing a nasty trick on the unsuspecting homeowner, this phenomenon revealed yet another defect in the mortgage middlemen structure – three primary forces encouraged, if not required, servicers to game homeowners in this way.

First, ratings agencies played a large part in dual-tracking.[50] Mortgage servicing companies compete for business and one way they make themselves attractive is by having a stellar score assigned to them by one of the national credit ratings agencies. In some ways, ratings agencies provide some of the most significant oversight when it comes to the mortgage middleman industry.[51] Just as credit ratings agencies determine the ratings for the various bonds issues from a pool of mortgages, they also judge servicers based on, among other things, their general solvency. These scores not only set the general terms for any borrowing that the servicer might need to undertake but also dictate the likelihood that the firm can obtain servicing rights on a given pool of mortgages.[52] Ratings agencies give better scores to those firms that do not delay foreclosure.[53] So, the quicker servicers move toward the foreclosure process the better score they receive, thus signaling to the market that they are a more desirable and efficient middleman for managing a given pool of mortgage loans.

Second, the pooling and servicing agreement between the trust and the servicer basically required dual-tracking.[54] The agreement with the trust that holds the mortgages typically mandates that the servicer pursue a foreclosure even if it is simultaneously working with the homeowner on a loss mitigation package. What made the process all the more muddied was that two different offices within the mortgage servicing company handled the process – one for foreclosures and one for loss mitigation – and they rarely communicated well (or at all) with each other.

Third, Fannie Mae and Freddie Mac, as well as other government mortgage insurance programs, often require that a foreclosure be completed within so many days after a delinquency. Sometimes these deadlines vary from state to state.[55] For instance, the maximum number of days is 540 in Louisiana, 1,230 in D.C., and 330 in Missouri.[56] Failure to adhere to these guidelines results in funds being withheld from the servicer. Thus, it is almost necessary to start foreclosure proceedings at the same time a loan modification process begins to avoid potentially missing the deadline.

LOAN MODIFICATION IS NOT AN OPTION

The servicers decision whether to attempt a loss mitigation comes down to analyzing competing NPV data. NPV is the value that the MBS investors would receive if it utilized a foreclosure versus going with some type of loss mitigation option. If the value resulting from the foreclosure is higher, then the NPV calculation would lean in favor of proceeding ahead without pursuing some sort of workout. Loss mitigation should only be implemented by the servicer if it will produce a higher NPV for the MBS investors. To help servicers in making these calculations, the mortgage middlemen are supposed to consider factors such as whether the homeowner would default again after the modification takes place, whether the homeowner would catch up on his or her payments in the ordinary course without the need to modify the loan, and the extent to which the loan would need to be discounted to achieve a meaningful modification of the payment amount.[57]

However, consumer advocates note that the value of the mortgaged property plays the primary role in this determination. Moreover, attorneys representing homeowners in distress have observed that the NPV calculation is a black box, leaving consumers and their advocates with little ability to verify the calculations.[58] In a 2009 report by ProPublica, when a loss mitigation employee at the mortgage servicer CitiMortgage entered an 83-year-old widow's information into the firm's NPV calculator the computer responded with "NPV Test: Failed." This meant that the homeowner would not be getting her loan modification. Yet, the CitiMortgage employee admitted in an e-mail that "I am unable to come up with a reason for the denial."[59] In fact, during the height of the foreclosure crisis, a number of consumer lawyers presented evidence that some servicers were not even performing the NPV calculation at all.[60]

For servicers working in the private-label market, the calculation of NPV is even more reliant upon the servicer's discretion, including which formula is used and what factors play into the calculus. The standard is a general one: that the servicer should "use standards of prudent mortgage servicing" (whatever that means).[61] Comparatively, Fannie Mae and Freddie Mac provide greater guidance to their servicers on how to deal with the NPV analysis for GSE-backed loans.[62] The GSEs not only monitor their servicers' practices more closely (although still with some flaws), but they also provide their middlemen with software to help in making the NPV calculation. But, servicers still have significant discretion in the GSE context as well, and in the wake of the crisis they would typically steer toward the option that would take the least amount of time and effort – and would result in the greatest amount of reimbursable expenses.[63] Still, mortgage servicers attest that the modification rate is higher for Fannie- and Freddie-backed loans.[64]

But for the private-label folks, neither the pooling and servicing agreement nor any government regulations attempt to provide guidance or impose restrictions on how this all-important analysis is undertaken.[65] That means servicers had (and to some extent still do have) the power to manipulate the process, considering factors that may not be aligned with either the interests of the homeowner or that of the MBS investors – such as compensation for the servicer, time expended in dealing with the loan, and the likelihood of recovering servicer expenses.

Generally, the servicer might incur less time and costs by merely moving ahead with a foreclosure, rather than trying to work with a homeowner on modifying the loan (even if keeping the homeowner paying is better for some if not most investors).[66] When modifications did come, they were not quick endeavors – they could last anywhere from 7 to 11 months for some servicers.[67] But sometimes servicers would determine that a loss mitigation option would be more in their interest, not necessarily because it would result in the homeowner getting his or her payments back on track but because it will result in greater fees for the servicer. Specifically, as discussed in the preceding text, certain loss mitigation options can increase the costs of the loan by adding past missed payments of interest into the principal and by piling on default and administrative fees. Thus, a homeowner might be given a forbearance and the ability to pay less for a period, but only to later see the monthly payments return to a higher, unsustainable amount and with a larger principal number. In the end, the result is still foreclosure but with more secured debt and less equity for the homeowner. And still at other times, servicers – particularly Bank of America – would drag the homeowner along through the loan modification process, as well as contemplate foreclosure of the property, but ultimately do neither, thereby leaving the homeowner in limbo.[68]

In the aftermath of the crisis, as mortgage defaults flooded the market, industry groups and regulators became increasingly critical of mortgage servicers and their inability to help distressed homeowners find a way forward through a loan modification. An April 2008 report by the Conference of State Bank Supervisors (the national group for all state banking regulators) said that servicers were moving "too slow" in processing and achieving loan modifications.[69] At other times, "[S]ervicer communication and coordination kept many distressed consumers in the dark about available options to avoid foreclosure."[70] When servicers did begin the process of helping a homeowner work through a loss mitigation effort it typically only happened after the individual was already delinquent (meaning a monthly mortgage payment is past due) or in default (generally meaning that a payment is 30 days or more past due).[71] An attempt to work through a loan modification or other loss mitigation process would be much more fruitful (for the homeowner and for the investors) if it was attempted closer to the time that the homeowner initially defaulted. The more missed payments build up, the more difficult the loan modification becomes.

LOSS MITIGATION GONE WRONG

Even once loss mitigation efforts were started, homeowners decried the incredibly long period it took to achieve any sort of significant progress. National groups like NeighborWorks America reported in the middle of 2008 that the period between submitting a loss mitigation application and receiving a response (one way or the other) was ever-increasing in length.[72] Distressed homeowners routinely decried the fact that servicers often lost their paperwork and frequently failed to return phone calls and e-mails. Stories from the trenches noted that because filling out the loss mitigation application and gathering (and analyzing) all the necessary paperwork usually took such a long period, it was often the case that (due to dual-tracking) by the time everything was complete the foreclosure was already too advanced to stop.

Servicers were also not eager to employ more ambitious, consumer-oriented approaches to dealing with distressed homeowners. It was often reported by mortgage industry groups that servicers would have a difficult time getting in touch with homeowners or getting homeowners to call them back, usually due to a fear by the homeowner that there was nothing that could help them or that speaking with the bank would make the situation worse or accelerate the loss of their home. Servicers for Fannie Mae/Freddie Mac mortgage-backed securities were better about addressing this situation than those in the private-label/subprime market. GSE-related servicers would sometimes hire firms to help counsel homeowners and spread the word about loss mitigation options. The private-label market (the home of most subprime borrowing) rarely engaged in these efforts because it feared the expenses related to such efforts would not be reimbursed.

HOW SERVICERS GET PAID

Another critical factor in understanding the mortgage middlemen and their failure to materially help homeowners in the wake of the financial crisis is knowing how they make and use their money. In goods times, giant mortgage servicers are able to take advantage of economies of scale to process payments, handle escrows, and disburse uniform, electronically generated notices and statements with simple ease. Scaling resulted in a great deal of industry consolidation over the years. In 2008, the five largest mortgage servicers (all commercial banks, including Bank of America, Wells Fargo, Chase, CitiMortgage, Residential Capital, and IndyMac) were handling about 60 percent of the residential mortgage market.[73] But loss mitigation efforts are time intensive and require a great deal of labor – something that the routine, assembly-line process of mortgage servicing was not well equipped to handle.

Servicers completely lacked the staff, training, guidance, or technology to effectively deal with so many defaulting homeowners seeking help to stay in their homes. Because housing markets rise and fall in cycles, during the boom mortgage servicers found it more profitable to automate as much of the servicing process as possible and thereby reduce their need to invest in human capital.[74] This resulted in a dearth of trained staff capable of handling those periods when the market took a downward turn. Investing in necessary training and resources to address market drops was simply not a priority for the upper management of mortgage servicers, and thus they were woefully underinvested when the foreclosure flood arrived.[75]

Principally, servicers are paid based on a set fee that is derived from a percentage of a loan's unpaid principal balance.[76] Practically speaking, the servicer takes that percentage from the monthly payments made by the homeowner, before then passing on the remainder to the investors' trustee. As far as claims to the monthly payments go, servicers get first priority to these payments. In terms of types of mortgage credit products, subprime loans are the most lucrative, earning an annual fee around 50 basis points (or 0.50 percent).[77] Consider the following example: The servicer of a loan with a $100,000 principal balance in a given year could expect to earn approximately $1,000 in servicing fees for that period (0.005% × $100,000 × 2 years = $1,000). As the principal balance of the loan is paid down, the servicing fee declines as well. For comparison, fees for prime loans with fixed interest rates are 25 basis points and those with adjustable interest rates are 37.5 basis points.[78]

If you were a mortgage middleman, you can easily see which is more profitable. Perhaps equally noteworthy, the MBS investors are typically unaware of the precise structure that provides for the servicer's compensation. "Even the sometimes substantial fees paid to servicers in foreclosure are often invisible to investors."[79] Because the fees servicers are owed are derived from the outstanding principal balance, there is an economic incentive for the servicer to stretch out the loan modification as long as possible.[80] The more late fees and penalties get piled on the less likely any payments made by the homeowner will go toward reducing the principal. As the principal remains the same, the middleman maintains its fee levels. Thus, there's a motivation for the servicer to draw out the modification process as long as possible. While the cost of making advances to the investors might be high, this might be outweighed by the fees being earned on the principal. When it comes to subservicers, the principal servicer will typically pay a fee to the subcompany on a per loan basis.[81]

Yet another way that servicers earn money is by floating the income they receive from homeowners by making short-term investments before the funds must be disbursed.[82] In other words, if a homeowner makes a payment by the first of the month, it is often the case that the servicer will not have to send the principal and interest payments to the trustee (for the MBS investors) until toward the end of the month. That means that there are a few weeks in between where the servicer has a bunch of cash on hand. Many mortgage middlemen will put that cash into short-term, high-grade investments, pulling out the principal at the end of the period when it's time to forward the money to the investors.[83] The interest earned on that money is kept by the servicer as profit. These firms can do something similar (although over a longer period) with insurance and property tax amounts that are escrowed each month but not payable until typically the end of the year. This can end up being big money. For instance, Twomey and Levitin note that in public filings for Ocwen Financial Corporation (a major and notorious mortgage servicer) it was revealed that in 2007 the firm held $677 million in escrow accounts for its homeowners.[84] Investing those amounts yielded the company $30 million (which ended up comprising 9 percent of its total servicing income that year).

Lastly, sometimes servicers earn income based on fees charged to homeowners in default. For instance, late monthly payments usually trigger a late fee or some other charge (typically about 5 percent of the monthly payment). Also, bounced checks and agreements to modify the mortgage loan are also frequently accompanied by fees. If these fees are paid by the homeowner, then the servicer can often keep them. While it may not seem like much, these loan-related fees can add up. Ocwen Financial reported that in 2008 about 18 percent of its total servicing income that year came from such fees.[85]

Servicers have engaged in some pretty dodgy practices when it comes to these sorts of fees. For instance, Twomey and Levitin again note that Countrywide Financial (at one time the country's largest mortgage servicer) was hit with a $108 million penalty from the Federal Trade Commission due to the fact that it overcharged borrowers for such fees.[86] What this middleman got into the habit of doing was after a default occurred the company would have the grass cut on the property and the home inspected, all under the auspices of protecting the investors' collateral. The defaulted homeowner was concomitantly charged for these services. However, Countrywide wasn't hiring third-party vendors to do these tasks. Rather, it created subsidiary companies to perform the services, which would in turn place a premium markup on their services (frequently by as much as 100 percent). Countrywide would then pull these fat fees up from its shell service companies, reaping big profits.

In another case in which Katherine Porter studied foreclosures in Chapter 13 bankruptcy cases, it was discovered that that a particular servicer claimed that a borrower owed in excess of $1 million on a home loan.[87] But when the improper fees and charges were removed, it was later discovered, however, that the real amount was only $60,000.[88] Dubious fees that get added on to the borrower's loan include "$145 in something called 'demand fees,' $137 in overnight delivery fees, fax fees of $50 and payoff statement charges of $60." Servicers would nickel and dime homeowners for every little thing after a default occurred – and each dollar and cent would make the principal balance all the bigger.

As noted from the FTC example with Countrywide, the ability to charge fees and then keep them (if the homeowner pays) was such a powerful incentive for some servicers that they came to charge fees that the loan agreement or mortgage with the borrower didn't authorize. As Levitin and Twomey note, "Financially distressed homeowners are unlikely to notice unauthorized fees." Indeed, "Even if they do, they lack the financial and emotional wherewithal to fight them and get little benefit from avoiding them."[89]

As you can see from the servicing fee structure and with default fee incentives, going the loss mitigation route (which might result in the homeowner staying in the property) adds costs to the servicer that are not contemplated in the fee structure with the trust – or at least the fee is not increased to take loss mitigation into account. The servicer's employees have to communicate with the homeowners, collect information from them, perform an evaluation of the home, assess the collateral, and determine whether the missed payment is just a blip that can be remedied or if the homeowner has instead hit some major life event that has altered his or her economic situation. Lastly the servicer must perform the all-important NPV calculation.

Against the backdrop of this labor-intensive process, servicers report that finding employees who are skilled in dealing with loss mitigation situations is difficult. As one can imagine, not only must the person have some knowledge of mortgage finance, but he or she must also be able to act as a sort of counselor. The agent will be dealing with the homeowner at the point of greatest stress, often accompanying emotional and sometimes even mental suffering. These individuals command higher compensation and are often difficult to recruit. Because of this, most servicers often employ loss mitigation staff that are untrained and undercompensated for the important work they perform. Because investments in technology and highly skilled staff are only needed in times of financial crisis when defaults are high, executives running these mortgage middleman firms have preferred to go the easy (and cheap) way when it comes to resource allocation and human capital investment. Despite the fact that many of the larger servicers failed to adequately invest in their staffs and technological resources to sufficiently deal with homeowners in distress, these same servicers handled the largest share of subprime loans.[90] Perhaps it is because of this, and the perception that despite a loan modification most of homeowners will default again, that the management and parent firms of mortgage servicers declined to make such investments in their loan modification capacity.[91] Instead, outsourcing and off-shoring functions such as loan administration, default advising, and customer service became the norm.[92] In 2014, the servicing giant Ocwen off-shored 75 percent of its servicing staff, most operating from Uruguay, India, and the Philippines. Nationstar Mortgage off-shored 33 percent and CitiMortgage farmed out 26 percent. The ratings agency Fitch cautioned that the use of off-shoring results in servicing staff being too reliant on scripts, which results in them providing mechanical responses that are not adequately responsive to consumer needs when they deviate from the norm.[93]

Yet another aspect of the economics of the mortgage middlemen has to do with paying the MBS investors in the event of mortgage loan defaults. As mentioned previously, merely because the homeowner defaults does not necessarily mean that the investors will not get paid. The mortgage middlemen pick up the tab when homeowners default, meaning that the servicer is responsible for making principal and interest payments to the MBS investors even when monthly mortgage payments from borrowers are not forthcoming.[94] The cash significance of this can be monumental, depending on the kind of securitization. If the mortgage loans are part of a GSE securitization, the servicer must continue to do this until either there is a loan modification of some sort and the homeowner starts paying again, or else the home is sold in foreclosure and the proceeds from that process are realized.

The cost of covering these interim payments to the investors can take a serious chunk out of the finances of the servicer.[95] In fact, they can often be the servicer's most substantial expense.[96] Sometimes the cost of covering these payments can become so burdensome, it spurs the servicer to move quickly toward resolving the default (through either a workout or foreclosure).[97] For example, in 2008 Ocwen Financial – squeezed for capital and forced to make substantial investor advances – started to rapidly modify defaulted loans by forgiving loan principal.[98] By getting these loans back into the "performing" category, Ocwen was relieved of having to make the investor payments itself. But more frequently than not, aggressive loan modification was not the result. Because a loan modification can take a longer period to complete, while a foreclosure can be quick (particularly in nonjudicial foreclosure states), there was yet another incentive for servicers to favor going after the home.

There are, however, at least some expenses that servicers can recoup from the MBS investors or the trustee. Generally, costs related to title searches (which are part of both a foreclosure and a loss mitigation process) are reimbursable. Sometimes property maintenance fees are also reimbursed.[99] Yet, many pooling and servicing agreements limit recoupment or cabin it to only one series of costs. For instance, data indicate that investors frequently agree to reimburse foreclosure-related pass-on costs at a higher rate than they do pass-on costs related to loss mitigation.[100] These further incentivize servicers to proceed down the foreclosure route. Recall also that pooling and servicing agreements are not uniform, which can result in wide variation.[101] A servicer might handle a number of loans for a host of different subprime mortgage investor pools, thus hampering any attempt to create uniform processes. While it is true that GSE-backed mortgage loan pools utilize a more harmonized pooling and servicing agreement across the Fannie/Freddie marketplace, the subprime pools (dominated by the private-label industry) did not.

GSE VS. PRIVATE-LABEL MARKET IN HELPING HOMEOWNERS

Although one can see some common attributes (and problems) across the servicing market, there are some distinctive features that have defined servicing of mortgage-backed securities issued by Fannie Mae and Freddie Mac as opposed to those issued by the private-label market (being mostly subprime or jumbo loans).[102] First, when dealing with servicers seeking to engage in loan modifications, Fannie and Freddie have authority to act on behalf of all the investors of their mortgage-backed securities (and there are no intrapool tranche conflicts because Fannie and Freddie generally do not divide their pool into tranches to begin with).[103] The GSEs also provide incentives for their mortgage middlemen to engage in loan modifications – both monetary and reputational. Programs like Early Indicator, Risk Profiler, Workout Prospector, and Early Resolution together provide incredibly hands-on and helpful tools for servicers in working through a loan modification – including how to conduct a complete NPV calculation – and dealing with homeowners who have become delinquent on their payments.[104] Yet, these programs are still problematic because the accuracy of the NPV calculation depends on the quality of the data used to make the decision.[105]

On the industry profile side, the GSEs (somewhat like credit reporting agencies) provide scores to servicing firms based on their performance. Better scores mean that the servicer will be first in line for further GSE work in the future. On the financial side, servicers can earn extra fees when they complete successful loss mitigations. This includes giving financial tools to help servicers deal with junior mortgage or lienholders whose participation might be necessary to achieve an orderly modification, refinance, or short sale. One particularly strong economic incentive used by Fannie and Freddie during the stormy days of 2008 was when they agreed to substantially increase fees given to servicers when they completed successful modifications. For instance, Freddie said it would pay "$500 for a repayment plan, $800 for a loan modification, and $2,200 for a short sale."[106] These economic incentives helped encourage servicers to invest the time and resources necessary to develop robust loss mitigation departments within their organizations. Federal Reserve researchers have noted that servicers report having a much easier time managing GSE mortgage pools than those in the private-label arena, mostly due to the fact that there is a "single set of guidelines that make it easier to apply rules and approve exceptions."[107]

First, there was very little market incentive for servicers of subprime loans to do a great job for reputational reasons.[108] One would think that having a good name on Wall Street would lead to future servicing business. However, in the wake of the crash this simply was not the case. There was widespread belief in the industry that the chances of having a huge portfolio of subprime loans to service in the future was nil. In 2008, it was fairly obviously to everyone that some kind of financial reform was coming and that the heyday of making high-cost, risky subprime loans was coming to an end – or at least it wouldn't reach the levels that it had before. Because the business model of servicing subprime loans was essentially headed down the toilet, there was no reason to compete for future business – and thus no real reason to strive for excellence in servicing the loans that were quickly going into default.

The specter of tranche warfare among the MBS investors also discouraged the middlemen from acting too quickly or with much resolve in handling loss mitigation issues. As noted in the preceding text, senior MBS tranche investors have an economic incentive to favor foreclosure because it will ensure payment, while junior/equity MBS tranche holders will prefer a loan modification because foreclosure might ultimately leave them with nothing. However, even this rationale escapes some logic. Senior debt holders should still prefer a workout because, if the loan is modified to an amount that the borrower can pay, the long-term effect is to ensure continued performance of the loan, which benefits the senior tranches as well as more junior debt holders. This is particularly true because the value of homes continued to decline in the aftermath of the crisis, signifying that the value achieved from a foreclosure sale would not be significant and therefore not always resulting in a win for the senior tranche folks.

Another factor driving the mortgage middlemen away from loss mitigation options came in the form of the repeat-offender rate for defaults – one of the primary factors used in making the NPV calculation. In other words, if the chances are high that the homeowner will simply default again not long after the modification occurs, then it might be better to just proceed with a foreclosure now rather than limping along for a short period. Federal researchers note that about 18 percent of all subprime loans undergoing modification in 2008 went into default a mere few months thereafter.[109] Of course, a high recidivism rate can hardly be surprising. Subprime loans, with their predatory features, surprise payment schemes, and lack of any serious underwriting (indeed, sometimes with no underwriting at all), were built to fail. Without significant write-downs that resulted in monthly payments being dramatically rescaled to the ability of the homeowners to pay, it was basically inevitable that a default would reoccur. Indeed, as former FDIC chairperson Sheila Bair details, very often the high recidivism rate decried by servicers as a reason to pursue foreclosure was the result of less than meaningful loan modifications on the front end.[110] Data from 2010 indicate that loan modifications that resulted in capitalized arrearages (essentially, meaning that the loan principal increased) were consistently the largest category of modifications.[111] This would mean that the modification increased the homeowner's principal balance and monthly payment, making him or her owe more in pure principal on the loan than before the modification. Without a real modification involving a reduction in the interest rate or an extension of the term resulting in decreased monthly payments (rather than merely providing temporary relief), there could be no other future for homeowners with subprime loans than falling behind yet again.

It's not exactly surprising, considering the way servicers are compensated, that many loan modifications did not result in making the principal balance lower (but rather making it higher). Recall that mortgage middlemen are paid based on a percentage of the outstanding principal balance of the loan, which means the scales are also tipped in favor of adding late fees and penalties to the principal, lengthening the repayment term, lowering the interest rate, or suspending the requirement to make payments for a period – rather than making permanent reductions in the principal portion of the loan.[112]

Also, unlike with Fannie and Freddie, the private-label investors generally do not provide additional compensation to servicers for doing loan modifications with homeowners.[113] The general feeling among these bondholder groups was that the administrative fee that servicers collected as part of their general servicing duties should have been sufficient compensation for all servicer-related activities (including modifications). Again, because loan modifications are more labor intensive and take more time and resources, servicers are incentivized to go straight to the less costly and less time-consuming process of foreclosure (indeed, the process of seizing and selling someone's home can be quite quick in nonjudicial foreclosure states where servicers need not go to court). Some commentators have noted that there are incentives built into the system for the servicer to vigorously pursue a loan modification, such as the fact that the servicer must cover payments to the investors pending the foreclosure and that the ability to get the borrower back on track in making sustainable payments ensures that the servicer can earn future fees from servicing the loan.[114] However, these inducements have not, in practice, seemed to have served as a driving factor in directing general middleman behavior.

Ratings agencies and bond insurance companies also played a role in subprime loan modifications. Sometimes the consent of these parties was required before proceeding with a modification. In one report, UC Davis's John Patrick Hunt studied 65 pooling and servicing agreements governing the largest subprime securitizations in 2006.[115] The dataset revealed that of all the agreements where a modification by the servicer was even permitted, 52 percent provided that the consent of the relevant rating agency was needed for any loan modification to occur. Another 32 percent in the dataset required the bond insurance company to give its permission if the modification would result in changes to more than 5 percent of the loans. Thus, these two important players in the securitization game enjoyed substantial influence over how middlemen engaged in loss mitigation, typically based on their varying (and sometimes opposing) interests as to the type of loan and the type of modification.[116]

Finally, another frequently seen feature of subprime loans that made them challenging for servicers to modify had to do with the presence of junior mortgages.[117] As noted previously, one of the particularly predatory practices of the subprime market was to mortgage a given piece of real estate to the hilt. That meant taking out a loan at 80 percent of the value of the home, and then taking out yet another mortgage loan against the remaining 20 percent. The homeowner had no equity in the home, and if there was any downward market fluctuation in housing prices then he or she would have negative equity.

For context, in 2006 the percentage of adjustable rate subprime mortgage loans with second mortgages nationwide was just more than 35 percent. The same percentage of fixed rate subprime loans was just less than 14 percent.[118] However, neither of these figures considers second mortgages that were placed on the home at some point after the original, first mortgage was taken. Indeed, it was very common for individuals, after acquiring a home and building up equity, to then use that equity to take out a subsequent mortgage loan for making home improvements or for other purposes.[119] These were known as home equity lines of credit (HELOCs) or home equity loans (HELs).[120] This means, as Federal Reserve researchers have noted, that the actual number of homes with junior mortgages is much higher than the preceding numbers indicate.[121]

The significance of the second mortgage is this: Many servicers feared that under state law a modification of a mortgage that was too significant could constitute a court deciding that this was a new mortgage altogether. The danger of this was that the loan, secured by the first mortgage, would then become secured by a mortgage that would take a new priority ranking. Thus, the second mortgage would become first and the first would become last. Considering the decline in home values and the losses taken on foreclosure sales generally, losing that first position would have been catastrophic for the servicer (or, more specifically, the MBS investors).

Now, as any real estate lawyer knowledgeable about mortgage law would know, the chances that a diminishment of loan principal, lowering of the interest rate, or lengthening of the repayment period would cause a loss of ranking or result in a recasting of the mortgage is fairly laughable (or at least extremely unlikely). Those who studied the issue in 2009 note that they had "not found any instances in the current foreclosure episode of junior lienholders successfully promoting their claim over a senior lienholder."[122] Then again, it speaks to the larger issue of a lack of resources, training, and knowledge on the part of mortgage middlemen when it came to loss mitigation. This loss of priority argument provided yet another reason (a subterfuge, some might say) for why a loan modification was not possible or desirable.

What servicers would try to do when faced with this priority dilemma was to get the junior mortgage lender to agree to the modification and also agree that the first mortgage would remain superior. To entice junior mortgagees to agree, sometimes servicers would offer them money. For instance, Fannie and Freddie would compensate secondary mortgage holders to the tune of anywhere from $1,000 to $5,000 for their agreement.[123] In truth, this was a great deal for the junior mortgagee because a foreclosure of the property would likely have yielded them nothing anyway. This was a chance to at least extract some money from the deal. However, as you might imagine, the time and energy required for a servicer to contact, negotiate, and then coordinate the consent of the junior mortgagee was not insignificant. Again, the easier route would be to opt for foreclosure.

HOW TAXATION AND ACCOUNTING HELPED CAUSE SERVICER MALFUNCTION

Without getting overly technical, there were also some tax and accounting reasons offered by the mortgage middlemen regarding why loan modifications were difficult. Pools of mortgages serviced by middlemen are subject to Real Estate Mortgage Investment Conduit (REMIC) rules and Financial Accounting Statement 140 (FAS140). Prior to 1986 there were some very real tax drawbacks for those investing in MBSs.[124] The payments made by the homeowners were taxed when they reached the mortgage pool level (the trust discussed in the preceding text) and then they would be taxed again when they were distributed to the investors. Because no one likes double taxation, particularly Wall Street firms that invested in MBSs, Congress was lobbied to change the rules. The result of these efforts was the creation of a special tax designation for which certain entities could qualify – a REMIC. If your entity qualified as a REMIC, then the tax at the trust level was eliminated. After its passage, almost all new issuances of mortgage-backed securities were done through the use of investor-friendly REMICs.

But there were some important rules that had to be followed for the mortgage pooling entity to qualify as a REMIC. One of the most significant rules was the requirement that the pool of mortgages be static and that the entity only be used for passive investment purposes (sometimes called the "brain dead" requirement because the entity is not supposed to be engaged in active business endeavors). For instance, a REMIC must acquire its pool of residential mortgage loans within a mere three-month period from the date it is created. And importantly, because the trust can only operate in a passive way it "has no powers to vary the composition of its mortgage assets."[125]

Investors and servicers have generally been very leery about getting too creative in dealing with mortgage loans held in a REMIC pool because a violation of the REMIC rules can result in some pretty severe penalties. Specifically, because it was said that the pool of mortgages in a REMIC had to be "static," many argued that it would violate the REMIC rules for a handful of loans within the pool to be modified and thus made nonstatic. The result was that Fannie and Freddie often engaged in the practice of taking loans they modified out of the pool altogether. Private-label market servicers could not do this because of tranching, which made beneficial ownership of the loan too difficult to trace, thus making it too impractical to remove the mortgage loans from the pool. Servicers of these loans often raised the point that the overall fear of throwing a wrench in the trust's REMIC status played heavily against modifying a loan.

Happily, in 2007 and 2008 the IRS, as part of a larger government effort to combat the foreclosure epidemic, issued much needed guidance, generally making clear to MBS parties that as long as there was a "significant risk of foreclosure" on the loan and as long as the property securing the loan remained owner occupied, then the REMIC's classification would not be impaired by a modification of the loan.[126] This removed a significant roadblock that had been used by servicers and trustees in resisting calls to engage in aggressive loss mitigation activities. Many consumer groups, however, noted that the rules were already clear before the IRS took action and that servicers could modify loans that were in default or when default was foreseeable prior to the IRS changes.[127]

The second part of the antiloss mitigation equation dealt with accounting. The Financial Accounting Standards Board (FASB) is a nongovernmental body whose mission is to create and constantly improve generally accepted accounting principles (GAAP). Despite being a private entity, FASB's pronouncements have the force of law by virtue of the fact that the Securities and Exchange Commission (SEC) makes compliance with FASB rules mandatory for all publicly traded companies.[128]

FAS140 is a special accounting rule that applies to entities that own pools of securitized assets (like residential mortgage loans). The rule provides that a person who transfers an asset is allowed to treat that asset as being off its balance sheet.[129] This means that, to the bank transferor's advantage, it need not maintain capital against the loans any longer. So the sponsor of a securitization (the entity that purchases a bunch of mortgage loans from originators) can transfer those loans to the special purpose entity (the trust that will hold the pool of mortgages) and thereby remove the assets from the sponsor's balance sheet, even if the special purpose entity is entirely a creature of the sponsor. On the other side of the transaction, those investors who purchase securities backed by the mortgages in the pool are insulated from the claims of the sponsor's creditors. The process essentially puts a shield around the mortgage loans (and their revenue streams) when it comes to people who are owed money by the sponsor. In this way, the pool of mortgages is said to be "bankruptcy remote" from the sponsor – the sponsor's creditors cannot reach the pool of mortgages because it is made, legally speaking, too remote.[130]

As you can imagine, the ability to take advantage of FAS140 was almost just as important to MBS investors as the ability to maintain REMIC treatment of the trust. One provides a significant tax advantage and the other provides bankruptcy protection and a shield from competing claimants to the money. But here again, servicers and trustees often claimed that FAS140 served as an impediment to a muscular loss mitigation system. Here, as with the REMIC rules, there was a component of FAS140 that required that the special purpose entity hold the securitized assets in a passive way such that "holding the asset or instrument does not involve its holder in making decisions other than the decisions inherent in servicing."[131] Other specific changes to the loan, such as adding new debtors, additional collateral, or new lines of credit all constituted violations of FAS140.

What constituted a decision "inherent in servicing" was used to push back against strong encouragements to modify loans, with servicers arguing that changing loan terms or providing a suspension in the requirement to pay might constitute an impermissible form of decision making. Although it was always the case that FAS140 did indeed allow loan modifications, the servicer could only do them if it provided fairly significant documentation – such as why the default occurred, loss of employment, and the inability to refinance (among others).[132]

Fortunately, in mid-2007, at the request of then chairman of the House Committee on Financial Services, Congressman Barney Frank, the Securities and Exchange Commission issued a statement clarifying that "[w]hen a loan is delinquent ... FAS 140 implementation guidance provides that a servicer may have discretion in restructuring or working out a loan ... without calling into question off-balance sheet treatment for the loan."[33] This clarification also provided a reduction in the amount of required documentation. Yet, this change too failed to achieve the burst in loan modifications for which lawmakers had hoped.

THE HIDDEN ARCHITECTURE REVEALED

As noted in the preceding text, although most homeowners think of their servicer as their "lender," that is far from the truth. There is a complex, and frequently invisible, series of parties and transactions that exist on the other side of the curtain. Of these parties, the servicers – the middlemen between the homeowner and the true owners of the mortgage loan – play a hugely outsized role. Surprisingly, despite their immense importance in the constellation of homeownership and housing finance in the United States, they proved themselves to be immensely ill-equipped to handle the duties and responsibilities that fell to them in the aftermath of the financial crisis. As loan after loan went into default, the middlemen found what was once a fairly simple and routine task – servicing the loan – had turned into the multifaceted and labor-intensive undertaking of trying to deal with an ever-increasing volume of delinquent mortgages. In the face of this task, servicers were either paralyzed by conflicting incentives and clashing legal positions or else were eager to take the path of least resistance that would yield the heftiest fees. Homeowners were entirely at their mercy.

PART II

Foreclosures, Middlemen, and Homeowners in Crisis

4

The Most Important Document You've Never Read

The uniform residential mortgage contract rests at the heart of American housing finance. Widespread homeownership throughout this country would hardly be possible without it. This all-important instrument helps facilitate the flow of housing credit across the country and provides access to the resources necessary for many Americans to own their homes. And importantly, mortgage servicers derive a tremendous amount of their power (one might say it is the source of most of their power) from this document when it comes to dealing with the homes of financially distressed Americans. Yet, despite the mortgage contract's great importance, it has gone mostly unnoticed by law and policy makers. In all the reforms that followed the crisis, the mortgage contract was left untouched.

To truly understand the role played by the mortgage middlemen in the foreclosure disaster, you need to understand the mortgage contract, what authority it confers on servicers by homeowners (whether homeowners realize they are doing so or not), and how this all-important document got to be the way it is today. The key words here are *standardization* and the *secondary market*.[1]

HOW GOVERNMENT GOT INTO THE HOUSING FINANCE BUSINESS

Essentially, it all started with the FHA. While the government has always had a hand in housing, the FHA, an agency within HUD, has played perhaps the most significant role – and this is certainly true when it comes to the uniform residential mortgage contract. As noted by housing finance scholar David Reiss, the FHA can be best conceptualized as "a specialized insurance company that guarantees the payment of mortgages made by private lenders (banks and other mortgage lenders) who provide loans to developers and homebuyers."[2] The FHA was created in 1934, shortly after the Great Depression – another period in America's history during which the people of the United States were under significant financial distress. During this period, homeownership was nothing like it is today – mortgage loans were not easy to come by in the least. Loan-to-value ratios required around 50 percent, to 60 percent, which required enormous down payments.[3] Also, the practice of a person making equal monthly payments comprised of principal and interest that was fully amortized over the loan period (meaning that the last monthly payment would retire the debt) was not the norm. Instead, interest only, periodic payments with large lump sum amounts due at the end of the term were hallmarks of many mortgage loans at the time. This meant that the only way for someone to afford to purchase a home was to refinance the mortgage loan (i.e., take out a new loan and pay off the existing one) prior to the time the balloon payment was due – often multiple times over. The Great Depression took that possibility off the table, which had horrendous effects on households. As President Hebert Hoover put it:

> The literally thousands of heart-breaking instances of the inability of working people to attain renewal of expiring mortgages on favorable terms, and the consequent loss of their homes, have been one of the tragedies of this depression.[4]

By 1933, between 40 percent and 50 percent of all mortgage loans were in default, and the housing financing system was nearing complete collapse.

But even with the ability to refinance these balloon mortgage loans, homeownership was out of reach for most Americans. Consider the homeownership trend over time. In 1890, right before the turn of the century, the homeownership rate was about 47.8 percent. It hovered somewhere between 45 percent and 47 percent from the period between 1900 and 1930.[5]

The FHA's mission, however, was to bring reform and fresh air to housing finance in America. To do this, the agency sought to change the type of loan products that were offered. It wanted to create a market of mortgage loans that had longer repayment terms and required a very low down payment. But the FHA did not seek to do this by becoming a mortgage lender. Instead, the FHA created economic incentives so that the private lending market would start issuing loans on these favorable terms. It did this by lowering the credit risk for private lenders by providing insurance on the mortgage loans they originated, as long as those loans conformed with certain homeowner-favorable terms.

As noted in the preceding text, lenders wanted to make sure their borrowers could pay (particularly before the advent of the secondary mortgage market). But by participating in the FHA program, a private lender could make a loan without the need to be overly concerned that the borrower might default and therefore cause a loss. Instead, the FHA would issue a mortgage insurance policy that would protect the private lender from bearing the economic brunt of the default, provided that the borrower qualified for the program and that the loan contained the desired terms and conditions.

Once launched, the use of "FHA loans" became very popular.[6] Getting an FHA mortgage loan from your local bank now allowed the would-be homeowner to provide a lower down payment than would otherwise be required under the lender's conventional underwriting standards. Also, different than before, weak or low credit scores did not automatically disqualify the individual.

Indeed, the FHA program was meant to open up homeownership to a whole swathe of the American public – particularly those who were of moderate means. This meant that insubstantial employment or modest income levels were allowable.[7] Most importantly, a higher debt-to-value ratio was permissible with an FHA loan. This meant that the homeowner's equity could be much lower than what was needed before.

Most importantly, however, the FHA heralded the arrival of the secondary mortgage market. Because an FHA-backed mortgage loan carried with it a government guarantee, lenders that originated these loans could easily sell them to other lenders and financial institutions at a discount and thereby acquire an immediate return. Instead of waiting to collect the principal and interest (the profit) over the often-lengthy loan period, the guarantee of payment brought about a ready group of buyers for these loans. The lenders could sell the loans at a discount and thereby increase their own liquidity, and then could make additional mortgage loans to other aspiring homeowners.

To make the system work where a loan was originated and then sold (i.e., the secondary market), the federal government decided to create special entities that would be solely charged with buying up government-backed loans. These special purpose corporations were the Federal National Mortgage Association, the Federal Home Loan Mortgage Corporation, and the Government National Mortgage Association. Or, as they are more commonly known today, Fannie Mae, Freddie Mac and Ginnie Mae, respectively. Their jobs were generally to purchase these loans from private lenders and provide more liquidity to the mortgage market, as well as provide a securitization platform.[8] By doing this, the government hoped to provide yet another incentive for the private sector to expand credit even further.

As discussed in prior chapters, the GSEs (Fannie Mae and Freddie Mac, chartered in 1930 and 1970 respectively) are the most powerful of the three entities when it comes to housing economics.[9] These congressionally created entities are mandated to expand the availability of mortgage credit, specifically by targeting certain income groups. However, they are not public bodies as presently constituted. Indeed, they are expected (and required) to operate like private companies. This means an important aim for both must be profit making and increasing shareholder value.[10] Also as described in prior chapters, these entities pioneered securitization as well. Through their loan purchasing and securitization activities, over the years the GSEs have become the largest and most substantial generator of homebuyer credit in the United States.

Despite the efforts of the GSEs and the FHA to expand opportunities for homeownership in America, the U.S. housing market was anything but coordinated. This is most evident in the critical documents that form the foundation of a home purchase.

THE BIRTH OF THE UNIFORM MORTGAGE CONTRACT

As Forrester and Carrozzo note in their important works on the standard residential mortgage, uniformity of documents in the housing finance world was quite unheard of prior to 1970.[11] Despite attempts by large financial institutions operating in various states, as well as professional and trade groups, to create some uniformity, the various nuances of state property law often served as significant roadblocks.[12] Each state had slightly different laws, practices, or customs when it came to dealing in the sale of real estate, particularly residential real estate. This resulted in the contracts used to effectuate home sales varying to one degree or another. Indeed, the lack of uniformity made the process of pooling and securitizing mortgage loans very difficult. Investors in mortgage-backed securities were, as previously noted, essentially purchasing economic rights to a pool of many mortgage loans. However, the ability to deal with those loans effectively hinged on some level of uniformity as to rights, terms, and conditions among all the loans in the pool. Variations, even if only slight, between the loans could cause legal difficulties down the road, such as if a portion of the mortgage loans required certain actions be taken prior to a foreclosure while others did not. The problem was more than just a small bother. Federal Reserve Board Governor Maisel noted at the time that most mortgage contracts "lacked the degree of homogeneity required for active trading in the secondary market."[13] Something had to be done if the federal government's housing accessibility goals were to be met over the long term. An economic crisis would soon provide the needed push.

Although not on the same scale as the Great Depression, an inflationary period in the late 1960s brought about a mortgage credit crisis. During this period, interest rates were low, and so investors needed somewhere to move their money to get better returns. Investor attention turned to nonmortgage-related investments. This was bad news for banks, which relied on investor funds to make new mortgage loans. This resulted in a credit problem as banks suddenly lacked the funds necessary to continue making new home loans. Even with the government's FHA guarantee, these institutions couldn't make new loans if they did not have any cash on hand to do so. The housing market was suffering tremendously. A Congressional Report at the time noted that the number of new residential constructions during a given month (often referred to as "housing starts") was at its lowest level since the conclusion of World War I and that the country had not seen interest rates at such a level since the American Civil War.[14]

Again, policy makers decided that the way to address the problem was to help banks gain more liquidity. To do this, in 1970 Congress passed and President Nixon signed the Emergency Home Finance Act. This law was aimed at making the secondary mortgage market more robust and expansive than it had been in the past.[15] As the masters of the secondary market, Fannie Mae and Freddie Mac responded to the legislation by getting to work on trying to make the secondary market a liquidity machine for American mortgage lenders. The GSEs announced that their first task in this endeavor would be to create a "standard mortgage form."[16] Both entities recognized that before anything else could be done to expand the capabilities of the secondary mortgage market, the mortgage document had to be harmonized across the industry.

However, the process of creating such standardization was not easy. Obviously, the success of the endeavor was dependent on this being a group effort – a combination of industry and consumer advocates. A large group of lawyers and housing advocates from various sectors came together to begin the work of drafting this all-important document, but the voices often clashed as interests frequently failed to align.

At the time, despite the variation, most all mortgage contracts contained provisions that were favorable to lenders. This was largely due to the fact that the typical residential borrower had very little bargaining power when applying for a home loan. If borrowers objected to provisions that they thought were unfair or overreaching, banks would simply turn the borrowers away in favor of other eager loan applicants. Because the borrower would no doubt rather accept the term and purchase the home than walk away and start all over again, the lender always emerged the victor. As representatives for the financial services industry came to the table to discuss standardization, the draft mortgage documents they submitted were decidedly pro-lender. Consumer groups, in turn, provided drafts that limited the lender's rights or remedies against the borrower and also bestowed protections on the homeowner. Both groups heavily objected to the other's changes.

One bit of testimony was particularly prophetic. During a congressional hearing over the latest form of the mortgage, consumer rights attorney and several time U.S. presidential candidate Ralph Nader cautioned that the committee was about to take a major step in reshaping homeowners in America. Whatever was decided upon when it came to this uniform document would shape mortgage law in all 50 states. He also noted, with great prescience, that in enacting this uniform mortgage contract and creating such a massive degree of standardization, "What is now a face-to-face relationship between two people in the same locality will become an impersonal relationship through agents between a person and a bulk buyer of investment paper."[17]

After much testimony, many public hearings, and a great deal of debate, Fannie Mae and Freddie Mac developed and jointly published a single form to be used in all GSE mortgage-related transactions. The document was heralded as being bent toward the borrower while still mindful of the creditor. It was a compromise. As Julie Forrester notes, the form has changed some over the years, but it remains largely the same today as it was when the document was first issued in the 1970s.[18]

Once the uniform mortgage contract was completed its use spread quickly.[19] Fannie Mae and Freddie Mac were the biggest players in the secondary mortgage market, and they set the rules of the game.[20] Both entities announced that they would only purchase home loans that were secured by mortgage loan packages that used their particular forms.[21] Thus, all those originating banks and financial entities that wished to increase their immediate liquidity by selling their mortgage loans to Fannie and Freddie were forced to immediately switch over to using the uniform contract.[22] In fact, even financial institutions that originated home loans but did not necessarily contemplate selling them on the secondary market nevertheless issued loans using the GSE uniform mortgage contract.[23] The ubiquity of the uniform instrument throughout the housing finance market is a testament to the power that the GSEs and the secondary market play in mortgage lending nationwide.

Importantly, most of the early work of the consumer groups who sat at the table and advocated on behalf of homeowners during those heated hearings and meetings in 1970 remains in place.[24] Homeowners of today still enjoy the good work of these individuals each time they take out a home loan and sign the accompanying mortgage document.[25] Forrester points out that just as significant as the terms that were included in the uniform mortgage contract are those that were left absent from it.[26] She argues that provisions that are frequently seen in "take-it or leave-it" contracts of adhesion are fairly absent from the residential mortgage.[27] These include waivers of a right to a trial by jury, arbitration clauses, and waivers of notice and other rights of the borrower.[28] Forrester also notes that although residential mortgage transactions are similar to other types of consumer transactions in that the consumer has no opportunity (or at least not a meaningful opportunity) to negotiate the terms of the deal, the creditor does not have the ability to unilaterally set the terms of the deal on a case-by-case basis because all lenders are forced to use the same, preordained document.[29]

To be sure, standardization of the mortgage contract has played a tremendous role in the housing finance market in the United States. It has allowed for a system of reliable securitization of mortgage loans that, in turn, increases the liquidity of financial institutions and thereby augments their ability to provide more credit and increase homeownership. Similarly, it has been argued that standardization has resulted in mortgage contracts that are fairer to consumer debtors when compared with the terms found in commercial mortgage loan documents and the other consumer finance agreements.[30] Yet, the foreclosure activities that followed the financial crisis proved the point that the mortgage contract left much to be desired.

In truth, the mortgage contract was and remains tremendously one-sided. Despite a handful of protective niceties, homeowners give away the farm entirely to lenders when they put ink to paper. The terms of the mortgage contract, while perhaps not "as bad" as they could be, are still incredibly harsh and overreaching. The very moment that someone purchases a home by accepting the deed, that same person essentially turns the property over to the lender.

THE UNIFORM MORTGAGE CONTRACT TODAY

To understand this, consider just a few of the standard mortgage contract's more aggressive provisions. The first of these is perhaps the most egregious to homeowners – one that the average American would likely be shocked to learn exists. Section 7 of the uniform Fannie/Freddie mortgage allows the lender to unilaterally enter onto the property of the homeowner for the vague purposes of making an "inspection." The only limitation on this right is that the inspection must be reasonable in both time and manner. Importantly, there is no requirement that the lender notify the homeowner that such an inspection will take place. In the event the lender decides an inspection is needed (regardless of the fact that the borrower has kept up with his or her monthly payments and has otherwise abided by any other obligations under the loan) it may send its agents to physically come on to the property and conduct an examination. The following provision describes the right:

> **Lender's Inspection of Property.** Lender, and others authorized by Lender, may enter on and inspect the Property. They will do so in a reasonable manner and at reasonable times. If it has a reasonable purpose, Lender may inspect the inside of the home or other improvements on the Property. Before or at the time an inspection is made, Lender will give me notice stating a reasonable purpose for such interior inspection.[31]

What would perhaps astonish most homeowners is the second part of this clause – that the lender also has the ability to inspect the *inside* of the home and other improvements on the property. The thought that the lender, without being prompted by a default or other failure to abide by the terms of the mortgage or the loan, would have the unilateral right to enter a person's home, garage, or other home-related structure would and should shock most homeowners. When one considers the inviolate nature of one's home (the proverbial castle), the cavalier bargaining away of such security and safe refuge is momentous from a legal perspective.

The clause does, however, provide that the homeowner must be provided notice of such an "interior inspection," but the provision gives no minimum time frame for such notice. Rather, the notice can even be made "before or at the time an inspection is made." Imagine an inspection agent for your lender knocking on the front door one day and declaring that he or she is there to inspect every room in your house, and, oh by the way, this serves as your notice. The reason you may ask? Because the lender thinks it's reasonable. What is considered a "reasonable" excuse for a lender's agent to inspect your bedroom? The mortgage document does not say. There is no illustrative list or set of guidelines in the document that would reveal how mortgage lenders are to determine what is reasonable. And indeed, it is worth noting that nothing in the provision requires the homeowner to be home during these inspections. If the door is locked, can the property be broken into? Is the lender's agent allowed to access the property however he or she sees fit? One would imagine that the mortgage would at least provide some limiting language as to the manner of entry. No such guidance on any of these matters can be found in the mortgage document. The provision is designed entirely in favor of the lender and is exercised at its discretion.

The unspoken purpose that underlies this clause is the notion that the borrower cannot be trusted with the home. The lender should have the right to inspect the property at will because the borrower surely cannot be trusted to maintain the property and keep it in good repair. Thrown to the wind is the fact that the property serves as a place of sanctuary, security, and human integrity – a concept that is otherwise given great policy and legal weight under various provisions of American law.[32]

Another (and perhaps the most) egregious provision in the mortgage is section 9, which deals with the rights that a lender has upon a default or other failure to comply with the mortgage on the part of the borrower. Unlike the inspection provision discussed in the preceding text (which applies regardless of a default), this clause aggressively shifts the power and control over the property to the lender after one occurs.

Importantly, the rights that spring to life in favor of the lender under these clauses do not merely hinge on a monetary default. It does not matter if the homeowner is completely current on his or her monthly installment payments. Rather, the language is more broadly drafted to include the violation of any and all "promises and agreements" contained in the mortgage. The clause also includes other triggers, such as the filing of a petition in bankruptcy, the mere pendency of proceedings by third parties claiming an interest in the property that is averse to the lender, or the initiation of proceedings for the enforcement of municipal liens. Abandonment of the property, with no definition and regardless of the timeliness of payments or other obligations, also triggers these rights, as well as the death of the homeowner and the initiation of proceedings to probate a will. If there is *any* such failure, a default occurs and a host of rights – many of which are extremely hostile and often overreaching – become available to the lender:

> **Lender's Right to Protect Its Rights in the Property.** If: (a) I do not keep my promises and agreements made in this Security Instrument; (b) someone, including me, begins a legal proceeding that may significantly affect Lender's interest in the Property or rights under this Security Instrument (such as a legal proceeding in bankruptcy, in probate, for Condemnation or Forfeiture (as defined in Section 11), proceedings which could give a Person rights which could equal or exceed Lender's interest in the Property or under this Security Instrument, proceedings for enforcement of a Lien which may become superior to this Security Instrument, or to enforce laws or regulations); or (c) I have abandoned the Property, then Lender may do and pay for whatever is reasonable or appropriate to protect Lender's interest in the Property and Lender's rights under this Security Instrument.

Lender's actions may include, but are not limited to: (a) protecting and/or assessing the value of the Property; (b) securing and/or repairing the Property; (c) paying sums to eliminate any Lien against the Property that may be equal or superior to this Security Instrument; (d) appearing in court; and (e) paying reasonable attorneys' fees to protect its interest in the Property and/or rights under this Security Instrument, including its secured position in a bankruptcy proceeding. Lender can also enter the Property to make repairs, change locks, replace or board up doors and windows, drain water from pipes, eliminate building or other code violations or dangerous conditions, have utilities turned on or off, and take any other action to secure the Property. Although Lender may take action under this Section 9, Lender does not have to do so and is under no duty to do so. I agree that Lender will not be liable for not taking any or all actions under this Section 9.[33]

Such broad contractual authority includes the power to "do and pay for whatever is reasonable and appropriate to protect the Lender's interest in the property," which leaves much to the creditor's discretion. Unlike with section 7, this provision conveniently provides an illustrative list of such "reasonable" acts. But, lest one think the authority granted by section 9 is limited, the limiting principal of reasonableness is described as the vague and broad power to "protect" the value of the asset and secure and repair the property as the lender may deem necessary.

Importantly, in exercising its rights under section 9, the duty to give notice before entering the premises is dispensed with, as this clause allows the lender to enter and change locks, board up windows, turn off the utilities, and "take any other action" to secure the property. Indeed, what broader authority could a lender possibly desire? It seems nearly limitless.

HOW FORECLOSURES WORK

Notably, all this power devolves to the lender prior to any foreclosure proceeding taking place. The importance of this can hardly be understated and merits a bit of an explanation about how foreclosure law works in the United States.

Historically, the law of mortgage foreclosure allowed mortgagees who defaulted on their loan obligations to nevertheless retrieve the property from the hands of the foreclosing lender by paying the amount due.[34] This was called the *equity of redemption*, meaning that even after the payment date had passed (and thereby caused the borrower to technically forfeit his or her rights to the property) the borrower maintained an equitable interest in the real estate and could get it back by simply making the necessary payment. However, to balance this right of redemption with the interests of creditors, the courts in England developed a way to cut off the borrower's right. Courts would say that a borrower's right in equity to pay the amount due and retrieve the property was foreclosed (terminated) if the payment was not made within a reasonable period.[35]

Today, that process of cutting off the mortgagor's right to redeem (i.e., the foreclosure process) provides a method of having the property (let us say, the home) seized from the owner and then sold (either under the supervision of the court or by contractually appointed trustee) through some form of auction. The proceeds from the sale of the property are then handed over to the creditor in an amount sufficient to satisfy the debt. Provided there are no other creditors waiting in line, any remaining funds after the mortgagee takes its share are then handed back to the owner. Most importantly, if there are any other mortgages or liens against the property that are junior in rank to the foreclosing creditor's mortgage, they are terminated. Thus, the purchaser of the property at the foreclosure sale receives title free and clear of any other encumbrances. The property gets a new lease on life.

The actual method of foreclosure is essentially broken up into two categories in the United States: judicial foreclosures and nonjudicial foreclosures. The judicial foreclosure process, which dominates, involves a full court proceeding involving all the relevant parties. A nonjudicial foreclosure removes the involvement of the court and allows a private third party to sell the property.

From the homeowner's perspective, those states that use the judicial foreclosure process provide at least the benefit of an impartial mediator in the form of the judge. Further, the actual process of selling the property is conducted by the sheriff or some other public official. Also, because the foreclosure must be court ordered, the lender must abide by all of that state's procedural requirements, including things like filing the suit within a particular geographic location and providing proper notice to the homeowner of the lawsuit.[36] Also, although it is not typical for the distressed borrower to file an answer to the lender's petition for foreclosure, borrowers do have the opportunity to formally contest the foreclosure or the debt before the judge. And, importantly, the plaintiff-lender still has the burden of proof, at least in theory if not in practice, to prove all the essential elements necessary to make out a valid foreclosure claim (including that ability to enforce the debt/promissory note).[37] This includes the obligation to produce the original version of the promissory note or otherwise account for why it cannot do so.[38]

Because a foreclosure can have significant economic consequences on a homeowner (such as the impairment of credit and the loss of a valuable asset, much less the possibility of continued liability if money is still owed to the lender after the foreclosure is complete), judicial foreclosure laws attempt to give the borrower some special protections.[39] These include requiring that the property be professionally appraised prior to the foreclosure sale so that there will be a benchmark for the home's market value. Further, state law in these jurisdictions can also require that there be a minimum bid amount, without which the auction cannot proceed to an ultimate sale. And lastly, legal mechanisms are sometimes put in place that prevent the lender from pursuing the homeowner for the amount of the loan that might remain due on account of the money produced from the foreclosure sale not being sufficient to satisfy the full amount of the debt. Some of these special rules are also found in nonjudicial foreclosure states, as well.

Nonjudicial foreclosure states, while still governed by a number of statutory requirements,[40] are far more creditor friendly. In these jurisdictions (which comprise roughly half the states), a creditor need not go to court at all to foreclose on the property. Usually the only advantage to going through the judicial process in these states is so that the lender can go after the homeowner for any deficiency that remains after the foreclosure sale. Even in these jurisdictions the borrower is entitled to many protections. These include providing notice to the homeowner that he or she has defaulted and posting notices of the upcoming foreclosure sale at the court house, in public places, and in local newspapers.[41] Although there is no public official like a sheriff who conducts the sale, the lender is not allowed to oversee the sale. Rather, a third party that is independent of the lender must supervise the process.

Of course, we have to trust that foreclosing lenders will respect all these various legal protections afforded to homeowners under state law. There is no judge or sheriff supervising the process and demanding that certain procedural and substantive requirements be fulfilled by the lender. This is indeed a major flaw in the nonjudicial foreclosure process.

Lastly, three different theories underpin the law of mortgages, and these theories have some very real practical consequences for homeowners.[42] The first theory – the lien theory – stands for the proposition that the lender's interest is merely that of a security right. The lender does not acquire ownership of the property when the mortgage is given – ownership remains with the homeowner. The lien theory is the most prevalent. Under this theory, possession of the property remains with the homeowner unless or until it is taken through a proper foreclosure action. Prior to this process taking place, the homeowner is entitled to remain in the home and the lender cannot interfere (at least as far as mortgage theory goes).

The second theory is called the *title theory*. Under this theory (which is the original theory of mortgages but now the minority view among U.S. jurisdictions), the lender acquires title to the property when the mortgage is given. The homeowner retains only an ambiguous form of title until the mortgage is released upon payment of the debt. Importantly, courts have variously held that, in states that use the title theory, the mortgagee is entitled to some form of possession of the property, even prior to a default by the homeowner.

Finally, some states adopt an intermediate theory whereby the right to possession serves as the distinguishing feature.[43] Under this theory, the right to possess and occupy the property is exclusively with the homeowner. However, once a default has occurred the right to possession then shifts to the lender. As a general matter, the lien theory states can be found to the west of the Mississippi River (with some exceptions) and the title and intermediate theory states lie to the east.[44]

In either the title or intermediate theory states (and sometimes even in strange cases, in lien theory states), a lender can take possession of the property prior to the foreclosure. This is often called the "mortgagee-in-possession" doctrine. Courts validate this rule, as mentioned previously, by drawing on ancient mortgage law – much of which is from medieval England – to justify the lender's right to possess the property of the borrower. Even in lien theory states, where the lender should certainly not be entitled to possession until after the foreclosure takes place, courts have analytically twisted themselves into knots to find a way to justify early possession by the lender. They will harken back to "the old rule, existing when a mortgage actually passed title to the property" to justify the contemporary survival of a concept that, today, would likely surprise most property owners.[45] It is generally supported by the notion that the owner might allow the value of the property (i.e., the lender's collateral) to deteriorate – the owner/borrower cannot be trusted. Moreover, the owner that has defaulted, so the notion goes, might trash the property and then abandon the premises. But what is most significant about the mortgagee-in-possession concept is that it has mostly been applied, with some limited exceptions, to only commercial mortgage loans. In other words, the doctrine has been applied in instances where the property is a shopping center, a condominium building still held by the developer, or some other commercial space that constitutes income-producing property.[46]

With that background on mortgage law, we return to the mortgage contract. Section 9 (and to some extent section 7) of the standard mortgage embodies this idea of homeowner mistrust by memorializing the idea of the mortgagee-in-possession in the mortgage contract but in the residential context – in the home. Focusing again on section 9, the triggering of this clause – which according to the language of the mortgage could be caused by the most innocuous of offenses – essentially amounts to a forfeiture of the borrower's possessory rights in the property.

It is important to remember that one cannot think about these concepts in the abstract; this is not merely any random property of the owner. This is the home. It is the place where the family resides, where one seeks sanctuary, and where one shares the most intimidate moments of life.

In light of these immediate, harsh, and relatively unpredictable rights springing to life in favor of the lender (or rather, the servicer), one wonders whether a man's home truly is his castle. Ancient mortgage concepts embodied in the modern mortgage contract (and blessed by government policy in the way of Fannie Mae and Freddie Mac) require the homeowner to bargain away his or her rights at the very moment they are acquired. The lender acquires not only a unilateral right to come on to the property (and even enter the home relatively unannounced) under section 7 but also section 9 equips the lender with a host of aggressive rights that, without exaggeration, allows the mortgagee to dispossess and (as Chapter 6 will show) even torment the financially distressed homeowner. Such being the case, is homeownership really what we think it is? Does the law match our societal expectations of what others can and cannot do in our homes? Indeed, this begs the question: Is one ever really secure in one's home when a mortgage lender is involved? The answer can often be no.

5

Lost and Sign on the Dotted Line

The issues created by mortgage servicers for homeowners in financial distress were not limited to merely those dealing with physical entry and possession of the property. While dispossession (preforeclosure) was certainly a problem, the actual foreclosure process was also riddled with problems. As described in Chapter 4, whether a servicer was foreclosing in a judicial or nonjudicial foreclosure state, the laws of that state still generally required that the foreclosing party prove that they had the right to foreclose on the home and that the debt connected with that foreclosure was due (and correctly calculated). And one would think that proving such a thing – particularly for a large, sophisticated financial institution with access to resources and legal advice – would be quite easy. But, as it turns out, securitization had laid waste to even the most minimal efforts by lenders and related financial institutions to maintain an accurate account of the paperwork or information relative to a borrower's loan, much less rights to the mortgage itself.

A TALE OF THE NOTE AND ITS MORTGAGE

At the crux of this breakdown was the process of how mortgage loans are realistically transferred. As previously discussed, securitization involves multiple transfers of the mortgage loan from one party to another.

The story would go something like this: Chris and McHenry would take out a loan from their local lender – likely from a bank or through a mortgage broker – to facilitate the purchase of their new home. At the time Chris and McHenry receive the loan they will sign two very important documents: the promissory note and the mortgage that secures it.

Chris and McHenry will go home and not think again about those documents except for making the monthly installment payments that are required to avoid a default and subsequent foreclosure on the property. The lender, however, will care very much about the note and the mortgage. First, the mortgage document will be filed into the official land records of the county where the home is located. This is done so as to ensure that the mortgagee gets the benefits of priority over subsequent mortgages or other rights in the property that might arise thereafter. The note is immensely important because it embodies Chris and McHenry's obligation to repay the loan, so the lender will keep it in a safe place. In the olden days, our lender would just keep the note in a vault or some other safe location for the duration of the loan's term. Chris and McHenry would repay the loan eventually (usually at the end of 15 or 30 years) and then the original note would be stamped "paid" or "cancelled" and returned to Chris and McHenry.

But, these are not the days of old. The secondary mortgage market and particularly securitization dictated that the loan should hardly remain on the books of the lender for more than a few days. The loan would be sold to another party, which would begin the securitization process. The actual process of "selling the loan" involved ownership of the promissory note being transferred from the lender to the buyer. Because the note was almost always classified under commercial law as a "negotiable instrument," the lender was required to "indorse" the note over to the buyer.[1] This generally involved signing the back of the note (like the way one indorses the back of a check) and then handing the note over to the buyer. That was the first part.

As for the mortgage, property law has long stated that "the mortgage follows the note."[2] That means that when the underlying obligation (the debt/note) is transferred, any security (i.e., like a mortgage) is automatically transferred as well. This makes sense, given that the mortgage cannot exist without the obligation to which it is attached. But, despite this long-standing rule, the lender would often execute a document called an "assignment of mortgage," which stated that the rights to the mortgage were being transferred from the lender to the buyer. This document was then recorded in the same land records where the mortgage was also on file. In theory, this series of steps would be repeated every time the loan was transferred until it was finally placed in a special purposes vehicle, with many hundreds of other loans, and the mortgage-backed securities were issued to investors. In a typical securitization there would be anywhere from four to five transfers.[3]

Over time, mortgage originators and other parties involved in the securitization process grew weary of paying county recording officials the fees that were required to file assignments of mortgages into the land records. They also complained of dealing with the administrative chaos that sometimes occurred in certain registry offices across the country. Recall, of course, that legally this act of recording the mortgage assignment was typically not necessary, but that finer point seemed to have escaped these supposedly sophisticated financial firms.[4] By this time they had become wed to the idea of recording some kind of assignment of the mortgage.

ENTER THE PHANTOM TRACKING SYSTEM OF MERS

In the early 1990s a small group of mortgage finance players gathered together to conceive of a new way to track the transfer of mortgage rights from person to person without having to deal with provincial country recorders (and their fees). As Christopher Peterson writes, in October 1993, a task force of industry professionals published a paper arguing that a central electronic registry should be created to handle the issues of mortgage transfers.[5] This effort resulted in the powerful Mortgage Bankers Association of America, in conjunction with the accounting firm Ernst & Young, studying the issue and coming up with a way for mortgage finance firms to avoid dealing with country land recorders altogether. This resulted in the creation of a Delaware corporation named Mortgage Electronic Registration Systems, Inc. (MERS) in 1995, the goal of which was to lower the cost of doing business for mortgage servicers.[6] Ownership of the MERS corporation rests with its users – financial institutions operating in the mortgage lending space – who pay annual fees to be members.[7]

The idea behind the system was that one single entity (MERS) would own all the mortgages across the entire country. Gone would be the days of having to record something that evidenced the transfer of rights in a mortgage from one party to another. This, of course, made mortgage transfers much cheaper because the sometimes substantial recording fees that would otherwise go to local land records were eliminated. It did not take long for the entire mortgage finance system to buy in to the MERS system. By 1999 both the GSEs and the private-label market had embraced MERS wholeheartedly.[8]

Under the MERS system, the transfer narrative described in the preceding text regarding Chris and McHenry's loan changes. Now, the mortgage document would list the lender as the party making the loan but would list MERS as being the "nominee" of the lender, as well as would list MERS as being the actual "mortgagee." This means that the lender's name appears as the party entitled to seek payment under the promissory note (i.e., the loan/debt), but MERS is the party in whose favor the mortgage exists. Simultaneously, MERS is the nominee of the lender. Importantly, the idea of a "nominee" is not a technically a legal term. We often think of a party's "agent" or "legal representative," and there exists a well-established body of law governing those concepts. However, a nominee is an ambiguous term with no foundation, either under the law or in the mortgage contract, that would reveal the precise nature of the relationship between the lender (who holds the right to enforce the debt) and MERS (who holds the security interest in the home).[9] Indeed, if the mortgage is ancillary and dependent upon the debt for its very existence, it seems problematic to have one person own the debt and another person own the mortgage. Courts, as we shall see further, found this problematic as well.

Picking up with our story, Chris and McHenry walk away from the closing having signed the promissory note and the mortgage. The mortgage is recorded as before and the promissory note is sold (and hopefully negotiated) over to a buyer to start the securitization process. However, instead of now executing an assignment of mortgage and recording it in the appropriate land records, the lender and the buyer will contact MERS and pay a small transaction fee for MERS to indicate on its electronic ledger that this mortgage loan is now owned by the buyer.[10] Nevertheless, on the face of the land records in the country where the property is located, MERS remains the official mortgagee of record.[11]

In a securitization, ownership of the mortgage loan will change a number of times before it finally is placed in the trust for the benefit of the MBS investors. So, not only would the physical promissory note need to be transferred (and ostensibly negotiated to the new owner), but MERS would have to be notified to transfer the mortgage as well – although, under long-standing legal authority in many jurisdictions, the mortgage and the note could not be separated anyway.[12] But, indeed that is exactly what MERS aimed to have happen. A senior vice president for MERS wrote that for "servicing companies to perform their duties satisfactorily, the note and mortgage were bifurcated."[13]

THE RELATIONSHIP BETWEEN MERS AND THE MORTGAGE MIDDLEMEN

Another complication arose – the mortgage servicer. MERS was also supposed to keep track of who the loan servicer was at any given time. This was important because MERS, being the mortgagee of record, received service of legal documents related to the home. So, when MERS received mail relating to Chris and McHenry's mortgage loan, MERS was responsible for making sure that the servicer for their loan received this documentation. Servicing rights on a particular mortgage securitization pool could change hands multiple times. This necessitated the registration of yet another assignment relative to the loan within the MERS system. Of course, the servicer is acting as the agent and representative of the trust (i.e., the investors) in dealing with the homeowners and their loans. But, MERS is also acting in some kind of ambiguous representative capacity – as the nominee of the owner of the loan – which was originally the lender that made the loan but now would be the trustee on behalf of the MBS investors.

At the time of its blossoming, officials with MERS stated that the new system represented "a dramatic change in mortgage loan practices."[14] And that "[a]djusting to [the] change may not be as difficult as it first appears." In fact, they argued that "this change should ultimately benefit lenders, title insurers, consumers, and their counsel."

Needless to say, it did not take long before the system started breaking down. The first problems arose when it came time to foreclose on mortgaged property. On the face of the mortgage the party listed as the mortgagee was MERS. Therefore, it seemed logical that a court would find that the only party that could foreclose on the property was MERS. But of course, MERS was not the party that was entitled to enforce the underlying obligation. It was the person who had the right to enforce the promissory note. Then again, the party that was charged in this whole scheme with conducting foreclosures was neither the owner of the loan (the trustee) nor the mortgagee (MERS), but rather the servicer – our mortgage middleman.

Things became messy fast. First, some states allowed servicers to move forward and foreclose on the property in the name of MERS without producing any documentation from MERS. Then, courts began requiring that MERS execute an assignment of the mortgage in favor of the servicer – which MERS was happy to do – for the foreclosure to proceed.[15] But in other cases, courts required that the actual party that owned the debt (i.e., the trustee/investors) join in the foreclosure action as a party to the litigation.[16] Because this was typically difficult or undesirable from the investors' standpoint, the trustee would then have to transfer ownership of the loan from the pool over to the servicer. And even then, when the servicer was both the owner of the loan and the party with the rights of the mortgagee, courts would still sometimes find that the jumble of transfers back and forth between parties combined with the fractured way in which the whole system was set up from the beginning rendered the foreclosure hopelessly defective.[17]

NOT LETTING A LITTLE STATE LAW GET IN THE WAY

What made the whole system even more hopelessly complicated and doomed to fail was that the engineers of the MERS system and those who facilitated the securitization system more broadly fundamentally failed to understand the law behind the enforcement of promissory note debt and accompanying mortgages on real estate.

First, the Fannie Mae/Freddie Mac standard residential promissory note (which everyone used) is universally classified by every court to have ever addressed the issue as being a negotiable instrument.[18] This means that it is subject to the intricate rules of the Uniform Commercial Code (UCC). Importantly, the UCC states that ownership of a promissory note is one thing, but the ability to enforce the note is another. This means that while someone may be the owner of a note, they may not necessary have the legal right to enforce it.

The fundamental distinction lies in the concept of being a holder or having the rights of a holder.[19] A holder is someone who has the right to enforce the note, regardless of whether he or she owns the instrument. Generally, a holder is the person who is named as such in the note. The holder can then make someone else a holder by either negotiating the instrument over to him or her (usually by signing the back of the instrument [called an indorsement], like one would sign the back of a check, and then passing possession) or by merely transferring one's right in the instrument (which would include the right to enforce the instrument) to the new owner along with, again, handing over possession of it. Because the actual legal transfer of ownership of a note might be difficult to prove, it is more desirable to have possession of a note that has been indorsement over to you. This prevents having to produce other evidence showing that you are really entitled to enforce the debt.

Under the UCC, without the ability to enforce the note, one cannot enforce any accompanying mortgage.[20]

As you can see, although MERS was concerned with the rights in the mortgage, who was a mortgagee of record, and how the mortgage got transferred, the important document in the entire mortgage lending and securitization process is really the note. Without the note and the ability to enforce the note, the mortgage is useless. Also, it is possible to separate who owns the note (and thus is entitled to the money that results from payment under it) and who is entitled to enforce the note (i.e., retrieve the money from the debtor). So, in an ideal situation, the trustee (the owner of the loan and as the representative of the mortgage-backed security holders) should be the owner of the loan, while the servicer (charged with collecting payments and foreclosing) should have the rights of a holder.

Securitization and MERS made such a clean and clear path to structuring mortgage finance and managing mortgage loans impossible to follow. First, mortgage notes were only sometimes indorsed and handed over to the transferees in a given securitization.[21] Indeed, it was not uncommon for promissory notes to get completely lost in the process.[22] Even after the loan was supposedly sold off in the secondary or the private-label market to be securitized, sometimes the originator (our original lender in the Chris and McHenry hypothetical) would still have the note somewhere in its offices or vault.[23] At other times, the note might have made it to the buyer of the loan, but not on to any subsequent issues or arrangers that supposedly acquired the loan down the line. Instead, the loan might end up (as was often the case with loans sold to Fannie and Freddie) in some far-off storage facility.[24] In one case out of Palm Beach County, Florida, JPMorgan Chase, as servicer, attempted to foreclose on the home of Ricardo Lopez.[25] When faced with a call to produce the note, the servicer's attorney at first asserted that she had the original note, only to then backtrack and state that it was in fact a copy. Then, the attorney reported that the note had been destroyed, only to turn around again and announce that the original had been found. Upon further inspection, it was discovered that this too was a copy, as the signature of Lopez was in black when, as evidenced by the other loan documents, he had signed using blue ink.

And, shockingly, at other times the physical note would have been destroyed[26] (sometimes in so-called paperwork reduction initiatives) and only a scanned electronic copy would exist.[27] This act could produce the most disastrous results for the investors because, under the UCC, the intentional destruction of a promissory note can result in the debt being cancelled altogether.[28]

The significance of this cannot be understated. One public interest lawyer in Florida noted that about 80 percent of the foreclosures filed in her area did not include the original promissory note.[29] Even without an indorsement, a person cannot become a holder without being able to show that they acquired the note from someone who was a holder and that they have physical possession of the note.[30] But servicers did not have physical possession of the note because it was often lost or no longer existed. The securitization machine was so fast and furious – particularly in the subprime, private-label market – no one cared to pay any attention to keeping the paperwork together or making sure that long-standing principles of commercial law were being followed. The goal was only to produce more and more subprime mortgage-backed securities to try and quench the insatiable thirst of institutional investors. When the system came crashing down, servicers – the parties charged with dealing with the homeowner, collecting the debt, and foreclosing on the home – very often had no idea where the original promissory note was or if it even existed. Therefore, the servicer had almost zero chance to show that it had the right to enforce the debt against the homeowner and thereby foreclose on the property.

As one scholar noted, when taking out a home loan the lender "overwhelms the new homeowner with legal paper, after legal paper, after legal paper that the borrower must sign or the loan will not go through."[31] No matter how minor a missing dot on an "i" or a missing cross of a "t" might be, the lender will badger the homeowner until everything is just as the financial institution so desires. Therefore, "[I]t's not unfair that at the other end of the transaction when banks are attempting to take someone's home [that] they ought to be required to follow the law then too."[32]

So, if the notes could not be produced, and commercial law requires production of the note to enforce the debt, you might wonder how we had a foreclosure crisis in the aftermath of the financial crash at all. The answer to that question lies in a special rule under the UCC that allows a creditor to enforce a promissory note even if it has been lost or destroyed.[33] To do this, the lender can use what is frequently known as the "lost note affidavit." To use this method, it must be shown that the note has been either destroyed or lost (or stolen) such that it can no longer be reasonably located and obtained. And some courts even require (at least before the 2002 amendments to the UCC, which were only adopted in roughly a dozen states) that the foreclosing party show not only that the note had been lost or destroyed but also that the creditor had possession of the note at the time the loss or destruction occurred.[34] In so many cases, the servicer never had possession of the note to begin with so there was no way it could show that the note was lost or destroyed while in the custody of the servicer *itself*. Indeed, even in those cases in which this requirement was excused, it was still necessary for the servicer to show that it obtained ownership of the lost or destroyed note from someone who *did* possess it at some point. That, of course, was a real problem considering that the note had been passed from person to person in a long chain of entities that formed part of the securitization process.[35]

LOST PAPER AND FORECLOSURE BREAKDOWNS

Despite these long-standing rules on enforcing mortgage notes and how lost or destroyed notes were handled, at the start of 2010 news outlets across the country started reporting tales of litigation against servicers accusing them of submitting false or faulty paperwork in connection with foreclosure proceedings.[36] The most egregious examples of this dealt with the so-called robo-signing scandal. This scandal was caused by two things. First, mortgage servicers, faced with a multitude of loan defaults, were unable (or else were too rushed to try) to locate the original mortgage notes that were necessary to commence a foreclosure. Second, major questions arose as to whether the servicer had the right to foreclose on the home at all. This issue existed because, as noted previously, MERS was listed as the "mortgagee" on the face of many mortgage contracts. Other problems persisted as well, such as those dealing with broken chains of title in mortgage transfers from one securitization party to the next.

The issue of the severance of the mortgage from the note became very important. Many courts questioned whether the act of naming the person entitled to be paid under the promissory note as one person (the loan originator) and naming the person entitled to enforce the mortgage as another person (MERS) resulted in an impermissible separation of the note and the mortgage.[37]

Foreclosing attorneys working on behalf of the servicer engaged in all kinds of legal acrobatics to try and prove they had the right to foreclose on people's homes. As Chris Peterson points out in his important work on MERS, the entity would argue that it was, in its capacity as a nominee for the lender, only acting in the position of an agent on behalf of a principal.[38] But this of course is problematic because, while that may be true, the actual mortgagee was listed as being MERS (not the lender, with MERS acting as agent of the mortgagee). This was a problem because the language of the mortgage does not support the principal-agent argument. But at other times, MERS would argue that it was independently the mortgagee with the power to foreclose (acting on its own behalf).

Despite the problems in each argument, it is most extraordinary that MERS did not just pick one and run with it. Instead, MERS would assert either argument variously in foreclosure litigation across the United States – sometimes inconsistently within the same judicial district. Peterson also points out the strange way in which MERS engaged with servicers to accomplish this confusing litigation strategy.[39] Despite its massive importance in the housing finance sector, MERS as a company has very few employees. MERS would designate foreclosing attorneys or employees of the mortgage servicer for the applicable loan as being some kind of minor corporate officer (like an assistant corporate secretary or a corporate assistant vice president). This resulted in a system where "MERS has adopted a company policy of naming thousands of individual employees of other companies and law firms 'certifying officers' of MERS."[40] Servicers who need a corporate appointment by MERS need only to have gone to the MERS website and filled out a form that results in the company spitting out a corporate resolution with the servicer's name listed and duly appointed.[41] Voila! To make things even more official, a servicer could even order a MERS corporate seal for the incredibly low price of $25.

Courts soon started to show some skepticism in the way MERS and servicers were trying to stick a Band-Aid on this flawed system of mortgage and loan structuring. For instance, the Kansas Supreme Court stated that it had no clue how to properly interpret the meaning of MERS serving as a "nominee" for the lender. That court observed that "[t]he parties appear to have defined the word in much the same way that blind men of Indian legend described an elephant – their description depended on which part they were touching at any given time."[42] Other courts held that if indeed MERS was the independent mortgagee, rather than an agent for the lender, then MERS held no right to enforce the security interest at all because it lacked the ability to enforce the actual debt.[43] In one particularly scathing, but insightful, indictment of the servicer/MERS foreclosure strategy, a Miami judge stated that of the tens of thousands of foreclosure suits filed in her court in the prior year, "almost every single one of them[] represents a situation where the bank's position is constantly shifting and changing because they don't know what the Sam Hill is going on in their files."[44] Some courts admonished servicers and MERS by enjoining the foreclosure or rejecting their ability to enforce the note.[45] But, in many other cases, courts found ways to validate the foreclosure despite the confounding system that big banks and the mortgage finance industry had created.[46]

Mortgage servicers soon realized that the mortgage-lending industry's system was completely defective when it came time to foreclose. The many broken parts and missing pieces could ultimately leave servicers unable to foreclose through the traditional legal process. In those instances where the original note could be produced, it lacked the necessary indorsements to make the servicer a holder and thereby gave it the ability to enforce the debt. To deal with this, servicers would sometimes "produce" separate documents called *allonges* that would indicate that the indorsements had been obtained, just in a separate but related document.[47] The authenticity of these documents was frequently called into question. In one foreclosure case in Kentucky, the court noted that it was troubling that the foreclosing party initially stated that the note was unavailable, but then suddenly, out of the blue, came up with a note and every accompanying attachment needed to indicate that the servicer had all the rights necessary to proceed.[48]

In another representative case, Wells Fargo, acting as servicer, attempted to foreclose on a piece of property in Rock Round, Texas, that was encumbered by a deed of trust mortgage.[49] The debtor challenged the foreclosure on the basis that Wells Fargo lacked sufficient legal authority to foreclose in connection with the promissory note, to which Wells Fargo responded by pointing to the original note and a copy of the deed of trust mortgage that were included in the foreclosure lawsuit. However, that original promissory note and the deed of trust were made payable to a lender by the (curious) name of "Mortgage Factory, Inc." That note bore an indorsement by Mortgage Factory to an entity named ABN Amro Mortgage

Group, Inc., and there was also the copy of a recorded "assignment of lien" document whereby Mortgage Factory also assigned the deed of trust to ABN Amro. Lastly, the foreclosure documents included a yet another document titled "assignment of deed of trust" whereby ABN Amro transferred all its "beneficial interest in" the deed of trust and the note to MERS, which was acting as nominee for Washington Mutual Bank, FA. Lastly, the pile of lawsuit documents contained an "assignment of mortgage" whereby MERS transferred its right to "a mortgage" (not the deed of trust or any promissory note) to Wells Fargo.

The bankruptcy court dealing with this case looked with a skeptical eye at this chain of paperwork. First, how could Wells Fargo claim to have the right to enforce the promissory note when it was indorsed to ABN Amro, which had subsequently transferred its rights in the note to MERS (or rather Washington Mutual Bank). No rights in the note were ever transferred to Wells Fargo. Further, it seemed equally unlikely that Wells Fargo could claim to have any rights under the deed of trust because the "assignment of mortgage" was quizzically signed by a certain John Kennerty acting on behalf of MERS (on behalf of Washington Mutual), yet who was also an employee of Wells Fargo at the time! The court noted that there was no evidence that Washington Mutual Bank had ever authorized MERS to assign its interest in the deed of trust to Wells Fargo.

If you are confused by this case, then you should be. The flow of paperwork makes zero sense, and, indeed, the judge used the term *fraud* more than once in his opinion to describe the circumstances around Wells Fargo's behavior. In similar cases, it was not unusual for a servicer to suddenly come up with a necessary assignment or endorsement when it was time to foreclose and appropriate documentation became necessary. These became known as "tah-dah indorsements" because they arrived just in the nick of time.[50]

JUST SIGN IT, WHATEVER IT SAYS

To deal with these tremendous structural and record-keeping problems, servicers looked to the lost note affidavit procedure. Servicer employees started submitting written statements whereby the servicer would swear to the court that it had the right to enforce the note and (either in combination with the bootstrapped corporate designation by MERS or even without it) also had the right to enforce the mortgage against the home.

Of course, what is implied behind the lost note affidavit procedure is the fact that the servicer had conducted the necessary due diligence to ensure that the information to which it was swearing in the affidavit was indeed correct. To do this, the servicer would have to go through various documents, assignments, MERS records, and records contained in the various state recording systems to ensure that title to the note could be validated, the mortgage had not been severed from the note it secured, and the right to enforce the note existed in a successor-in-title that, at least at one time, had possession of the note. In the context of securitization (particularly in the subprime private-label market), this was an impossible task.[51] The notes had been long lost (or even destroyed in what many securitization parties foolishly called *paperwork reduction initiatives*) and evidence of the actual transfer of the notes (or the mortgages for that matter) was either inconsistent, partial, or nonexistent. In many cases, no amount of due diligence would have resulted in a servicer being able to truthfully attest that it had the legal right to foreclose.

Nevertheless, servicers found a way around these legal roadblocks. They would assign the task of investigating these mortgage loans to a small handful of employees who would then sign the necessary affidavits attesting to the legal right to foreclosure on the property. It did not take much time for a paper mill to ensue. These servicer employees would begin signing the affidavits without conducting any due diligence at all – asserting the servicer's right to collect on the loan and foreclose on the borrower's home without even the slightest clue as to whether this could be proven. This practice became known as "robo-signing" because the servicer employees would simply sign affidavits, almost in a robotic fashion, with relatively little if any care as to the authenticity or truthfulness of their contents.[52] Often times a servicer would "employ only one person to sign up to 10,000 foreclosure affidavits per month."[53] One employee of Wells Fargo cranked out about 500 foreclosures a day using this process.[54] While some courts would force foreclosing creditors to at least show that they attempted to find the lost note, many took the affidavits at face value and allowed the servicer to proceed with the foreclosure.[55]

The first robo-signing litigation started in Maine in 2010 when retired bank attorney turned public interest lawyer Thomas Cox took the case of Nicolle Bradbury[56] and discovered obvious irregularities in the foreclosure file. He soon discovered that a single employee for the servicer, GMAC, had prepared nearly 400 foreclosures cases per day and that, despite the assertions in his sworn affidavits, the allegations in these cases had not been reviewed by the employee or anyone else.[57] After this information went public, litigation spread like wildfire to a host of other states across the United States.[58] Consumer watchdog organizations and homeownership advocates denounced the practice. They argued that it stemmed from the very same types of fraud, neglect, and greed that served as the principal drivers of the financial crisis in the first place.

HOMEOWNERS STUCK IN THE MIDDLE

Now, to be clear, the problems presented by the MERS system and robo-signing do not suggest that homeowners should necessarily be excused from paying their debts. These individuals indeed borrowed money to purchase a home and therefore should be required to repay those amounts. The problem is that a homeowner would not know who to pay.

Notably, there is not just a little injustice in the way the mortgage lenders harangue homeowners over paperwork details when they try to take out a loan but then ask courts to look the other way when those same lenders (or rather their servicers) cannot seem to find the paperwork. As one federal court stated, "Financial institutions, noted for instating on their customers' compliance with numerous ritualistic formalities, are not sympathetic petitioners in urging the relaxation of an elementary business practice."[59]

But more fundamentally, this defective system can cause serious loss for homeowners. This is particularly true when homeowners are called upon to pay twice in instances in which multiple parties claim the ability to enforce the debt. Under the UCC's system for promissory notes, it is possible for a borrower to pay one party, thinking that he or she is fulfilling the obligation that is owed, but then be called upon again later to pay a second time (double liability) to someone who has the right enforce the note.

Consider the following example: homeowner's promissory note is assigned from Party A to Party B. However, despite the dictates of federal law, homeowner is not informed of the transfer. Being none the wiser, homeowner makes a payment to Party A. About a week later, Party B sends a notice to homeowner saying that he or she is in default for failure to make the required monthly payments. Homeowner will of course argue that the payment was already made, only to be met with the assertion by Party B that the homeowner paid the wrong party. Under normal circumstances homeowner would be able to assert the defense of having already paid when the money as sent to Party A. However, if Party B qualifies for the special status under the UCC called being a "holder in due course" then homeowner is precluded from raising this defense. What this means is that although homeowner already paid the monthly amount and thereby thought he or she was acting in accordance with his or her obligations, the transfer of the note and the holder in due course doctrine essentially prevent the homeowner from defending his- or herself. Hence, the homeowner will be required to pay twice.

Now of course, homeowner can certainly seek recourse against Party A to get the mispayment back, but that will cost money and time. Party A may give homeowner the runaround or use delay tactics. Imagine now that homeowner is in financial distress and has already defaulted. Now, homeowner hopes to stay in the home by making a late payment to Party A, only to later discover that Party A has sold the loan to Party B. Now homeowner is in a financially vulnerable position and may have very few resources to try and recoup the wrongfully paid amount to Party A. As Dale Whitman notes, the risk of double enforcement of a promissory note under the holder in due course rules of the UCC is very real and should give homeowners pause before treating with a party that cannot affirmatively substantiate that it has the definitive right to enforce the note.[60]

The related robo-signing practice also created issues. In perhaps one of the most egregious examples, some servicers would commence foreclosure actions against homeowners who owed no debt at all. For example, a retired police officer named Warren Nyerges and his wife Maureen purchased a home in Florida and paid in cash. Then, in February 2010, Bank of America's servicing arm filed a foreclosure action against them.[61] The couple naturally owed Bank of American nothing, and the two were forced to hire an attorney to defend themselves against the foreclosure. Clearly, if Bank of America had done even the most minimal amount of due diligence before filing the lawsuit then they would have known that Warren and Maureen did not have a mortgage with Bank of America.

The homeowners eventually prevailed in the litigation, but not before incurring $2,500 in legal expenses, in addition to court costs. To make matters worse, the court ordered Bank of America to reimburse Warren and Maureen for these costs, but the bank failed to respond to any of the couple's letters or phone calls. In a rare example of homeowner justice, the couple had their attorney obtain a court order instructing a sheriff's deputy to go a local Bank of American branch and remove "cash from the tellers' drawers, furniture, computers and other property" of the bank to make Warren and Maureen whole. The bank quickly came up with the required funds and handed a check over to the homeowners, pointing the finger at an outside attorney for not having sent the money sooner.

The MERS system also makes it hard to know for sure who had the right to enforce the note and thereby who the homeowner could speak with about trying to do a workout. During the time when foreclosures were at their height and servicers were nonresponsive or were refusing to work with homeowners, MERS engaged in a policy of refusing to disclose to any information about the ownership of home loans.[62] Homeowners and lawyers for homeowners could not be sure of exactly who was the party to negotiate with to attempt a workout when the servicer refused to talk.[63] In other instances, the foreclosing party (the servicer) would assert that it was the proper party, but a homeowner who wanted to avoid the possibility of paying twice would naturally want some kind of verification. With the note lost or destroyed and in the absence of any kind of documentation showing that the servicer had the right to treat with the defaulting party, financially distressed homeowners with few resources and facing the loss of their homes were trapped in a most uncertain and precarious position. Moreover, without the ability to discover the true owner of the loan (i.e., the name of the securitization trust that held the loan and the identity of the trustee), a homeowner had no way of challenging a servicer's assertion that it could not negotiate any kind of workout to avoid loss of the home.

Another problem that MERS created dealt with clear title to property. When things work well, a homeowner who pays off a loan is entitled to have the mortgage cancelled of record. The reason for this has to do with making title to the property marketable. While it is true that once a loan is paid off the legal effects of the mortgage cease, from a practical standpoint the land records of the county where the property is located will still reflect that a mortgage encumbers the property. This means that when the homeowner attempts to sell the property to someone else the buyer will be able to point to the continued existence of the recorded mortgage as a reason to refuse to go through with the sale. The existence of the recorded mortgage creates a so-called cloud on title. Normally a lender will record a document into the public records once the loan is paid off that indicates that the mortgage is no longer effective. However, often times the lender will forget or neglect to have such a document filed – particularly when the servicer does a poor job of keeping up with the loans it manages. This means that the homeowner (perhaps years after the loan has been paid off) will need to contact someone to have the mortgage cancelled. One would think, at least in theory, that having a centralized entity like MERS would make this process easy for homeowners. Because MERS keeps track of who has rights to the loan, the homeowner would need only contact MERS to have the cancellation accomplished.

Unfortunately, frequently this process was not so easily achieved. Principally, the MERS record-keeping system was riddled with inaccuracies as to who owned the loan and who had servicing rights to it. A homeowner might have significant problems getting in touch with the right company to get the cancellation done. On the other side, the system also put MBS investors at risk because MERS was often found to accidentally cancel mortgages when the loans were still outstanding. As Alan White has noted, in 2011 the Attorney General for the State of New York sued MERS for having erroneously filed mortgage cancellation documents into the public records on incorrect properties.[64] He notes that when MERS (really the servicer) discovered the problem, they would then file sundry and questionable legal documents against the homes to try and fix their error on the backend (a process that caused homeowners ample grief and forced them to incur legal expenses to fix the problem).[65]

THE NATIONAL MORTGAGE LITIGATION SETTLEMENT

As more information came to light about the shoddy foreclosure practices of these many servicers, lawsuits by government agencies against wrongdoing firms came in waves. In April 2012, the attorneys general of 49 states, as well as HUD, filed suit against several of the country's largest mortgage banks – Citigroup, JPMorgan Chase, Wells Fargo, Ally Financial, and Bank of America.[66] The government plaintiffs sought civil damages from these giants, premised on the fact that their "misconduct resulted in the issuance of improper mortgages, premature and unauthorized foreclosures, violation of service members' and other homeowners' rights and protections, the use of false and deceptive affidavits and other documents, and the waste and abuse of taxpayer funds."[67] The claims therefore encompassed not only the origination of subprime mortgages but also importantly the illegal and fraudulent practices of mortgage servicers in dealing with distressed homeowners and handling properties facing foreclosure. In February 2012, the mortgage banks reached a $26 billion settlement with the states and the federal government.[68]

MERS TODAY

In the end, the systemic breakdown in the MERS system of record keeping contributed to the major weakness already inherent in the mortgage servicing system. The enormous number of mortgages that were originated, packaged, and sold, followed by the massive number of foreclosures resulting from the crash in 2008, revealed the major defects in the mortgage tracking system. What resulted was chaos as servicers, listed as neither lender, nominee, nor mortgagee in the mortgage document or in the loan documents, sought to enforce notes that either lacked any evidence that the servicer had the right to seek collection and foreclosure at best, or that had been long ago lost or destroyed at worst. The widespread use of MERS as a recording proxy muddied title to property and made a system that had long been the backbone of real estate transactions in the United States (a single, transparent system of recorded interests in property) into a tracking scheme that was shrouded in mystery and very often riddled with inaccuracies and inconsistencies.

6

Break-In Foreclosures

There should be due process .... When people borrow money to buy a house, they don't anticipate that someone may one day drive by their home and make a determination on their own about whether it is vacant or not, and then possibly change their locks and go through their stuff. That is a scary proposition to me.[1]

> The Honorable Pamela A. M. Campbell Judge, Sixth Judicial Circuit Court State of Florida

One of the worst abuses of the foreclosure crisis – and one that has shockingly been given little attention – deals with the way mortgage middlemen use third-party property contractors to deal with homes facing foreclosure.[2] Recall that as the housing crisis unfolded massive numbers of home loans went into default. Servicers were confronted with a new and unfamiliar volume of properties for which foreclosure was a necessity.[3] In the past, portfolio lenders and then servicers had handled the management and preservation of their mortgaged property. Even after the height of the crisis had passed and foreclosure rates started to decline, servicers still had to deal with the tremendous backlog of homes awaiting foreclosure or those properties that, because of their substantially diminished value, could not be successfully sold at a foreclosure sale.[4]

To deal with these problems, the mortgage middlemen started to increasingly hire third-party contractors to assist them in managing these foreclosed or about-to-be foreclosed properties on the servicer's behalf.[5]

ENTER THE MORTGAGE MIDDLEMAN'S MIDDLEMAN

These firms, which collectively call themselves the "mortgage field services industry" and claim expertise in the management and preservation of real estate, would take charge of a large swathe of distressed properties to ensure, both postdefault/preforeclosure and postforeclosure, that the homes were preserved and maintained. A contractor might visit a property as often as once a month or more to make sure that there is no sign of damage, deterioration, or vandalism during the foreclosure period. Interestingly, however, the actual labor performed under these agreements is almost never untaken by the property contracting firm. Rather, the firm hires additional third-party subcontractors who are allocated various portions of the job.

While many industries across the country were crippled or severely hurt during the financial crisis, the mortgage field services industry soared.[6] In 2010 alone, Safeguard Properties (a Cleveland-based property contractor with operations in every state and that is said to inspect 1.5 million homes per month)[7] had 900 employees, used 10,000 contractors, and produced $600 million in income.[8]

The crisis created a very lucrative cottage industry for property preservation service providers. New, smaller property contractors – not knowing much about what they were doing but seeking to get into the game – started popping up and trying to compete with the larger, more established firms like Safeguard. This led to increased layers of middlemen: contractors hiring subcontractors hiring sub-subcontractors to do the actual work. But, as the stacking-up became more elaborate, the profit margins became thinner. This, in turn, created incentives to cut corners. One Maryland contractor stated that "[t]here can be two or three companies between you and the bank taking chunks of this money out for doing nothing but shuffling paperwork."[9] The farther down the chain you go, the less money (and care) you are likely to find.

THEN THINGS STARTED GOING AWRY

In mid-2012, a flurry of articles began cropping up in newspapers and media outlets across the country telling stories of people returning to their homes at the end of a long day to find that all their belongings had been taken and their property damaged.[10] The story went something like this: the homeowner would find the break-in and investigate what happened. Soon thereafter, the homeowner would discover that it was not a random criminal off the street that had been the intruder and caused the damage, but rather it was a property management contractor, hired by and operating at the direction of the homeowner's mortgage servicer, who had committed the acts. The contractor (or often the contractor's contractor) had been charged by the mortgage servicer with cleaning out and securing the premises until such time that the property could be sold at foreclosure – this is known as a *break-in foreclosure*. Typical cases involved instances where the homeowner was delinquent on his or her mortgage loan but where negotiations were pending with the servicer for a workout or forbearance. Then, the servicer would send a contractor out to the home to conduct an inspection to see whether the property had been abandoned. The contractor, despite evidence that the property was still inhabited, would deem it abandoned and clear out the home, winterize the premises, and padlock the doors. The homeowner would then arrive back at the property later that day and discover not only the break-in but also that a foreclosure was imminent.

As time progressed, stories continued to surface in the news media about homeowners in distress being ejected from their homes by these property contractors acting on behalf of the homeowner's servicer. In the summer of 2012, lawsuits had been filed in roughly 30 states against these property management firms and often their servicers.[11] Most shockingly, this behavior occurred only a year and a half after the April 2012 national mortgage settlement, which was supposed to impose new rules for how servicers managed their third-party vendors (like property contracting firms). By 2012, foreclosure abuse had a new face – a large and powerful group of servicer-engaged property contractors armed with the servicer's wide-ranging authority and, as described in the following text, often with little training or care for the properties they inspected or the people who called these properties home.[12] To make matters worse, included among those servicers that engaged these aggressive third-party property management firms were the same mortgage giants who were parties to the national mortgage settlement.[13]

THE WORLD OF SERVICERS AND THEIR PROPERTY CONTRACTORS

To understand the break-in foreclosure phenomenon, you have to understand a few things about the relationship between the mortgage middlemen and their third-party contractors – and particularly how the relationship is rife with incentives for abuse. In theory, the arrangement is typical of the many situations in which a contractor or third-party vendor is hired to perform a task that the principal does not wish or is not equipped to carry out.[14] However, for an industry that often complains about having too little direction from investors regarding how to handle loss mitigation, servicers provided the same lack of guidance to their contractors about how to handle homeowners in distressed situations.

In general, servicers, especially during the height of the foreclosure crisis, feared that a defaulting homeowner would walk away from his or her property and leave it abandoned to the elements or to criminal activity.[15] In doing so, the property could become greatly damaged and subsequently decline in value. Abandoned property can pose health and safety risks for communities, can become a haven for criminality, and has the effect of depressing adjacent property values.[16] This, in theory, could explain servicers' drive to actively police abandonment of their mortgaged properties, and even their use of property contractors to do the policing.

Although the possibility of the property losing value is a significant driver, the securitization scheme discussed earlier creates additional incentives for aggressive policing of properties. When a servicer agrees to manage a pool of mortgage loans, it enters into a pooling and servicing agreement that sets forth a number of promises – called *representations* and *warranties* – that the servicer makes to the trustee. The trustee is the entity that holds all the pooled loans on behalf of the securities investors. One of these promises is that the homes that secures the loans will be maintained in good condition and, to that end, that the servicer will conduct quality inspections to ensure quality maintenance. If a servicer fails to do this, then the trustee can force the servicer to purchase the loan that is connected to the poorly maintained property.[17] You can imagine, then, that if a host of mortgaged properties are not properly maintained, and the trustee calls on the servicer to purchase the relevant loans from the pool, this can be a major drain on the servicer's financial health. And for nonbank servicers that already lack capital reserve requirements, such a call can bring about major solvency issues – it could even make a servicer go broke.[18]

To protect against that risk, servicers charge property contractors with traveling to the mortgaged property in question, inspecting the premises – which is, legally and practically speaking, still owned by the homeowner – from the street without entering on to the premises, and determining whether the property was still occupied or if it had been abandoned by the troubled homeowner. If the contractor determines that the property is abandoned, then the firm (or its subcontractor) is supposed to "secure the property by boarding up the doorway, turning off the water and winterizing the home, and placing lockboxes or padlocks on the door."[19] These preservation activities sometimes even involve removing personal property and other effects from the home. Also, these periodic inspections and services often continue "throughout the foreclosure process and after the mortgage lender purchase[d] the property in the foreclosure auction."[20]

HOW PROPERTY CONTRACTORS GET PAID

The compensation structure for the mortgage field services industry plays an important role in how these firms operate and why they seem to frequently engage in abusive activity. When thinking about the payment structure, it is useful to think about who is doing the paying. As of December 2017, Fannie Mae and Freddie Mac securitizations made up just less than 60 percent of the total mortgage market and unsecuritized mortgage loans that are held by banks, credit unions, and the GSEs comprised about 30 percent.[21] That left just less than 5 percent for securitizations stemming from the private-label market. Considering their majority position, it is helpful to look at how Fannie and Freddie compensate property contractors for those who service GSE loans when trying to understand the incentives that can lead to abuse.

Between 2011 and 2012, Fannie and Freddie spent $91.2 million on their servicers in connection with preforeclosure property inspection and preservation activities.[22] As previously mentioned, the GSEs issue many hundreds of pages worth of servicing guidelines that help direct the practices and activities of the servicers with whom they do business. With respect to preserving mortgaged property, these guidelines include instructions and matrices for how often a servicer should cut the grass, inspect the property, and make home repairs (among many other topics).[23] For example, according to Fannie Mae's 2014 guidelines, in those instances in which the servicer was allowed to bill Fannie Mae for inspection expenses, the inspection of the home's exterior was reimbursed at $15 and an inspection of the interior of the home earned $20.[24] Repairing a garage door was reimbursed at $100 (not per repair, but for the entire life of the loan). Window repairs got $25. For cutting the grass, there are different schedules for the initial cut and then for subsequent cuts, all depending on the square footage of the yard (less than 10,000 square feet earned $100 on the first cut and $80 thereafter).

When it comes to clearing out trash and debris, the numbers grew small quickly. Removing garbage from the inside and outside of the house earned the servicer $40 per cubic yard, but with a cap of 10 cubic yards for the life of the loan (or $400 total). For moving the homeowner's personal property off the premises, it was $20 per cubic yard, but again subject to the same loan-life limit. What is most surprising is that, despite the effects of inflation, these 2014 reimbursement amounts have by and large remained the same through 2017.[25]

Recall, of course, that this is what Fannie Mae will reimburse the servicer. The servicer will then pass the work on to a contractor who will pass it along to at least one additional (sometimes more) subcontractor to do the work. Each contractor takes a cut, leaving additional contractors down the chain with less money. This results in incentives to find and create work, especially work that sits on the high side of the payment schedule. Also, it is important to remember that this only concerns instances in which Fannie Mae and the servicer have agreed that the relevant GSE will reimburse the servicer for certain preservation expenses. This is compared to some servicing agreements that force the mortgage middleman to internalize these preservation costs as part of its normal servicing obligations.

Even with these numbers in mind, it is important to remember that not only does the servicer hire (and pay) a contractor to do the actual work but also that there is a great deal of layering between the servicer that orders the work to be done and the person who ends up physically going to inspect the property. The further one goes down the chain, the thinner the profit margins become. Considering how small the preceding reimbursement numbers can be, the actual cash that goes into the hands of a subcontractor can be quite small. For Angie Montgomery of Cincinnati, who is one of those subcontractors that does the work of going to the property, that means somewhere between $3 and $4 per visit if she has to inspect the interior of the home.[26] She covers the cost of gas, insurance, and maintenance of her car herself.

DETERMINATIONS OF ABANDONMENT AND ACTS OF PRESERVATION

You might be wondering at this point how these property contractors – complete strangers to the homeowner – have the authority to come on to (or even into) someone's home, all prior to a foreclosure. Would not this be trespass of some sort?

The answer to that question lies with, as noted in Chapter 4, the mortgage contract. Provisions in the mortgage contract – particularly sections 7 and 9 – authorize servicers, or their agents, to engage in acts of preservation of the mortgaged property. This contractual authority is typically broad and far-reaching. It stipulates that if the homeowner intentionally or through his or her negligence allows the mortgaged property to be damaged or subjected to deterioration, then the mortgagee or its agent has the authority to enter onto the premises.

Also, as you will also recall, the mortgage contract allows the servicer or its agent to enter the interior of the premises if there is reasonable cause to do so. The homeowner must be given notice, but the mortgage does not detail when that notice must be given, its form, or what must be included. Lastly, once the homeowner has missed a payment or otherwise failed to broadly fulfill his or her obligations under the mortgage contract, the servicer is given a host of options, including the boarding up of windows, turning off of utilities, clearing out of the premises, and winterizing of the home. All this is done with an aim toward protecting the property (the loan collateral) from harm. It presumes that the homeowner is abusing the property or otherwise permitting the home to fall into disrepair.

ABUSE AND FRAUD

Unfortunately, the incentives and payment structure, combined with nearly unfettered discretion and a lack of guidance, led to countless stories of mortgage servicers, through their third-party contractors, undertaking a much more aggressive and, in many cases, unauthorized approach to dealing with foreclosed properties. Indeed, it turns out that the mortgage field service industry – the mortgage servicer's man-on-the-ground that is said to have brought in $2 billion in revenue in 2012 – is plagued by numerous allegations of abuse, misconduct, and fraud.[27] Investigative reports reveal various lawsuits and police reports from across the country where property contractors, acting on behalf of mortgage servicers, have been met with the following allegations – all under the auspices of property preservation: emptying out homes that were still occupied by their owners; tossing away jewelry, family photos, heirlooms, and coin collections; and even disposing of one family's pet cat.[28]

And far from being preserved, sometimes the homes were in worse condition after the servicer's contractor left the premises. Mimi Norris, who owns and operates a small Ohio firm that engages contractors to do home inspections and repairs, stated that "'I've walked into houses that [a different contractor] was supposed to take care of that were in horrible shape ... I have gone to inspect properties reported as vacant that were still occupied. This happens too often.'"[29]

In one report out of Tampa, Florida, homeowner Deanna Tedone alleged that she returned to her home at the end of the day only to find that a contractor, sent by her servicer U.S. Bank, had smashed holes in the walls of her house.[30] The purported reason was that he was inspecting the property for Chinese drywall, all in an effort by

U.S. Bank to protect its collateral.[31] Although Tedone had indeed fallen behind on her mortgage payments, she stated that neither U.S. Bank nor its contractor contacted her prior to the visit. The so-called inspection left debris and rubble scattered about the home, which Tedone said diminished her ability to sell the property at a short sale and thereby avoid damaging her ability to obtain other forms of credit in the future.

In 2013, Marie "Mitzi" Osborne, a recent widow, was facing foreclosure but was continuing to live in her Arkansas farmhouse.[32] In a 2013 lawsuit filed against Safeguard Properties and one of its subcontractors, Osborne stated that she came home one day to discover that the lock to her gate was broken off and her doors had been padlocked. Once she gained entry, she reported that her home had been "ransacked" and "[a] grandfather clock was missing, along with an antique gold mirror, several televisions and family photos."[33] The home was clearly not abandoned. Osborne stated that family members and workers were frequently going in and out of the house and there was much evidence of an active daily life on the property.

Mitzi Osborne was not the only widow to face off against a mortgage servicer. In August 2005, Mimi Ashe of Truckee, California, lost her husband.[34] Shortly after his death, she stopped making payments on the home mortgage loan and the servicer, Bank of America, began negotiations with Mrs. Ashe to do a workout. Eventually, Bank of America foreclosed on the property, but the servicer and Mrs. Ashe continued to exchange e-mails and phone calls to explore a loan modification and a rescission of the foreclosure.[35] Shortly after the foreclosure notice was posted to the front door, but while the home was still fully furnished and contained clothes and other household items within, Bank of America allegedly sent a contractor to the property on two occasions to "trash out" the premises. Items that were taken included Rolex watches, home videos, and, most tragically, the urn containing the remains of Mrs. Ashe's late husband, Robert.

In another account, Majorie Principe of Illinois claimed that she returned home one day to find that her bank's contractor had "taken her furniture, books, savings bonds, and electronics."[36] The Napolitanos of Maine entered into a successful loan modification with Bank of America, who they thought was their authorized servicer, but were later met with allegations of a loan default by a new middleman, Green Tree Servicing,[37] and a subsequent property invasion by Safeguard.[38]

A homeowner who had defaulted on his loan out of Cleveland, Ohio, purports to have been deprived of his clothing by a property preservation sweep, and an Atlanta man was arrested when he tried to "force his way back into his home after a Safeguard contractor locked him out."[39] For this Atlanta homeowner, the situation was particularly egregious, as it was discovered that the contractor had accidentally gone to the wrong house.

And homeowners are not the only casualties of these practices. Tenants of defaulting homeowners have also been victims. For instance, Nicole Corum of

Independence, Missouri, stated that she returned to her rented home – for which she was current on all rental obligations – to find that all her belongings were missing, including her seven-year-old son's toys, and the premises damaged.[40] Neighbors reported seeing a man emptying the house earlier in the day and, when confronted, answered that he had "an order. I work for Safeguard, deal with them." Upon calling Safeguard, Corum states that she was told that all her belongings were "out in the dump" and that Safeguard was not in the business of keeping things in storage that were the subject of a property preservation order.

A man named Innocent Obi met a similar fate.[41] He and his family rented an apartment in Chicago and were current on their rent. He alleged in his pro se complaint that one day in February 2010, he came home from work and found that the locks had been changed and several items of personal property were scattered about on the ground outside. Evidently his landlord had defaulted on the mortgage loan and the servicer, Chase Home Finance, sent a contractor (Safeguard) to "change the locks on the property, board up the unit, winterize it, and evict any person living there." Notably, a foreclosure had not taken place and there was no court order authorizing the entry.[42] Obi stated that he called the number left on the door notice, but no one answered. He and his five children had to find shelter for that night and several days thereafter. Obi reported that he had to miss work for the next few days to deal with the housing situation. He ultimately lost his job.

WHO INSPECTS THE INSPECTORS?

With all this abuse, property damage, and sometimes even theft, one might wonder why servicers are not doing a better job of making sure the contractors that they employ have the proper credentials and backgrounds for this sensitive type of work. The lack of care by servicers in this department is quite shocking considering what is at stake when a homeowner faces foreclosure and the reputational risk associated with being identified with such activities.

Recall that servicers engage contractor firms, which then often engage subcontractors to do the work. But they fail to ensure that those working "on the ground" on the servicer's behalf are fit to undertake the important work of managing someone's home when the owner is in financial distress. For example, the owner of Florida vacation rental property facing foreclosure filed a lawsuit against his servicer's contractor, Core Logic, when the owner's weekend renters reported that they returned from the beach one day to discover a number of items of personal property – including a laptop, iPad, and several bottles of wine – were missing from the premises.[43] An empty can of beer was also left on the kitchen counter. As it turns out, the employee of Core Logic, Victor Titenko, made a wrongful determination that the property had been abandoned by the owner. Titenko denied having taken anything, including the beer. Later, however, it was discovered that Titenko's fingerprints were found on the beer can. Further inspection revealed that he had been arrested six times in that state for an array of crimes including burglary and robbery, as well as attempting to sell stolen goods.

The prior story of Marie Osborne's Arkansas break-in foreclosure also relates to a lack of proper background checks by servicers. Daryl Cole, the owner of and inspector at the contractor company Cole & Sons, which had broken in, was a convicted sex offender who pled guilty to soliciting a 14-year-old girl in 2008.[44] And even when servicers inquire about the credentials and backgrounds of the property contractors they hire, it is not certain that they verify for accuracy. In 2013, it was reported that a leaked document from the complaint department of Safeguard Properties revealed that the company was receiving, on average, 85 complaints per month between August and January 2009 related to theft and damage to property.[45] The man who leaked the document, the former head of Safeguard's complaint department, was subsequently sued by the company for a breach of confidentiality.[46] If property contracting companies go through such efforts to keep complaint data hidden from public view, what other information do they work to keep secret?

To be sure, servicers carry much of the blame for these events. The watchdog agency for the GSEs reported that for the servicers used by Fannie Mae and Freddie Mac, many firms "inconsistently adopted requirements for inspectors to complete and pass criminal background checks."[47] In fact, in one 2014 study of GSE servicers, many stated that even if they do require such checks, they rarely confirm whether the contractor has passed. Other servicers in the report said they rely on the internal policies of contractors to handle background check requirements. And none of the servicers in the study said they ever required background checks for subcontractors of the prime contracting firm. In fact, many of these servicers do not even require that the name of the person who conducts the inspection be included in the report submitted to the servicer by the prime contractor.[48] When the identity of the ultimate subcontractor did appear, the report noted, it was often expressed as "either untraceable initials or their last names."

What all this means is that servicers often have no idea who is going to the property and interacting with the homeowner. In 2011, a contractor named Don Zilen was arrested in a suburb of Fort Meyers, Florida, for admitting that he dumped more than 10,000 pounds of garbage into the back yard of a home.[49] The trash came from two homes that Zilen had cleared out as part of so-called preservation activities.[50] It was speculated that Zilen was trying to save some money on paying trash yard dumping fees by depositing the garbage in the neighbor's yard. The owner of the firm that had contracted with Zilen, REO Proz, said at the time that while the company usually does background checks, "Sometimes we hired them on a whim."[51] As one industry consultant noted, "The bank almost certainly doesn't know anything about the individual chosen to represent them at the property."[52]

These stories (and the findings by the FHFA inspector general detailed in the following text) emphasize the fact that the mortgage middlemen are not engaging in the type of careful and proper background checking, monitoring, and compensating that is necessary to safely imbue these unknown individuals with the power – granted to servicers unknowingly by homeowners in their mortgage contract – to enter people's homes. Servicers evidently cannot rely upon their contractors to do this important work. For instance, a spokesman for Safeguard Properties stated that while the company does background checks for the owners of those it contracts with, it leaves it to the subcontractor to do sufficient checks on parties further down the chain.[53]

And it is not just finding evidence of criminality that supports a robust system for credentialing and checking the backgrounds of contractors. Servicers should be concerned about these individuals having the right training and temperament for this important job. Engaging with homeowners facing a loss of their home – usually because they are in financial distress stemming from any number of adverse life events – requires a careful hand. Nancy Cox of Clawson, Michigan, came to learn this the hard way. She came home to discover that her property had been visited by a property preservation firm. She alleged in a lawsuit that many of her possession were strewn about the front yard in pieces, accompanied by a chalk rendering of a clown face on her garage with the inscription "another job well done."[54]

Servicers have played a huge role in the breakdown of the property contractor system. The former owner of the Florida property preservation company REO Proz, Adam Reynolds, said "[c]ountless times" he received orders to forcibly enter and clear out homes that were clearly still occupied – with photos on the shelves and stocked refrigerators.[55] This suggests that the servicer might have had every reason to believe the property was not abandoned – perhaps even that the homeowner was interested in doing a workout. Reynolds even said that one time he "had an order sending me to a property that was never owned by any bank." This suggests that servicers are not even careful about knowing which property they even have a mortgage on before sending contractors out to conduct inspections.

The issue became so acute that in September 2013 the Illinois Attorney General filed suit against Safeguard Properties based on a series of successive break-in-style foreclosure actions spanning across the entire state.[56] The attorney general based her suit on violations of the Illinois Consumer Fraud Act. The state's petition requested that the court "permanently enjoin[] [Safeguard] from engaging in the deceptive and unfair acts and practices ... including a permanent injunction barring [it] from engaging in the business of advertising, soliciting, offering for sale, and selling property management and preservation services ... in the State of Illinois." This was in addition to requesting civil penalties in the amount of $50,000, another $50,000 penalty for each consumer fraud violation, and a final $10,000 penalty for each consumer fraud violation "found to have been committed against a person sixty-five years of age or older."

The petition went on to specifically list those acts, committed by Safeguard under the direction of the applicable mortgage servicer, that constituted unfair or deceptive trade practices. This included representing to homeowners that they no longer had a right to occupy their homes, as well as engaging in acts of intimidation to entice legal possessors to vacate the premises. The petition also alleged that Safeguard took unlawful possession of mortgaged homes, including through acts of breaking and entering legally occupied property, changing locks, depriving owners of access, and turning off utilities. And finally, the attorney general asserted that the company unlawfully removed the personal property and effects of many homeowners, all without proper judicial authority, as well as failed to train, hire, and supervise its subcontractors who engaged in these activities on Safeguard's behalf.

In response to the lawsuit, Safeguard's chief executive officer sent a letter to the company's mortgage servicing clients and stated that the contractor had a "rigorous procedure of checks and balances to verify occupancy prior to securing a vacant property."[57] As to allegations of poor hiring or supervision, Safeguard stated that it conducts "background checks of all contractors and crews, carefully monitor[s] the performance of inspectors, and take[s] immediate corrective action if policies are violated."

In June 2015, Safeguard and the Illinois Attorney General entered into a settlement where the contractor agreed to pay $1 million.[58] Almost the entire amount was set to be distributed to homeowners and tenants who suffered improper treatment by Safeguard or its subcontractors during the foreclosure process. Also, as part of the settlement, Safeguard agreed to reform its company practices and procedures and to set up a 24-hour hotline where consumers could report their complaints. Lastly, Safeguard agreed to no longer remove or otherwise dispose of nonperishable and nonhazardous personal property from a home facing foreclosure, unless the company had a court order to do so. A few months later in August 2015, Safeguard settled a similar lawsuit with the Maryland Attorney General related to comparable allegations of break-in foreclosure abuse.[59] The company again agreed to reform its practices and pay restitution to aggrieved consumers. Private litigation by individual aggrieved homeowners against the company remains legion.[60]

THE (LACK OF) GOVERNMENT RESPONSE

Considering all the lawsuits, police reports, and news articles on the issues of mortgage servicer and property contractor abuse, one might assume that government regulators would jump to action to protect homeowners and handle the situation. That, however, has been far from the truth.

That is not to say that the government lacked sufficient evidence of the problem. In 2012, the FHFA – the regulator and now conservator for the GSEs – and Secret Service agents conducted a raid on a property contracting firm in Hernando County, Florida, named American Mortgage Field Services.[61] The owner of the company pled guilty to fabricating three years' worth of property inspection reports and then submitting them to Bank of America, which was acting as a servicer for Fannie and Freddie.[62] In another report, one inspector was sent to property facing a foreclosure and reported that the grass was exactly eight inches high – for seven months straight.[63] It was revealed that the contractor had simply been submitting copied and pasted information from an old inspection report on to subsequent monthly reports without noticing. Sometimes the date was not even changed from monthly report to monthly report.

Also, in September 2012 the HUD inspector general did an audit on a preservation company named Innotion Enterprises, which was charged with maintaining homes on behalf of the federal agency. The audit revealed that of 96 properties that were surveyed in the Las Vegas area, nearly 40 percent failed to be preserved and maintained as Innotion had reported.[64] For instance, during a March 2012 visit by the auditors, it was noted that the front yard of one home had weeds growing four feet tall.[65] But, 13 days prior to the audit visit, Innotion submitted photos to HUD showing its inspector pulling weeds. When the auditors returned to the property a second time in April, the property was still significantly overgrown with weeds – suggesting that the photos were falsified or at least misleading. In another instance described in the audit, a contractor reported to HUD that he had installed a safety rail to the front porch of a home.[66] The auditors went to the property and discovered that the contractor seemed to have left off the nails and screws needed to hold the rail in place.[67]

Most significantly, in March 2014 the FHFA inspector general issued a report that sharply criticized the lack of government oversight in connection with the use of property management contractors by the mortgage servicers used by Fannie Mae and Freddie Mac to handle properties related to GSE securitization trusts.[68] The report noted that "[o]verall, several servicers reviewed during the audit did not have quality controls in place to ensure contractors provided accurate, complete, and consistent information in property inspection reports." The report further stated that many of the audited inspection reports revealed "inconsistent and inaccurate information; missing or blurry photographs; manipulated date and time stamps on the photographs; and unnecessary inspections that did not provide useful information about the properties." In one example, an inspector submitted photos showing different sides and various angles of a consumer's home, yet each photo had the same date and the exact same time (9:21 AM) – suggesting that either the individual had acquired the ability to bi-locate or else he had manipulated photo information.

The audit also revealed instances in which the inspections conducted by these firms, and billed to the servicer, were perfunctory at best. In one account, a contractor submitted bills to a servicer for 12 separate inspections of a home that was located within a gated subdivision.[69] But because the inspector never gained access to the neighborhood, all his inspections were conducted from outside the gated community by peering through a fence. To the extent servicers studied in the audit did engage in any type of meaningful evaluation of their contractors, it came in the way of scorecards whereby the servicer would ostensibly rate the contractor for its good work. But, the content and quality of these scoring mechanisms varied greatly from servicing firm to servicing firm. In some scorecards that were the subject of the inspector general's audit, the focus was not on the quality of the property inspection but instead on the timeliness of the inspection (i.e., how fast they got out to the property once the call was put in).

And lastly, the inspector general found that "[t]he pre-foreclosure property inspection industry is largely unregulated" and that "there are no specific federal or state laws that govern property inspections of homes securing mortgage loans in default" that includes standards for servicers "to require their inspectors to maintain minimum education requirements, experience level, or qualifications."

However, despite this quite damning report and series of findings, the response from the FHFA was that it would direct the GSEs to "assess and manage risks related to property inspections" but that "[t]he [FHFA] does not believe the report findings and examples of deficiencies provide compelling support for the imposition of uniform standards."[70] In other words, the government did not plan on doing much of anything about this problem.

PART III

Solutions and Moving Forward

7

Regulating Mortgage Servicing

Corruption, embezzlement [and] fraud, these are the characteristics which exist everywhere. It is regrettably the way human nature functions, whether we like it or not. What successful economies do is keep it to a minimum.

        Alan Greenspan, former chairperson of the Board of Governors of the
        Federal Reserve System[1]

Mortgage servicing – one of the most important components of the architecture of American housing finance – was deeply broken during and after the financial crisis and in many ways remains so today. A number of aspects of the mortgage servicing business cause very unique problems when it comes to the protection of homeowners and to the stability of servicers. The structure of mortgage servicing within the housing finance system (and securitization specifically) combined with the way firms in this space are compensated creates a variety of misaligned incentives when it comes to protecting consumer interests and mainlining financial stability.

For homeowners, they have no choice in who their servicer will be. This means that homeowners can neither make thoughtful choices about who manages their loan nor steer away from firms that engage in shoddy or harmful activities. Our system of mortgage finance would be safer and healthier if steps were taken to redesign the mortgage servicing framework and then reinforce its most important parts so that it not only delivers a better experience for homeowners but also provides a bulwark against future market downturns. The first step in that process is to properly regulate the mortgage servicing industry.

WHO REGULATES THE MORTGAGE MIDDLEMEN?

Historically, the mortgage servicing industry has been subject to a patchwork of state and federal regulations. Even after the financial reforms that followed 2008, the industry's regulatory framework remains both overly complex and underdeveloped.

Part of the reason for these defects is due to the fact that different kinds of financial institutions engage in mortgage servicing. Sometimes servicing is done by banks and sometimes by more general nonbanks. Thus, because financial institutions are subject to different regulatory regimes, the monitoring and regulating of their mortgage servicing activities by government officials varies.

The Federal Reserve oversees state-chartered banks that are members of the Federal Reserve System. The FDIC has authority over state-chartered banks that are not members of the Federal Reserve System. Additionally, all state-chartered banks are supervised by state banking supervisors. For banks that are federally chartered, supervision rests with the Comptroller of the Currency within the U.S. Department of the Treasury or with the National Credit Union Administration (NCUA).[2]

In addition, all FDIC-insured banks are subject to oversight by the FDIC in its role as insurer of deposits.[3] The Federal Reserve also has authority over bank holding companies, including those that have nonbank affiliates.[4] In the most recent change in financial oversight, Congress created the Consumer Financial Protection Bureau (CFPB), which has authority over multiple types of financial entities including mortgage servicers of all stripes. This includes mortgage servicers that are not affiliated with a bank.

Mortgage servicers must also abide by rules that are not necessarily dictated by a governmental entity, but rather by bodies that form an integral part of the securitization process. For instance, Fannie Mae and Freddie Mac, which securitize loans they purchase, have their own servicing guidelines.[5] Similarly, loans that are securitized in the private-label market are subject to servicing rules that are dictated by private securitization trusts or issuers. And finally, because mortgage-backed securities are rated, the ratings agencies have some level of influence over how mortgage servicers operate due to reputational and securities scoring.

As this panoply of regulatory regimes reveals, there is tremendous pressure on mortgage servicers to satisfy many masters. From this perspective, compliance costs can be high if only to make sure a servicer knows what rules mean and how they will or might be applied. This is to say nothing of dealing with enforcement actions, investigations, or reporting requirements. On the flip side, when it comes to mortgage middlemen who are negligent in their duties, firms can take advantage of the ill-defined rules and overlapping authorities to game the system.

To understand why mortgage servicing would benefit from a federalism partnership model, it is necessary to get a clear picture of the regulatory history and current state of affairs. In doing so, we can divide the discussion into two segments – regulation of servicing before Dodd-Frank and regulation thereafter. Seeing how the regulatory ecosystem developed helps us understand not only why the current system doesn't work but also the political possibilities of reforming it.

MIDDLEMAN REGULATION BEFORE DODD-FRANK

The principal federal statutes that govern mortgage servicing from the consumer rights perspective are the Real Estate Settlement Procedures Act (RESPA) and the Truth in Lending Act (TILA). RESPA was passed by Congress in June 1974 and authority for managing the act was initially assigned to HUD.[6] Originally, RESPA's enactment was motivated by two principal goals. The first was to end the opaque process of obtaining a mortgage loan. This was done by requiring a number of disclosures be provided to home purchasers to help them make informed credit decisions. The second purpose was to make it unlawful for lenders, real estate agents, and other parties involved in the transaction to engage in practices that drove up the cost of buying a home, such as with referral fees and kickbacks. Although RESPA is limited in scope to only so-called federally related mortgage loans, the definition is so broad that it basically embraces all mortgage loans made in the United States.[7]

After RESPA was passed, HUD promulgated Regulation X, which is a series of rules that implements and interprets the act. Many years later, in 1990, Congress passed that National Affordable Housing Act, which was aimed at strengthening the federal commitment to decent, safe, and sanitary housing.[8] For our purposes, the act amended RESPA and imposed regulations on those companies that serviced mortgage loans. These new rules required that home buyers be given disclosures relative to the transfer of servicing rights to their loan from one firm to another. It also imposed an obligation on servicers – as the generators of a borrower's loan statement – to provide itemized, detailed information about escrow amounts, both at the time of the closing of the loan and each year thereafter. This was the first time that federal legislation significantly stepped into the mortgage servicing space. The timing of this is not surprising considering that, as noted in Chapter 1, it was not until about this time that securitization truly took off.[9]

During the period of deregulation that characterized part of the Clinton administration, Congress passed the elaborately named Economic Growth and Regulatory Paperwork Reduction Act of 1996.[10] Its goal, as the title suggests, was to require that a number of federal agencies conduct a review of relevant regulations every 10 years with an aim at spurring economic growth by eliminating outdated, unnecessary, or overly burdensome industry rules. But, one of the results of the act was again to amend RESPA – this time to reduce the disclosure obligations imposed on mortgage servicers.

The biggest pre–Dodd-Frank change to RESPA came in the dark days of 2008 when HUD, faced with a deteriorating housing market and having failed at an earlier 2004 reform of the relevant rules, issued the so-called RESPA Reform Rule.[11] The Reform Rule made a number of changes – many of them substantive – to Regulation X. When it came to mortgage servicing, the focus was, as in the past, on disclosures. The Reform Rule attempted to streamline the way disclosures were provided by mortgage servicers to consumers, as well as to update escrow accounting requirements.

The Reform Rule, however, left much work undone. First, it was criticized for not doing enough to make the disclosure of important information clearer or simpler for home buyers.[12] If anything, it created more paperwork (that almost always went unread by consumers sitting at the closing table).[13] Some of the new requirements placed on servicers were extremely confusing, imprecise, and too complicated to implement with any level of certainty. The argument was also raised that some of the new disclosure requirements overlapped or contradicted other existing provisions of federal law – leading to an overall criticism that HUD had not properly coordinated with other federal agencies to ensure that the rule was coherent and not duplicative.[14]

RESPA is not alone in addressing mortgage middleman activity. TILA is the other major federal law dealing with mortgage servicers. The act was passed in May 1968, as part of the Consumer Credit Protection Act.[15] Its implementing instrument is Regulation Z, which was originally under the authority of the Federal Reserve Board.[16] The act, unlike RESPA, has not always been as directly related to mortgage servicing. The act and Regulation Z were amended a host of times in the 1980s and 1990s to include, among many other things, disclosures relative to adjustable rate mortgage loans – most significantly with the Home Ownership and Equity Protection Act of 1994 (HOEPA).[17] Servicing was not mentioned.

Further amendments were made to TILA in the mid-1990s to limit the scope of a mortgage lender's liability for noncompliance with the act's disclosure requirements – similar to the concurrent pullback in RESPA during these deregulatory years. Other amendments around this time tried to consolidate and trim credit transaction disclosures. But again, mortgage servicing was not central.

Then, as with RESPA, the 2008 crisis spurred the Federal Reserve to action in making additional changes to TILA law that were aimed at curbing abusive lending and foreclosure practices. In July 2008, the Federal Reserve created special rules that would apply to high cost mortgage loans, which had been a chronic target for predatory lending (particularly subprime mortgage lending). Additional safeguards against unfair, deceptive, and abusive practices for all types of mortgage loans were also a part of the package. The Mortgage Disclosure Improvement Act of 2008 added more provisions to TILA, which in turn required more amendments to Regulation Z to implement and reinforce them.[18] These changes expanded disclosure requirements to new types of credit products and incorporated a waiting period between when disclosures are furnished to consumers and when the credit transaction is completed. And importantly for homeowners, if the interest rate on a mortgage loan would change over time (like as with the notorious adjustable rate mortgage), then the disclosures would have to include examples showing how the monthly payment amount could change over time. Perhaps most significantly, disclosures had to include an express statement indicating to the consumer that there was no guarantee that a refinance would be available prior to the interest rate resetting.

As the crisis continued to unfold and the flood of foreclosures crashed forward unabated, Congress and regulators struggled to provide relief. In 2009, as an attempt to keep financially distressed Americans in their homes, Congress passed the Helping Families Save Their Homes Act.[19] The legislation amended portions of TILA to require that consumers receive a new set of notifications whenever their mortgage loan was sold or their servicing rights were transferred – specifically that the homeowner would need to receive notice within 30 days of the transfer date. This rule was important for consumers facing foreclosure because it was often the case, as noted in the Introduction, that servicers would assign their rights from one entity to another, sometimes switching from a general servicer to one that "specialized" in distressed mortgages, without the homeowner being fully abreast of the change.[20]

Yet, despite these changes in federal consumer-facing laws, servicing breakdowns continued. Some of this was the result of bad behavior, but at other times it was the result of the fact that servicing firms were not prepared and did not have the resources to manage the foreclosure pileup. Many of these regulatory measures came too late.

STATE REGULATION OF SERVICERS

Lastly, while federal law has played a primary role in how mortgage servicing is regulated from a consumer perspective, state law has also historically operated in this space. But, the role played by state-level regulators has been limited and often varied. First, not all states have regulated mortgage servicing (and a number still do not).[21] For those that do, the way in which these firms are regulated is basically limited to licensing rules.[22] To engage in mortgage servicing activities, a company must register with and obtain a license from a state's banking or financial services regulator.

Licensing requirements typically involve criminal background checks, credit report inquiries, the reporting of corporate organizational information, and the provision of information about professional experience and personal history.[23] Some states also require ongoing educational seminars and the administration of a written test prior to the issuance of a license. And lastly, the procurement of a bond, usually in an amount related to the total mortgage loan volume serviced in a given state, is frequently required.[24] Firms located in one state, but that operate in others, may be required to also obtain licenses in each state where they do business – those requirements vary depending on the number of loans issued and sometimes whether the firm has a physical presence in the jurisdiction.[25]

However, state regulatory coverage is limited. There are exemptions from licensure when the mortgage servicer is part of a federally chartered financial institution, like a national bank.[26] Because these entities are regulated by federal bank regulators, any mortgage servicing activities that they undertake are also covered by that same federal regulator.[27] This is the result of preemption principles whereby federal law in a particular area displaces any overlapping state rules.

In the aftermath of the financial crisis, a number of states enacted specific servicing laws and regulations in an attempt to address the foreclosure problem. As Levitin and Twomey note, some states required a meeting between the servicer and the homeowner in the way of a mediation conference before foreclosure proceedings could be commenced.[28] Other states added extra reporting requirements relative to loss mitigation efforts.

But again, the overall regulatory structure at the state level was and has been rather weak. Because most mortgage loans were and remain serviced by bank affiliates, these servicers escape state-level supervision altogether. To the extent servicers are subject to oversight by state banking officials, the oversight is disparate, depending on the politics and policy objectives of the particular jurisdiction.[29] Further, as noted in Chapters 4, 5, and 6, insofar as post-2008 changes to substantive foreclosure law tried to address servicing breakdowns, the results were mixed. Many servicers found themselves unable to effectively comply with new rules due to resource constraints.[30] And still others ignored the new rules altogether or else refused to make loan modifications because of supposed obligations under pooling and servicing agreements.[31]

POST–DODD-FRANK REGULATORY CONSOLIDATION (SORT OF)

By and large, as explained in Part II, mortgage servicing regulations did not do their job very well, both prior to and immediately after the crisis. They had little effect on the activities of mortgage servicers when it came to their financial soundness or their ability to effectively manage mortgage loans (and homeowners) in distress. These rules provided little guidance as to how servicers should handle loss mitigation activities, deal with homeowners in foreclosure, manage their third-party contractors, or how to behave when exercising the broad and aggressive rights granted to them under the mortgage contract. This is to say nothing of putting controls in place to ensure that they operated in a way that accounted for weaknesses in their business models during downturns. Mortgage servicers were described as sloppy and as having engaged in activities that were completely unacceptable.[32]

These shoddy activities were representative of significant market failures in the mortgage servicing industry.[33] Such breakdowns included, among other things, ill-trained and nonresponsive servicing staff. By some accounts, servicing staff ratios of loans to full-time employees ranged from one for every 100 loans to one for every 4,000 loans. A 2010 review of homeowner calls to a HUD-coordinated hotline revealed that more than half were from consumers who were unable to obtain information or even reach their mortgage servicer.

Servicers were discovered to have submitted false or deficient documentation in foreclosure proceedings and to have failed to properly manage their contractors and other important third-party service providers. When homeowners submitted loan modification applications, a General Accountability Office (GAO) investigation found that servicers often mishandled documentation and misled or failed to communicate with homeowners.

Other reports noted instances in which servicers were charging homeowners improper fees that they had no authority to impose or that were unnecessary. One such example dealt with force-place insurance. This is the process whereby the servicer would procure an insurance policy on the home because it had determined that the insurance held by the homeowner was insufficient (or did not exist) to properly protect the collateral in the event of a casualty loss, such as that caused by a fire, flood, or other event. The servicer would use the insurance to protect the collateral's value. The danger for homeowners, however, was that the authority to decide whether the current insurance was sufficient rested solely with the servicer – as did the power to select the new insurance policy.

Force-place insurance (i.e., insurance that is forced to be put in place by the servicer) is typically more costly than a policy that is obtained by the homeowner, who often shops around for the best deal (some report 10 times higher in cost).[34] The servicer has little incentive to do the same kind of aggressive quote gathering because the premium payments for the force-place insurance will be passed on to the borrower as part of his or her monthly installment. These forced policies are also generally more beneficial to the creditor than the homeowner, as they rarely cover owner liability or the loss of personal property in the home.[35]

Against the backdrop of these problems, it was obvious to postcrisis regulators that the mortgage servicing business was broken. After many amendments to federal law by Congress and federal agencies, lawmakers attempted to fundamentally change the mortgage servicing industry with the enactment of Dodd-Frank. First, the CFPB became the primary consumer regulatory agency in the United States. As part of that effort, authority over RESPA and TILA, including Regulations X and Z, were assigned to the CFPB. The bureau, armed with these new powers, immediately got to work trying to address the regulatory gaps in the mortgage servicing industry. The agency would only be partly successful.

THE CFPB RESPONDS WITH THE 2013 TILA/RESPA RULES

To reshape mortgage servicing, the CFPB had to make a series of amendments to federal consumer protection laws. The process started in early 2013 when the bureau amended Regulations X and Z.[36] These 2013 TILA/RESPA amendments did a host of things relative to servicers. First, they changed the notice requirement that mortgage middlemen must give to homeowners when their servicing rights are transferred to a new firm. The amendments also changed and clarified how a servicer was required to respond to homeowners when it came to settling disputes and handling consumer requests for information.

Additionally, the 2013 TILA/RESPA amendments tried to address the troublesome topic of how servicers handled the property tax and property insurance payments that are held in escrow on homeowners' behalf. The new rules also placed restrictions and gave direction to servicers when it came to force-place insurance, including mandating a reasonable basis for requiring insurance and sending three notices to the homeowner.

The 2013 TILA/RESPA amendments also tried to correct the many issues related to homeowners obtaining a successful workout or other resolution with servicers once a loan is delinquent. This included requiring that servicers maintain contact with homeowners throughout the loss mitigation process and requiring that the servicer try to contact homeowners early in the default process before their financial situation becomes too dire to rectify.

But, shortly after the 2013 rules were issued, it became clear to the CFPB that additional changes to Regulations X and Z were needed – particularly dealing with mortgage servicers due to the fact that problems with the industry continued to plague the country's housing recovery. A number of changes occurred in the summer and fall of 2013 to address consumer concerns and the industry's need for greater clarity.

These further amendments occurred in July[37] and September[38] of that same year, and then again in October 2014.[39] Some of the more significant changes dealt with the interaction of federal mortgage servicing rules and those that existed under state law. The rules also made additional clarifications and technical amendments with respect to the information requests and dispute resolution provisions of the January 2013 rule, as well as the rules about servicers intervening quickly after a default. And still, other changes dealt with the interests of successor parties to servicing/loan rights, bankruptcy proceedings, and clarifications on debt collection. The bureau also issued a compliance guide, feeling the need to give more particularized guidance to an industry now facing an avalanche of new rules.[40] And, yet again, in October 2014, the CFPB made definitional changes for so-called small mortgage servicing firms.[41]

As of this writing, the most recent series of rules for mortgage servicing – still at the federal level – began in November 2014 when the CFPB issued yet another proposal to amend the 2013 TILA/RESPA rules.[42] The goal of this amendment was to address nine specific subject matter areas that form core components of the work of mortgage servicers.[43] Aside from filling up countless pages in the Federal Register and subsequently the Code of Federal Regulations, this series of amendments, clarifications, and changes (likes those before them) represent the continuous rebalancing of the needs and concerns of the industry with those of consumer advocacy groups, as each attempts to use the latest rulemaking process to achieve their goals.

A final rule (with responsive changes) was published in October 2016.[44] The vast majority of the provisions went into effect on October 19, 2017. It is doubtful that this will be the last of the CFPB's rulemaking efforts in this space – each time adding additional complexity.

For even the casual observer, it should seem obvious that for all the bureau's good intentions, this frenetic rulemaking can only invite confusion and higher costs for the industry. Not only this, but the results and reactions to these rules have been decidedly mixed. Industry groups have decried the rampant rulemaking as "onerous" and note that firms are often given little time to interpret and apply the new rules that "necessitate programming and systems changes that are much more complex than a few computer keystrokes."[45] Meanwhile, consumer advocates argue that, despite improvements, there are regulatory "weaknesses" that call for further changes, such as with the use of limited kinds of data.[46]

WHY WE NEED TO CHANGE HOW WE APPROACH MORTGAGE SERVICING REGULATION

For all these many rules, one might think that mortgage servicing is now well regulated. Unfortunately, that is most certainly not the case. More regulation does not always mean good regulation. Further, the regulation of today is not necessarily sufficient to meet the regulatory needs of tomorrow, particularly in an industry that is going through significant changes.

Admittedly, a number of the rules – particularly those that recently went into effect in 2017 and 2018 – do address important areas where regulatory direction is needed. For instance, consumer advocacy and housing counseling groups raised the difficulty experienced by those who inherit mortgaged property after the borrower dies – specifically when it comes to ascertaining the status of the loan, getting the servicer to communicate with the heir, or applying for loss mitigation options. The postcrisis rules address these concerns. Similarly, homeowners in distress often complained of an inability to ascertain the identity of the owner of their loans from the servicers. To that point, the rules also mandate increased transparency. And, of course, there were endless tales of frustration and despair when loss mitigation applications were dropped or lost as servicing rights were transferred from one company to another. The new rules impose significant obligations on servicers in how they deal with homeowner loss mitigation activities. Some progress has been made.

These changes, however, function at the microlevel. There are some important, macro considerations that are missing from the conversation about regulating the mortgage middleman. These are also consumer-oriented rules. They do nothing to address the financial stability of mortgage servicers over the long term. A financially weak mortgage servicer is unlikely to be able to step up and comply with strong consumer protection laws when times get rough. The remainder of this chapter seeks to address these regulatory deficiencies and disconnects.

ACCESS TO MORTGAGE CREDIT

First and foremost, when thinking about properly regulating mortgage servicing (either by government power or through contract) we must take stock of the macro considerations that are missing from the current regulatory approach. It is fair to say that, since the 2008 crisis, obtaining a home loan is more difficult than it was in the past. However, that statement requires a bit of unpacking to see how the tightness of credit is connected to mortgage servicing – and why it matters.

First, the leading component of a consumer's credit profile is his or her Fair Isaac Corporation (FICO) score – the company that created the method of taking consumer credit reports (produced by companies like TransUnion, Equifax, and Experian) and turning that information into a score that reflects an individual's credit worthiness.[47] The FICO method assigns certain percentage weights to different types of information reflected in a consumer's credit profile. Specifically, payment history accounts for about 35 percent, the consumer debt of the individual is about 30 percent, the duration of a person's credit history is another 15 percent, and finally the different types of credit products that the individual used or acquired over time is about 10 percent. Using this formula, FICO assigns the person a score anywhere of from 300 to 850. Individuals who are offered subprime loans generally have scores below 660, and those who are offered prime loans have scores above 700.

Another important factor in assessing someone's creditworthiness is the loan-to-value ratio.[48] This is a financial phrase that assumes the loan is being secured by property (which is almost always the case in a home purchase) and seeks to determine the difference between the value of the mortgaged property and the amount of the loan. Along with the loan-to-value ratio is the debt-to-income ratio, which looks to the amount of the borrower's income (like wages and investment income) versus his or her overall debts (such as car loans, student loans, and utilities). And lastly, features of the loan play a significant role in the credit determination, such as the length of the repayment period and whether the interest rate is fixed or will adjust over time.

In a 2017 Urban Institute report by Laurie Goodman, housing policy analysts showed that many mortgage loans that should be made to borrowers with relatively low credit risk under the previously mentioned factors are, in fact, not being made.[49] The report notes that in 2001 there were roughly 5.7 million new or existing home sales. That number fell only slightly to about 5.6 million in 2015. Nevertheless, in that same period the number of home *loans* sank much deeper – from about 4.7 million to 3.5 million. So, home sales went down only 4 percent while new home mortgages went down 32 percent – quite a difference. Further, the report notes that while those prime consumers with a FICO score higher than 700 dropped about 1.4

percent between 2001 and 2015, the drop for those with scores between 660 and 700 was down about 20 percent, and (most alarmingly) those with scores between 660 (so-called subprime borrowers) fell almost 65 percent.[50]

So, what does this mean for credit availability? Goodman shows quite convincingly that lenders (particularly mortgage lenders) are being perhaps overly cautious when it comes to making home loans, often going beyond the highly safe underwriting guidelines required by the GSEs and the FHA. As she notes, "Fannie Mae may be willing to underwrite a mortgage [loan borrower] with a 620 FICO, but the originator requires a 660 FICO."[51] What is the cause of this shying away from less than stellar but still solidly credit-worthy borrowers? A main explanation is that lenders fear that such borrowers will be an expensive credit risk – that they are likely to default. This means that, from the originator's perspective, making the loan will be costly on the front end and managing the loan thereafter will be equally or even more expensive.

At first glance, it might seem that mortgage servicing has little to do with the access to credit issues described in the preceding text. After all, servicing is what happens *after* the loan has already been made. But, in fact, mortgage servicing has a great deal to say about who gets a mortgage loan *in the first place* – in large part, as Goodman notes, because of how it impacts costs. As a fundamental matter, certain types of loans are more expensive to service. We saw this in the fallout from the financial crisis. Of the 510 banks that failed in the years between 2007 and 2015, 66 of them had mortgage servicing arms.[52] Reports relative to many of these bank failures attributed mortgage servicing to being either a significant or contributing factor to the breakdown.

Because certain loans are costlier to service, mortgage middlemen charge more (i.e., require higher compensation) in exchange for managing such loans. This, as pointed out by a 2014 Urban Institute study, means that individuals with historically weaker credit profiles – even when they meet the conforming loan standards of the GSEs or conservative FHA loan requirements – can be priced out or denied credit pursuant to the lender's individual underwriting criteria.[53] This is a problem for communities of color in particular, as black and Latino individuals typically have weaker credit scores,[54] which in turn impacts the types of loans for which they qualify. Because of the massive drain on black and Latino wealth caused by the Great Recession, these communities are often denied credit or are offered loans that are very expensive. Between 2007 and 2010, Latino households lost 44 percent of their wealth and black households lost 31 percent.[55] White households, however, lost only 11 percent.

This boils down to the fact that servicers (and loan originators) consider black and Latino borrowers to, on average, constitute higher credit risks due to their FICO scores and other credit-worthiness traits. This is important because, from the mortgage middleman's perspective, servicing a delinquent loan is much costlier than one that is performing. By one account from 2013, the cost of servicing a defaulted mortgage loan was 15 times higher than the cost of managing one that was not in default ($2,537 compared to $156).[56] The Urban Institute reports that the cost difference between the two is rising at a rapid pace – the expense increased 264 percent between 2008 and 2013. Where do these extra expenses come from? Servicing a loan that is performing requires that typical overhead expenses and hard costs be accounted for, but nothing else. When a loan goes into default, however, expenses related to "collection, loss mitigation, foreclosure, [and] bankruptcy" are added on top of that, including any penalties that the loan investors impose for delinquency-related activities and foreclosure delays.[57]

So, in this way, mortgage servicers are passing the cost of managing loans to black and Latino borrowers – who may very well have perfectly acceptable GSE/FHA credit profiles but are nevertheless viewed as being a credit risk due to add-on factors – back to the lender such that the cost of credit is higher on the front-end. Thus, revisions to rules governing mortgage servicers must consider better ways to deal with delinquencies. If the cost of dealing with delinquencies can be better controlled, then this could lessen the pass-back effect of servicing costs to front-end originations when credit profiles are less than perfect.

A good first step, as indicated in the Urban Institute's 2014 report, was taken by the GSEs in diminishing penalty mechanisms on servicers when they fail to foreclose on property within a certain time period.[58] But this means there is still a tension, which requires thoughtful regulatory cooperation, between the interests of securitization trusts (whether held by the GSEs or the private-label market) and the interests of consumer advocates.[59] This tension between making money for the investors, on the one hand, and keeping defaulted individuals in their homes, on the other, makes it difficult for servicers to know in which direction to head. This, in turn, incentivizes them to increase the cost of servicing loans that have even the slightest potential to introduce this back-and-forth problem. If loans are only made to the most creditworthy of borrowers, then the delinquency issues are, ostensibly, taken off the table. But, this leaves many would-be homeowners, particularly in communities of color, left out.

Another way to handle the issue of servicing what loan originators and servicers consider "high-risk" borrowers is to provide government subsidies to servicers who manage loans to these particular individuals. The idea of providing compensation in this fashion is not new. After the crisis, programs where created whereby servicers were given money by the government to entice them to conduct loan modifications to distressed homeowners.[60] Mortgage middlemen were given $1,000 per loan modified and would get another $1,000 for each of three years thereafter as long as the homeowner did not default during that period. By providing a financial incentive for servicers to take on these types of loans, originators may then discover that finding servicing firms that will perform such duties at a reasonable cost (one that minimizes the impact on credit affordability) is easier to come by. This could, in the long run, loosen the credit box for underserved borrowers. Once a period passes whereby these loans perform well, originators might feel more comfortable and loosen their underwriting. Over time, the subsidy could be scaled down or eliminated as the credit market becomes more equitable.

THE GROWTH OF SHADOW BANK SERVICERS

The connection between access to credit and servicing is not the only macro consideration that should animate a regulatory overhaul. We must also recognize the fundamental shift occurring in the mortgage servicing industry toward nonbank firms (i.e., shadow banks). While nonbank mortgage servicers must abide by TILA (Regulation Z) and RESPA (Regulation X) requirements, that is not the same as having a designated prudential regulator as do banks that engage in mortgage servicing.[61] The shift from bank servicers to nonbank servicers is representative of the changing landscape of the industry. The losers in this shift have been traditional financial institutions – specifically federally insured banks.[62] While servicing by nonbanks represented only 6 percent of unpaid loan principal balances for single-family homes in 2010, that number rose to 7 percent in 2011, 14 percent in 2012, 24 percent in 2013, 29 percent in 2014, and as much as 31 percent in 2015.[63]

The movement away from mortgage servicing by banks is the result of a number of factors. First, some of it is driven by the significant expenses that come along with conducting mortgage servicing activities – not least of which includes settling lawsuits with federal agencies and attorneys general for foreclosure-related abuses – as well as the desire to refocus on other core lines of business. Second, after the crisis Fannie Mae created the High Touch Mortgage Servicing Program. This initiative was designed to facilitate (and incentivize) the transfer of mortgage servicing from banks (that were not handling the task very well) to specialty servicers (i.e., nonbank servicers) that had supposed expertise in managing troubled loans.[64]

Third, post-2008 changes to bank capital requirements made mortgage servicing a burden on bank balance sheets. These changes came with the third Basel Capital Accords (or simply, "Basel III"). The Basel Committee on Banking Supervision is an international body, established in 1974. Its purpose is to promote cooperation in the global banking community and to prescribe worldwide bank capital requirements.[65] This set of rules dictates how much money banks have to keep in their own rainy-day accounts.

In 2010, Basel III imposed a series of bank capital measures, stemming from financial crisis–related bank instability in 2008.[66] In essence, holding mortgage servicing assets (i.e., being engaged in mortgage servicing activities) increases a bank's capital holding requirements.[67] This means that since Basel III, it has become very undesirable for banks to be in the mortgage servicing business.[68] Shadow banks, however, are not subject to Basel III – because they are not technically banks. This means it is cheaper, from a regulatory standpoint, for them to service mortgage loans. Thus, as banks shed their mortgage servicing assets, nonbanks are able to take advantage of the regulatory arbitrage.[69]

The significance of this market shift can hardly be understated. In fact, there has been a veritable arms race among certain shadow banks for who can be the largest nonbank servicer. In the first quarter of 2012, the 20 largest servicers in the United States included only six shadow banks. By the second quarter of 2015, that number had risen to nine.[70] In October 2012, the shadow bank servicer Ocwen went into a bidding war at a bankruptcy auction (having pushed out Warren Buffett's Berkshire Hathaway) to acquire the mortgage loan servicing portfolio of Residential Capital LLC.[71] Ocwen prevailed by bidding $3 billion, which according to then stakeholder Wilbur Ross (now commerce secretary under President Trump) made Ocwen the fifth-largest mortgage servicer in the country. Ocwen then purchased all of the servicing assets of Ally Bank in 2013 (valued at $585 million), as well as some of OneWest Bank's servicing portfolio covering $78 billion worth of mortgage loans.[72] Ocwen is not the only shadow bank aggressively trying to dominate the market.[73] Nationstar purchased servicing rights from both Bank of America and Aurora Bank in 2012 and then went back to purchase more in 2013 – partially resulting in a threefold growth rate in a span of two years.[74]

These events are concerning because, as noted previously, while banks are subject to a number of capital requirements that serve as a cushion when downturns occur, nonbank servicers do not have similar mandatory reserves. As banks continue to offload their mortgage servicing assets to shadow bank entities, the need to manage the health, safety, and soundness of these nonbank firms becomes all the more critical.

A CROWDED BUT SHALLOW POOL

What is important to note from a regulatory, macro standpoint is that mortgage servicing – an industry already somewhat diffuse – is even less concentrated now than it was immediately before and shortly after the crisis.[75] In theory this is good because high concentrations within a given market often indicate that firms are too powerful – giving them the ability to manipulate the market as they wish because there are very few other options for counterparties to choose from.[76] The less concentration, the more competition between firms. In thinking about mortgage servicing this makes theoretical sense. The fewer servicers, the less options that a bank or securitization trust will have to manage the loans. This means that a few middleman firms can set the rules of engagement and, even when they do not perform well, are able to retain business because there is nowhere else for an unsatisfied counterparty to go. However, more servicers mean that trustees/investors can choose among many firms, which causes the firms to increase their value-add because competition is vigorous. But, if the ability of these small firms to gain market share is the result of cutting costs and charging little for their work, they will not be prepared for market downturns that require significant capital investments. In other words, a race to the bottom market works fine when the economy is doing well and the cost of servicing loans is low. The 2008 crisis taught us that when the market takes a hit, these thinly capitalized firms will not be ready to deal with distressed homeowners and a flood of foreclosures. From this perspective, the fact that the mortgage servicing market is so crowded becomes quite concerning.

The rise of shadow banks in the mortgage servicing sector is related to the lack of concentration in the servicing market. These large, shadow bank servicers include names such as PHH Mortgage, Nationstar Mortgage, Ocwen Financial, and Quicken Loans. Although banks still service the majority of mortgage loans (more than 75 percent), nonbank firms have a strong foothold in a very particular (and important) corner of the housing finance market – government-backed mortgage loans and FHA loans. The GAO reports that as of the second quarter of 2015, shadow banks serviced 35 percent of all Ginnie Mae–, Freddie Mac–, and Fannie Mae–related mortgage loans.[77] And, perhaps not surprisingly because they are able to service high-risk loans more cheaply than banks, nonbank servicers manage about 74 percent of the mortgage loans outstanding in the private-label market.[78]

The connection between nonbank servicer liquidity and Ginnie and the GSEs is, as described in Chapter 3, the fact that middlemen must continue to make payment advances to MBS investors, insurers, and taxing entities even when homeowners stop paying. The severity of this obligation, however, varies depending on whether the loan is securitized through the GSEs, the private-label market, or Ginnie Mae.[79]

If the loan is securitized by the GSEs or the private-label market, the servicer must make advances until it has been determined that the amounts advanced are not recoverable.[80] The obligation on the servicer is most severe, however, in the context of Ginnie Mae–backed securities. If there is a default, the servicer is obligated to continue making advances regardless of whether those amounts can be recovered by the servicer in any way.[81] The only way to stop the payments is by purchasing the loan from the securitization pool, which is often not economically efficient for the servicer to do.

The problem of having enough cash to meet these payment obligations was particularly acute for nonbank servicers in the private-label market. Ocwen, for instance, saw a large portion of its cash eaten up by the obligation to make advances when delinquencies were exploding.[82] As a share of Ocwen's total assets, the percentage consumed to meet these obligations went from 45 percent in 2006, to 59 percent in 2009, and all the way up to 79 percent in 2011. The CEO of Ocwen stated that "[i]f we are unable to fund additional advances, we could breach the requirements of our servicing contract."[83]

WHY BANK SERVICING WON'T MAKE A COMEBACK AND WHY WE CARE

Some believe that as the economy recovers and mortgage loans are made using more stringent underwriting criteria, as required under Dodd-Frank's mandatory "ability to repay" analysis, that banks will want to get back into the servicing game.[84] But, there are some reasons to be skeptical. Performing loans are still very costly to service, yet we do not know what accounts for these costs. If it is an issue related to technology and a lack of innovation, as I suspect it might be, then perhaps nonbank servicers are ostensibly better equipped to deal with those costs (at least in a low-default market) because they have less overhead and do not suffer the same legacy technology costs with which banks must currently contend.[85]

Legacy technology costs refer to technology investments that banks had to make years ago to compete (think enormous IBM computer that takes up a whole room) but that, despite being very expensive, quickly became obsolete. The best example of this would be the introduction in the 1970s of the mainframe-based system for computer processing.[86] A bank's central functions include handling deposits, extending credit, and dealing with corporate cash. The mainframe system was a new way to handle these functions more efficiently. But, the system was expensive, and banks had to make heavy investments (i.e., take on debt themselves) to pay for the upgrades. That was all well and good until technology made another sharp turn toward network computing and web-based programs – to say nothing of mobile banking and the more sophisticated online services that we enjoy today. Suddenly, the investments of the 1970s and 1980s were nearly outdated, but banks were still paying for them. So, banks again had to engage in spending (and borrowing) to make new investments. The "legacy" costs from these old systems, however, still hang around the necks of banks, making them less nimble and unable to innovate quickly (which again costs money). For this reason, it seems likely that shadow banks that do not have these same legacy costs will continue to flourish in the mortgage servicing sector.

But the promise of superior service and efficiency is misplaced. As with all cases of quick development, nonbank servicers are apt to experience growing pains as they continue to expand their market share. As firms, like Ocwen and Nationstar, rapidly expand their books of business, they may not be able to increase staff and invest at a rate that keeps pace with the work load. This is where one can see breakdowns in process and the potential for damage to homeowners.[87] Shadow banks are nimble because they lack the overhead of banks; however, banks have advantages in the servicing space because they are sophisticated when it comes to regulatory compliance – something that has long been a part of doing business for depository financial institutions. The lack of significant financial institution-type infrastructure within the nonbank mortgage servicing firm is a reason for regulators to be concerned about its growth.

Some signs of concern have already become evident in recent years, such as in 2014 when the New York State financial services regulator prevented Ocwen Financial from acquiring $39 billion worth of servicing rights from Wells Fargo.[88] The deal was halted on account of concerns over the capacity of Ocwen to handle the volume of work. And the CFPB has warned that, despite claims by nonbank servicers that they are better at helping homeowners in distress, the bureau received numerous complaints about "servicing interruptions and failures to honor loan modifications" by such nonbank firms.[89]

A strong shadow bank servicing sector is filling the gap left by large financial institutions leaving the servicing market. Because of this trend, the fair treatment of many homeowners depends on there being a strong and healthy nonbank servicing industry. When a nonbank has too much risk (i.e., is heavily exposed in the event the loans it services stop performing but the obligation to pay MBS investors continues) then the servicing, including loss mitigation efforts, falls apart. To make matters worse, sometimes the loans are transferred to yet another nonbank servicer. Servicing transfers are often where breakdowns in loss mitigation occur as applications are lost and homeowner phone calls don't get returned. Therefore, from a macro perspective that considers this market shift, requiring that nonbank servicers be adequately capitalized is important for the good of homeowners and investors alike. Banks already must maintain certain capital reserves to help them through times when cash is low, but expenses are level or make occasional jumps. Shadow banks do not have capital reserve requirements. So, when delinquencies are high, and cash coming in the door dries up, there is no savings account from which to draw. And having few resources makes helping distressed homeowners very difficult when, as a servicer, the firm also has an obligation to continue making payments to the MBS holders. Insolvency can be right around the corner.

THE BUSINESS MODEL OF SHADOW BANK SERVICERS

Another important aspect of shadow bank servicing pertains to who owns these firms. Most nonbank servicers are funded by private investors, who are seeking yield.[90] This fact is important because it says something about the goals and objectives of shadow bank servicing companies. Shadow banks (including shadow bank servicing firms) operate in the more traditional corporate duty sphere. Generally, American corporate law requires firms to maximize shareholder value – usually without regard to the risks to third parties.[91] This means that under normal circumstances a corporation is required by law to do what is necessary to make money for its owners, regardless of whether such activity imposes costs (externalities) on others.[92] Therefore, nonbank servicers, because of their private equity ownership, have different strategies than bank servicers when it comes to their investments and operation. Private equity firms focus on increasing cost efficiencies and, as the credit-rating agency Fitch notes, by benefiting from rising interest rates that discourage homeowners from refinancing their loans (thus keeping their servicing fees high).[93]

Banks are also corporations, but they operate in the highly regulated space that causes their management to balance shareholder value-maximizing activity with concerns about the safety and soundness of the entire banking system.[94] This is because banks, as Mehrsa Baradaran explains, are part of a social contract whereby they accept regulatory burdens in exchange for deposit insurance and access to funds on favorable terms from the Federal Reserve.[95] Also, a number of federal laws incentivize banks to keep consumer interests in mind. For instance, the 1977 Community Reinvestment Act encourages banks to focus their lending activities in low- to moderate-income communities. In exchange for doing so, regulators give favorable treatment to bank applications to open new branches or engage in merger or acquisition activities. Relatedly, banks have a long history of dealing with consumers as depositors, and therefore some of the customer-oriented norms that result spill over to their lending activities. Nonbank servicers with their private equity owners are less likely to have consumer interests in mind when making decisions – particularly if those decisions do not expand the bottom line.

Consider the example of Caliber Home Loans, a minor nonbank servicer purchased in 2014 by the $60 billion private equity firm Lone Star Funds. Caliber quickly became a major player in the mortgage middleman industry in just a few short years thereafter.[96] But, to the dismay of consumer advocates, reports indicated that after the acquisition Caliber was quick to foreclose and routinely denied loan modification applications.

To help address the issue of regulating nonbank servicers, at least with respect to loans owned by Fannie Mae and Freddie Mac, the GSEs have attempted to use their contractual relationships with servicers to handle the economics of nonbank servicing by imposing capital requirements. However, these efforts have been criticized as not going far enough, and they do not impact the private-label market (however small it may be as of this writing).[97] The efforts of the GSEs are also merely contractual, rather than regulatory, in nature. They thus carry a different set of remedies and occupy a different place in the hierarchy of law.

DESIGNING A BETTER WAY OF REGULATE MORTGAGE SERVICING

It's time to fundamentally change the way we regulate mortgage servicers by marrying consumer-facing rules and safety and soundness concerns under a coordinated state and federal umbrella. The current system is too fragmented and does not adequately reflect contemporary market conditions. State financial services regulators have their own licensing requirements (if they require servicers to be licensed at all), but they are more concerned with barriers to entry rather than long-term sustainability. The CFPB's rules address how mortgage servicers deal with homeowners from a consumer protection standpoint, such as with disclosures, loss mitigation, and communications. The CFPB's rules do not, however, speak to the core issue of how to make sure servicers are built and operate in a way that allows them to effectively abide by these consumer protection mandates on a consistent basis. The consumer rules assume that servicers have the financial capacity to meet their obligations. Also, federal banking regulators have their own prudential standards for mortgage servicers that are owned or operated through federally regulated financial institutions – introducing more variation and cabining. And finally, the GSEs have their own prudential-like requirements that are imposed when servicers manage Fannie- or Freddie-backed mortgage loans through contractually imposed capital and operating requirements. This whole structure is confusing and expensive for servicers to comply with and welcomes opportunities for mistake or manipulation. The following proposal provides the benefits of uniform regulation, under a federalism model, that incorporates consumer and prudential policies, without taking away the important role of the states.

POSTCRISIS FEDERALISM AT WORK

First, my proposal builds off an existing regulatory concept that was conceived after the financial crisis. The HERA of 2008, which was passed in the aftermath of the crisis, contained a section known as the Secure and Fair Enforcement for Mortgage Licensing Act of 2008 (SAFE Act). This legislation was created through the combined efforts of the Conference of State Banking Supervisors (CSBS),[98] HUD, OCC, the Federal Reserve, and the American Association of Residential Mortgage Regulators (AARMR)[99] (among others).

The purpose of the legislation was to deal with mortgage originators – those that make mortgage loans on the front-end. This was a natural point of concern because the making of risky loans was the first stop on the subprime securitization train. Addressing origination would go a long way to decreasing the chance of bad loans ballooning into catastrophic events for the economy.

The SAFE Act states that all mortgage loan originators must be licensed – either at the state or federal level. If the originator is employed by a federally insured deposit-taking institution (like a bank insured by the FDIC) or is a subsidiary of such an institution, then the appropriate federal regulator must oversee licensing. But, as a fallback, all other originators must be licensed by the appropriate state-level banking regulator. The law made no exceptions and created no loopholes – no firm originating mortgage loans could escape licensing at either the state or federal level. But, regardless of who did the licensing, all mortgage originators would be required to register with the newly created and unified Nationwide Mortgage Licensing System and Registry (NMLS). This system essentially created a single information center for all mortgage originators – a first of its kind.

When it came to actual licensing requirements, another goal of the SAFE Act was to create a level of uniformity across states as to the firms under their jurisdiction. To do this, the law stated that, like at the federal level, all state licensing requirements should entail criminal history checks, credit history inquiries, mandatory education and testing of applicants, continuing education, disclosure of information regarding a firm's net worth, and the procurement of surety bonds. This was done to bring a level of even-handedness to the licensing scheme, regardless of which state issued the license. And, at least originally, HUD had a role to play in this process. HUD was required to ensure that all state licensing schemes met these federal SAFE Act minimum standards. If HUD determined that a state's laws did not conform with these baseline requirements, then HUD could implement a licensing system for just that state – essentially stepping in to do what the state had failed to do. This helped keep states accountable.

After the passage of the Dodd-Frank Act, rulemaking authority for the SAFE Act was transferred to the CFPB.[100] This removed HUD as the compliance/oversight agency for the state-level regulators. Now, the CFPB makes sure states comply with SAFE Act obligations.[101]

The SAFE Act and NMLS system represent a coordinated effort at using our federalism structure to deal with the proper licensing of those that issue residential mortgage loans – a function that was at the heart of the financial crisis. The stated goals of the legislation and the single registry are to create minimum licensing requirements, develop uniformity in regulatory approach, improve the accountability of mortgage originators, fight fraud in the industry, and, importantly, enhance consumer protection.

In fulfilling the task assigned to them by the SAFE Act, the CSBS and the AARMR created and now operate the NMLS. The NMLS system is owned by a subsidiary entity of CSBS – State Regulatory Registry LLC. Any company seeking to apply for, amend, renew, or terminate a license to engage in the origination or brokering of residential mortgage loans must go through the NMLS system. The actual decision to issue a license, however, is made by the federal or state regulatory body (which, as noted, is guided by certain minimum standards).[102] The NMLS is merely the portal – albeit a uniform one – for that process. To promote harmony between state and federal actors, the CSBS created model state-level legislation that jurisdictions could enact and thereby be confident that their mortgage origination requirements met SAFE Act mandates. With the blessing of HUD (and then the CFPB), this legislation has been widely enacted in state houses across the country.

APPLYING A FEDERALISM APPROACH TO MIDDLEMAN REGULATION

The SAFE Act/NMLS system represents a unique approach to regulation of an industry – one that does not require states to yield to federal authority or for state laws to be preempted. Indeed, through a coordinated partnership, the system has operated successfully and has largely met the stated goals of the SAFE Act in bringing order to the regulation of licensing for those that issue the all-important residential mortgage loan.

The licensure of mortgage servicing firms would benefit from a similar federalism partnership approach. One of the benefits of the NMLS is that state financial services regulators have seized upon this national, uniform registry apparatus to expand its use to other types of licenses beyond merely mortgage originators. In 2012, the NMLS started handling licensing for consumer finance firms, payday lenders, money transmitters, checking cashing firms (collectively called "money services businesses"), and debt collectors, among others.[103] And a number of states now require mortgage servicing companies to also be licensed through the NMLS. For instance, a small number of states – such as California,[104] Nebraska,[105] Tennessee,[106] Vermont,[107] and Colorado[108] – require that a firm that services a loan for a borrower resident in that state must obtain a license through the NMLS.

What is needed is a similar state-federal partnership in the licensing of mortgage servicers that also incorporates prudential components. First, there should be federally mandated licensing requirements for mortgage servicers that include safety and soundness standards. These regulatory requirements would be created by state regulators and relevant federal agencies.

When it comes to the actual content of these new licensure requirements, they would in some sense be similar, at least in part, to the requirements imposed on mortgage originators. This would include requiring that certain servicing employees undergo a criminal background check, undergo credit history inquiries, take a qualifying written test, and receive continuing education annually. But as noted in the preceding text, these licensing standards would also incorporate a prudential component (further described in the following text). The prudential piece is important because it can promote a safe and stable mortgage servicing industry – something that is particularly important when it comes to nonbank servicers, which are growing in market share and can have serious liquidity problems. Although the CFPB regulates nonbank servicers, the CFPB is not a prudential regulator. As Angela Littwin notes, "The CFPB has no safety and soundness authority. Its examination procedures, for example, assess the risks that companies' practices pose for consumers, rather than risks to the companies' financial health."[109] The CFPB's supervisory activities with respect to mortgage servicers are therefore limited. Moreover, the CFPB is not well equipped to deal with the large number of servicers operating in the market place[110] and instead tends to focus more of their supervision on large firms.[111]

When it comes to formulating what prudential standards might look like, a good place to start is the Proposed Regulatory Prudential Standards for Non-Bank Mortgage Servicers that was released in November 2017 by CSBS. The proposal establishes baseline prudential standards for nonbank servicers that cover eight target areas: capital, risk management, data standards, data protection, liquidity, corporate governance, transferring servicing rights, and change of control matters. I would also suggest that such standards incorporate some key consumer-oriented rules, as suggested in 2011 by the National Consumer Law Center.[112] These would include mandatory homeowner-servicer mediation (as some states have adopted) and limitations on foreclosure-related fees, among others.

Once these licensing and prudential standards are enacted into federal law, model state legislation should be created to meet and operationalize these requirements for state-regulated servicers (like with the SAFE Act). Further, it should be mandatory for all mortgage servicers (whether state or federally licensed) to go through the NMLS for all registration, renewal, amendment, and surrender processes. Making this mandatory could help capture within the regulatory net those nonbank mortgage servicers that are not connected to a federally chartered bank or other regulated financial institution and that operate in states that do not require licensure. This new partnership system would also help avoid the regulatory variation effect, whereby different states take or could take varied approaches to licensing and regulating mortgage servicing. For federally licensed servicers, the rules would be similarly uniform regardless of where the servicer operated, due to the preemption of state law. But for state-licensed servicers, the federally mandated (although written in a partnership between state and federal agencies) requirements should give way to a reciprocal licensing framework within the NMLS. Thus, a servicer located in one state and licensed in that state through the NMLS should be given licensure status in other states where that same servicer does business.

This federalism framework serves as a foundation upon which an integrated regulatory system for *all* mortgage servicers could be built. Perhaps most importantly, developing liquidity standards that require mortgage servicers (particularly shadow bank servicers) to set aside stipulated amounts of capital as a cushion against market downturns will help make the nonbank servicing industry strong and healthy – which is good for consumers and our housing finance system as a whole. Admittedly, these changes might drive some industry consolidation, but that might not be such a bad outcome. As noted previously, the large but shallow pool of mortgage servicers can be seriously problematic in a market downtown. If a smaller number of servicers remain after the enactment of these prudential standards, then the market will be left with only those nonbank firms that have the financial health to weather economic downturns and maintain homeowner customer care.

Also, as part of this federalism partnership, a standing committee of the CFPB, CSBS, AARMR, and select federal regulators should be charged with the governance of the mortgage servicing licensure system. The committee would be similar in spirit to the way the UCC is curated on an ongoing basis. Because mortgage servicing is a dynamic industry, it is important that the regulatory framework (both the consumer-facing portion and the licensing/prudential portion) be updated on a regular basis and done in a coordinated manner. If not, otherwise laudatory financial regulation can become obsolete or can impede the industry's important functions when the architecture changes and the design morphs with the shifting housing market.

The UCC benefits from a standing committee – the Permanent Editorial Board of the UCC, which is a joint and apolitical body of the Uniform Law Commission and the American Law Institute – that monitors the commercial sector and makes proposed amendments to the UCC articles as needed. This coordinating committee on mortgage servicing would serve a similar function and would do so by creating a lasting infrastructural framework for a state-federal regulatory partnership. Further, the federal statute enacted as part of this process would create this coordinating committee as a governmental body that could issue regulations relative to mortgage servicers, thereby ensuring that the regulatory framework could be responsive to industry and market concerns and changes. Having the CFPB represented on this committee, as well as designating the bureau to serve as compliance watchdog over the state regulators as is done under the SAFE Act, will help ensure that TILA/RESPA rules are enacted with prudential considerations in mind. This would finally unite financial stability and consumer financial protection under a single regulatory regime.

Some of this coordination work is on its way to being accomplished. For instance, in 2013 the CFPB and the CSBS announced a framework for coordination and information sharing in their supervision of and enforcement work for financial institutions.[113] The framework establishes a process for harmonizing, to the extent possible, federal and state consumer protection, supervision, and enforcement when there is concurrent jurisdiction. The coordinating committee I suggest here would further crystalize the level of synchronization between this committee of state banking regulators and the CFPB. In the end, mortgage servicing is multifaceted. There are consumer protection, licensing, prudential, and contractual pieces. Moreover, servicing costs are high, which unnecessarily feeds into the tightness of credit. Coordination between servicers and state and federal regulatory partners around one table, using as close to one set of rules as possible, has to be the animating feature of how we approach mortgage servicing. The preceding proposal to create a federalism-partnership framework for regulating mortgage servicing of all kinds would be a powerful and effective step in that direction.

8

Reforming Mortgage Law and Practice

And the law of England has so particular and tender a regard to the immunity of a man's house, that it stiles it his castle, and will never suffer it to be violated with immunity.
4 William Blackstone's Commentaries on the Laws of England

Reforming the regulation of mortgage servicing is not the only step needed to give this important industry the change it requires and the support it needs. After all, licensing, prudential supervision, and consumer oversight can only go so far. The second step is to make some key changes to both substantive mortgage law and to several of the practices that pervade the mortgage finance industry.

REWRITING THE MORTGAGE CONTRACT

The first thing that needs to happen is that we must change the standard form mortgage contract.[1] The time has come for Fannie Mae and Freddie Mac – together with housing advocates and industry – to undertake a serious and informed review of the standard residential mortgage; a document that is now nearly 50 years old. The most significant areas that require change are sections 7 and 9 – the provisions that deal with property inspections and preservation.

A fresh look is warranted for a number of compelling reasons. First, to the extent these property preservation clauses are premised on owners being irresponsible with their homes in the aftermath or on the eve of a loan default, today's post-2008 borrowers are made to undergo an incredibly stringent and scrutinizing underwriting process before a home loan is made. Indeed, as noted previously, only the most credit worthy of borrowers can become homeowners as lenders are requiring credit backgrounds that exceed even what Fannie Mae and Freddie Mac require for conforming loans. Also, industry data shows that mortgage originators are issuing – almost exclusively – only the most vanilla mortgage loans with fixed and fully amortizing interest rates and only after conducting careful underwriting.[2] With such a change in the way loans are made on the front end, we can at least say that a more tempered mortgage contract is merited.

The second obvious reason that supports a change to these clauses in the standard mortgage contract stems from the massive amount of litigation regarding break-in foreclosures. While admittedly changing the mortgage contract would not systemically alter mortgage servicing or the mortgage field services industry, it does have the strong potential to diminish the chances for break-in foreclosure abuse. This is because the servicer's contractual authority to deal with consumers' homes prior to foreclosure is derived from these provisions – authority that is handed down from the servicer to the contractor industry. A change in the property preservation provisions of the Fannie/Freddie mortgage contract could help mitigate future scandals of this type.

Section 7 is the first provision that needs reform. As noted Chapters 4 and 6, it allows the servicer or its agent to unilaterally enter onto the property for the all-too-vague purpose of making an "inspection." The only limitation on this right is that the inspection must be reasonable in both time and manner. But, importantly, there are no requirements relative to how or when the servicer must notify the consumer that the inspection will take place. A homeowner might look out the window one day to find someone looking around the backyard – and there would be nothing illegal about it. Importantly, these rights exist although the homeowner is current on his or her monthly payments and is otherwise acting in conformity with other loan obligations.

But, more shocking still, the servicer can also enter and inspect the interior of the home. The thought that one's servicer, without even being prompted by a default or other failure to abide by the terms of the mortgage, would have the unilateral right to enter a person's home, garage, or other structure would and should shock most homeowners. Now, admittedly, section 7 does stipulate that the homeowner has to be provided notice of the inspection, but the provision is quite one-sided. It gives no minimum time frame for giving notice, instead it indicates that the notice can be given at the time the inspection takes place. This is tantamount to no notice at all. The provision is designed entirely in favor of the lender and is administered entirely at its discretion.

The unspoken truth behind this clause is that homeowners cannot be trusted with their homes. In essence, the mortgage servicer should have the right to inspect the property at will because the homeowner surely cannot be relied upon to keep his or her home in good repair. I argue that this clause (section 7) should be eliminated entirely, with some of its core functions combined with a revision to section 9 (discussed in the following text). Without first having some breach or failure to perform by the homeowner, the servicer should not have the ability to interfere with the owner's possessory rights in the property. If today's homeowner is required to meet such rigorous underwriting requirements on the front end when the loan is made, then mortgage contract provisions like these that assume the worst about the consumer are unjust and offensive. Moreover, if the servicer really does want to conduct some kind of inspection, then it can be done from the street and without coming on to the property. If indeed the homeowner is damaging the property, then the servicer can file suit and pursue general common law rights (such as under the doctrine of waste) that all creditors have with respect to collateral.[3]

But most importantly, the contract provisions in section 9 require extensive revision. Unlike the other provisions of section 7 discussed previously, section 9 significantly shifts property rights related to power and control over the property from the homeowner to the servicer – all without a foreclosure or other divestiture under the law taking place. These rights are not limited in that they are only triggered when a homeowner misses a monthly payment. Instead, the language broadly states that all that is required is a failure of the homeowner to abide by any and all of the "promises and agreements" in the mortgage, including the filing of a bankruptcy petition or the mere pendency of a proceeding by a third-party claiming an interest in competition with the servicer. Also, even if the homeowner is timely in all payments, the act of leaving the premises, if it can be broadly considered an "abandonment," triggers these rights in favor of the servicer.

These powerful contractual rights include the power to "do and pay for whatever is reasonable and appropriate to protect the Lender's interest in the property." And lest one think that this leaves far too much to the servicer's discretion, the clause conveniently provides an illustrative list of such "reasonable" acts. This list includes the nebulous power to "protect" the value of the home and secure and repair the property. Notably, the servicer's obligation to give notice to the homeowner is now dispensed with under this provision. Now, without the slightest notice, the servicer may enter the home, change locks, board up windows, turn off the utilities, and "take any other action" to secure the property as the servicer sees fit. Indeed, what broader authority could any creditor desire over the property of its debtor? And remarkably, all these acts may be exercised by the servicer prior to any foreclosure proceedings.

Now, we can readily agree that a servicer surely must be vested with the tools it needs to preserve the collateral in the event of a default. After all, the loan would never have been given without the existence of the mortgage. Also, damaged and deteriorating property has a host of negative consequences on adjacent properties and entire neighborhoods. And lastly, requiring a servicer to go through the lengthy and costly process of requesting that a court appoint a receiver for the property is not efficient.

But, the scope and potency of the rights described in section 9 of the Fannie Mae/ Freddie Mac standard mortgage contract go too far. We must balance the servicer's interest and duty to protect the collateral with the fundamental nature of the collateral in question. This is not a commercial office building, a retail space, or an industrial building. This is someone's home. The law imposes great significance to the home and American housing and economic policy has strongly emphasized ownership of one's residence. The sense of individual integrity, self-autonomy, and psychological and physical well-being has been keenly identified with the home.[4] The status of the home as a person's dwelling place – where children are reared, the most cherished memories are made, and life's most private moments are shared – merits different treatment and a heightened level of respect.

Ironically, a tenant under property law or a debtor under article 9 of the UCC enjoys greater security in property than does a homeowner vis-à-vis a mortgage servicer. Under landlord–tenant law, landlords can often only remove tenants who remain on the premises after the expiration of the lease term by going through an applicable judicial procedure.[5] States have created summary proceedings that allow landlords to accomplish this ejectment rather quickly,[6] but landlords in many jurisdictions may not engage in self-help by taking matters into their own hands.[7] Provisions in residential leases that provide otherwise are invalid.[8] And even in those jurisdictions that do allow landlords to engage in self-help, the right is limited. The landlord can only retake possession of the property without going to court if he or she does so peacefully.[9] This usually means that the entry is accomplished without breaking in or resorting to threats, such as when the tenants have since vacated the premises.[10] A landlord who changes the locks to the property while the tenant is away is often considered to have impermissibly engaged in self-help.[11]

In commercial law, creditors who have a security interest in personal property are allowed to engage in self-help and repossess the property after the debtor defaults. The quintessential example of this usually plays out in the context of auto financing.[12] Car owners who fail to pay their monthly auto loan may wake up one morning to find that their vehicle is gone – repossessed by the car dealership that made the credit sale.[13] However, secured creditors can only take matters into their own hands (and thereby avoid the time and expense of going to court and paying the sheriff to seize the property) if it can be done without breaching the peace.[14] Although that phrase is not defined in the UCC, courts have read it fairly expansively. For instance, a court in Georgia held that even the perception of violence is enough to violate the standard, such as where the creditor used offensive or insulting language during the repossession process.[15] Other courts have suggested that any protest by the debtor in the face of self-help activities,[16] even protests by a spouse or children,[17] are sufficient to create a breach of the peace. Also, breaking locks to doors or windows to enter the property constitutes a breach of the peace.[18]

A failure to abide by this "breach the peace" standard can result in damages, including statutory damages if the property is a consumer good.[19] Importantly, the creditor cannot avoid liability merely because a contractor or subcontractor is hired to perform the task. "[A] repossessing creditor is not relieved of liability for breaching the peace simply because it has employed an independent contractor to carry out the task of repossession."[20]

Yet homeowners do not benefit from these well-established and well-enforced standards when facing the break-in foreclosure activities of servicers and their contractors. The extensive and deeply troubling stories stemming from litigation and media coverage of conflicts between homeowners and their mortgage servicers and the mortgage field services industry evidences that the current state of affairs regarding property preservation law is rife with trouble and ready for reform. Ralph Nader, who participated in the drafting of the standard mortgage contract back in the 1970s, cautioned that the agreement granted too much power to lenders, and particularly "the power to invade the consumer's home for any reason, or no reason at all."[21] History has proven him right, and now is the time to correct this decades-old error.

REDRAFTING KEY MORTGAGE PROVISIONS

As a starting point, these broad-ranging contractual powers (both in sections 7 and 9) in favor of the servicer should only be triggered when there is a material threat to the value of the collateral – not merely upon a simple default or whenever the servicer feels like it wants to check in on the property. The servicer should be required to give notice to the homeowner that it is taking such action, although under the general rule this notice can occur at any time before or at the time of the act. This standard of "material threat" to value should satisfy both homeowner advocates and servicers. It creates an actual standard for the exercise of rights (which does not currently exist in section 7) and it places some controls on when rights can be exercised (which is ill-defined or absent in section 9). But, this standard does leave open the possibility that the servicer could, for instance, inspect the property or engage in acts of preservation even prior to a default on the off chance that the otherwise conforming homeowner is damaging the property.

Second, if the homeowner is still living on the premises (i.e., if the property is not vacant/abandoned), additional protections should attach to limit the servicers' rights already described. First, the servicer should have an obligation to give at least 24-hour notice to the homeowner before coming on to the property. Also, reasonable arrangements should be made so that the owner can have a chance to be present during the inspection or for whenever acts of preservation are being contemplated. And under no circumstances should the servicer be able to turn off utilities or empty out the contents of one's home when the homeowner is still in possession of the property.

Additionally, the contract should eliminate the use of mere abandonment/vacancy as an event that triggers the servicer's expansive rights. Some servicers will raise the argument that muscular provisions are needed to deal with instances whereby the property has been abandoned by the owner and left to deteriorate. I would argue, however, that the existence of a material threat to the value of the property addresses that issue, provided that the servicer can make a good faith argument that this is occurring. But, the mortgage contract does need a clear definition of abandonment for purposes of the servicer deciding whether a 24-hour notice and other protections must be given to the homeowner. Using the general term *abandonment* is too amorphous of a standard. Courts dealing with these cases are left to their own devices and have had difficulty determining when this occurs – sometimes using vacancy or relinquishment of possession as the yardsticks to varying results.[22]

One way to solve this would be to say that when facts and circumstances surrounding a mortgaged property indicate that the owner has relinquished physical possession and has no intent to return, then the property has been abandoned. This would be the standards-based approach. This could then be accompanied by a safe harbor whereby if additional facts were present then the property would be deemed abandoned/vacant. This would include things like overgrown vegetation, boarded-up doors or windows, or other specific facts indicating that the property is open or unprotected. Recall of course that the purpose of determining whether property is vacant/abandoned is for the servicer to know its limitations in exercising section 9 rights. But, many of the incidents of abandonment/vacancy will necessarily raise the potential for a material threat to the value of the property, thus triggering the rights in the first place. For instance, in *Kautsman v. Carrington Mortgage Services, LLC*, the homeowners fell behind on their mortgage loan payments.[23] Believing that they could make them up by renting out the home, they moved out and began to show the property to prospective tenants. Although it might have appeared at first blush that because the homeowners were living elsewhere and the furnishings had been removed, the property was vacant. That was not the case. Instead, they had merely moved out but intended to continue to exercise control over the property – control as landlords. This scenario does not, however, raise the issue of impairment of the collateral value of the home. Thus, separating the standard for triggering the rights from the concept of mere abandonment makes sense.

Lastly, I suggest that the exercise of section 9 rights be overlaid with an obligation not to breach the peace. This would impose a similar standard on servicers as that which already exists for UCC article 9 creditors and landlords. If the servicer (or rather its agent) believes the necessary acts of preservation cannot be accomplished without a potential breach of the peace, then the servicer should go to court and seek judicial recognition of its rights. The servicer should not, however, proceed in an environment that might result in intimidating or otherwise becoming engaged in a fight with the homeowner. Going to court does take time and money, but too much is at stake to do otherwise when the potential for violence is present.

In conclusion, I suggest that the mortgage contract should be amended by Fannie Mae and Freddie Mac (or under the authority of its conservator, the FHFA) to put these changes into effect. Doing so will, in part, help ameliorate the servicer-contractor-homeowner problem by reorienting the source of the servicer's authority over the home – the mortgage contract.

ACCOMPANYING STATE AND LOCAL GOVERNMENT LAW CHANGES

But, making these changes to the Fannie Mae/Freddie Mac mortgage are not enough. A number of state law and federal regulatory changes must accompany these contract revisions to make them fully enforceable and to bring legal harmony across different (but highly relevant) areas of mortgage law. First, American courts need guidance on how to deal with property preservation issues with respect to mortgaged property because they have reached varied results and based on shaky legal footing with respect to these issues. On the one hand, a small number of courts (and legislatures) have rejected the operation of these clauses altogether – instead requiring foreclosure.[24] For instance, the Washington Supreme Court was confronted with a servicer-contractor incident in *Jordan v. Nationstar Mortgage, LLC*.[25] The court said that "it is well settled that Washington [lien-theory mortgage] law prohibits lenders from taking possession of borrowers' property before foreclosure"[26] and the servicer "Nationstar effectively ousted Jordan by changing her locks, exercising its control over the property."[27] Thus, Nationstar (and its contractor) acted illegally in entering the property of the homeowner prior to foreclosure.

But other courts have more readily upheld the use of these preservation clauses. In *Kheder v. Seterus, Inc.*, the Michigan appeals court, when faced with a claim for trespass, noted that the owner had consented to such entry pursuant to the clause in the mortgage: "Keller Williams's actions were reasonable and appropriate to protect the lender's interest and were, therefore, authorized by plaintiffs."[28] In 2013, the court in *McCray v. Specialized Loan Servicing* was again faced with a trespass claim related to the changing of locks, shutting off of water, winterization of the home, and allegedly damaging a screen and front door.[29] The court went so far as to say that the homeowner "no longer had possession of the Property following her default on the loan" even though a foreclosure under the deed of trust had not yet been concluded.[30]

Some courts, like the one in *Jordan* and in other similar cases, say that these clauses are not operable because the state where the mortgaged property is located follows the "lien theory" of mortgage.[31] As noted in Chapter 4, this is where the creditor obtains only a security right – something less than a piece of ownership – when it takes a mortgage. Thus, ownership of the property remains with the homeowner and the creditor merely has a lesser property right. And while it is true that the *Nationstar* court and other courts that reject property preservation clauses are located in lien theory states, the power of the lien versus title theory argument is rather weak. For example, the Michigan case previously cited in which the court upheld the property preservation clause was operable took place in a lien theory state. Michigan does not follow the title theory, yet the servicer was nonetheless able to exercise its authority.[32] The Kentucky court in *Riley v. Wells Fargo* said it would uphold the entry and preservation clause in the mortgage if the servicer's acts were reasonable and appropriate, even prior to a formal foreclosure.[33] This was again despite the fact that Kentucky too is a lien theory state.[34]

In truth, it should not matter in the least whether a state follows the lien or title theory of mortgages – this is a person's home, whether he or she lives in Kentucky, Michigan, or Timbuktu. And a homeowner should not have to worry about his or her servicer breaking into the home just because of which state they choose to live. The law should be the same in this respect everywhere. The lien theory versus title theory of mortgages concept is an antique and, at least in residential mortgage lending, is not aligned with the significant policy choices we have made about homeownership nor is it consistently applied by modern courts.[35] Indeed, some courts in title theory states claim that despite the theoretical fact that the mortgage vests "the legal title in the mortgagee," the lender is nevertheless "not in a general sense the owner of the mortgaged estate before foreclosure."[36]

What this means is that whatever changes are made to the Fannie Mae/Freddie Mac mortgage with respect to how property preservation practices should work must be matched with how state law treats preforeclosure mortgage activity. To that end, the FHFA/GSEs should work with the Uniform Law Commission (ULC), and particularly the Joint Editorial Board for Uniform Real Property Acts, to develop a set of statutory amendments that could be made to a state's foreclosure statute. These amendments would include a codification of the standards, triggers, and safe harbors set forth in the preceding text such that a servicer would be able to conduct preforeclosure preservation activity, but where the homeowner's rights would be respected and scaled to whether the property is abandoned.

State law changes are needed along with local government law reforms. Many local governments require that mortgage holders protect and preserve vacant properties and conduct regular inspections (even predefault and preforeclosure).[37] And some of these municipal code provisions impose the duty on the lender when the property is merely vacant (but not necessarily in decline). The justification for these local laws is that absentee ownership can lead to property deterioration. That is true, but it is not that the absenteeism alone causes the damage – it is neglect. Abandonment is merely used as a heuristic for neglect, which is not always the case. Thus, I do not think abandonment should be the standard.[38] It might be the case that abandonment leads to a material threat to the value of the property, but abandonment alone leaves too many issues on the table. So, similar to how the standard residential mortgage should be changed to remove mere abandonment as a trigger for the servicer to exercise rights, so too should mere abandonment/vacancy be removed as a trigger to impose duties on servicers to engage in acts of preservation at the local government level. The ordinance structure relative to a servicer's obligation to maintain mortgaged property should be harmonized with the changes suggested for the mortgage contract, and state law changes can help with that effort.

ACCOMPANYING CHANGES TO FEDERAL HUD REGULATIONS

And lastly, HUD's own rules with respect to the servicers of FHA-insured mortgage loans must also be changed. HUD regulation requires that if there has been a default and the property is vacant/abandoned, then the servicer must take "reasonable action to protect and preserve such security property."[39] Specific HUD guidance as to this regulation states that the government will hold the servicer liable for any "damage or destruction" that results from a failure to protect and preserve the "vacant or abandoned property."[40] Clearly the purpose of this regulation is to protect the collateral value of homes that secure FHA-insured mortgage loans – and that goal makes sense for reasons already stated. But again, the focus is on abandonment, which must necessarily lead to damage or decay. It may very well be that one follows the other, but this formulation (like with some local ordinances) puts the cart before the horse. It would be better, as noted previously, to focus the obligation (and any subsequent liability) on situations in which the servicer allows a material threat to the value of the property to occur – regardless of whether the property is abandoned. Then, the servicer's rights will be scaled to whether abandonment has occurred. Thus, HUD rules should be adjusted to also be consistent with these amendments to the Fannie Mae/Freddie Mac mortgage contract.[41]

In the end, servicers need some ability to protect their collateral for the benefit of the investors that they serve. And, keeping mortgaged property in good repair benefits society at large because the negative externalities that flow from decaying and damaged property must be absorbed by adjacent property owners, communities, and taxpayers at large. But, the unfettered right to engage with someone's home with relatively few prescribed barriers is producing very harsh results for homeowners at times when they are in their most vulnerable state. Changing the language in a contract will not by any means totally eliminate bad actors – the law has its limits. However, giving some contours to when acts of preservation can occur and how homeowners should be treated in these instances is a good first step.

YOUR CONTRACTOR BREAKS IT: YOU BUY IT

Even if the mortgage contract is changed to temper the authority granted to servicers by homeowners when it comes to the home, contractor abuse can still happen. Because there is so much layering between the servicers and the ultimate subcontractor that performs the work, there needs to be more incentives on the part of the servicer to ensure there is necessary vendor oversight. The national mortgage settlement agreement required servicers to "adopt procedures to oversee foreclosure trustees, *independent contractors*, and its agents including foreclosure firms, subservicers, agents, subsidiaries and affiliates."[42]

These new third-party oversight standards included a servicer obligation to conduct appropriate due diligence as to the qualifications, expertise, capacity, reputation, complaints, information security, document custody practices, business continuity, and financial viability of any third-party contractors.[43] The settlement also requires servicers to warrant that any agreements, contracts, or policies between the servicer and the contractor delineate how adequate oversight will be operationalized, including measures to enforce contractual rights and remedies and to provide timely action with regard to failures in performance. In the event of a vendor's failure to perform the required obligations or its failure to meet the standards set forth by or imposed upon the servicer, the mortgage middleman must have a process for reviewing and addressing any customer complaints it receives in connection with these contractor firms. To ensure that covered servicers are meeting their obligations under the settlement, the National Mortgage Settlement Monitor and the internal review group conducts periodic tests and inspections for the five banks.

While this system may sound good, in truth it does not go far enough. Consider that the National Mortgage Settlement only applied to five financial institutions – Citigroup, JPMorgan Chase, Wells Fargo, Ally Financial, and Bank of America. While these firms certainly have servicing arms, they are also traditional banks. And recall that banks are shrinking their servicing operations, while nonbanks – shadow banks – are taking an increasingly large share of the mortgage market. Moreover, the monitoring of these five banks for compliance with the settlement came to an end in March 2016.[44]

Some nonbank servicers have also been swept into the joint state-federal mortgage settlement system in years since 2012 as a result of additional lawsuits filed by state attorneys general and several federal agencies. These nonbank servicers include American Home Mortgage Servicing, Homeward Residential Holdings, Litton, Ocwen Financial, SunTrust, and HSBC.[45] But that still leaves out many other nonbank servicers. In essence, the scattershot approach of regulating servicing vendor oversight standards through litigation settlements is not ideal. It leaves gaps in coverage and does not account for new entrants to the mortgage servicing market.

Since taking control over the consumer-facing aspects of mortgage servicing, the CFPB has also tried to address the vendor-oversight issue.[46] First, in April 2012 the bureau put out a bulletin[47] on so-called service providers to financial institutions falling under the CFPB's purview.[48] The bulletin took note of the fact that banks and nonbanks use contractors often, particularly when they need to rely on certain expertise that would otherwise require significant investment to conduct the activity in-house. But the bureau noted that the use of a service provider does not "absolve the supervised bank or nonbank of responsibility."[49] Further, the failure of a service provider to become familiar with consumer protection requirements or to enact internal controls can harm the consumer and result in liability to the contracting firm. The bulletin then explained the bureau's expectation that banks and nonbanks should have processes in place to manage their vendors, including measures to ensure that proper due diligence related to the firm is conducted; the bank/nonbank understands the service provider's policies, procedures, and internal controls (including ensuring the appropriate training and oversight of employees and agents); provisions relative to violations and abusive/deceptive practices are contained in the service contract; and the bank/nonbank performs regular monitoring of the relationship.

Then again, in its fall 2016 supervisory highlights publication, the CFPB warned of the need for regulated institutions to strengthen their service provider oversight programs.[50] In the summer 2016 issue of this same publication, the bureau warned of taking action against service providers.[51] And finally, in a more formal compliance bulletin and policy guidance publication in 2016, the bureau reinforced its expectations in the first 2012 bulletin regarding vendor oversight responsibilities, and warned that "exercise of its supervisory and enforcement authority will closely reflect this orientation and emphasis."[52]

But it has not been at all clear that the CFPB's warnings were directed at the mortgage field services industry. To date, there does not appear to be any readily available information relative to enforcement actions brought against property contractors directly. And, with the change in political ideology taking place at the CFPB as a result of the election of President Donald Trump and his installation of new leadership at the bureau, it is uncertain whether the agency can be relied upon to police servicers and their property contractor relationships.[53]

What this means is that the law has to provide sufficient avenues for aggrieved homeowners to take matters into their own hands through private litigation. The National Mortgage Settlement is limited to only certain servicers in terms of the vendor oversight obligations imposed on them, and it requires action be taken by governmental officials involved in the settlement for things like break-in foreclosure wrongs resulting from servicer-contractor agreements to be addressed. Further, the CFPB's movement in service provider oversight – going back to 2012 – has been slow in coming and, again, requires governmental action to address any wrongs that might result. Homeowners that suffer at the hands of servicers and their property contractors should not be forced to toss about in the changing political winds – they should have a means to defend themselves.

Law reform is needed to give private litigants a fighting chance. While many homeowners did not take break-in foreclosures lying down (indeed, hundreds filed suit against their servicers and their strings of contractors), these lawsuits have been met with differing levels of success.[54] Although the stories are all similar – tales of homeowners, behind on their payments and often still in negotiations with their servicer, experiencing varying levels of aggressive and intimidating behavior by property contracting companies hired by the mortgage middleman to perform certain inspection and preservation services – the litigation results often are mixed and inconsistent.

The lawsuits almost uniformly raise the legal issues of conversion of property, invasion of privacy, intentional infliction of emotional distress, breach of contract, general negligence, sometimes state consumer protection laws, and all of these in combination with agency theories to impute liability up the chain to the mortgage servicer.[55] However, there is no uniformity as to whether any single or combination of theories leads to a victory for the distressed homeowner. In many cases, courts are not eager to give homeowners much relief. In some cases, claims for conversion are denied because although the homeowner might be locked out of the premises by the contractor, the fact that they were able "to gain entry to the Homestead within a matter of hours" defeated the claim for conversion because the duration of exclusion was so brief.[56]

Courts also frequently dismiss claims for intentional infliction of emotional distress on the theory that the act was either not intentional or that although the acts of the contractor might have produced "general feelings of upset and defeat" these were not "substantial enough to qualify as emotional distress."[57] Other courts say that negligent infliction of emotional distress is only available in instances in which "there exists a special relationship where it is foreseeable that a breach of the relevant duty would result in emotional harm so extreme that a reasonable person should not be expected to endure the resulting distress."[58] And "[a]lthough the case involve[d] Plaintiff's home and possessions, the relationship was commercial and adversarial" so a sufficient duty was not owed.[59]

With respect to negligence, sometimes courts do find that the servicer and the contractor owe a duty to "act with care when identifying and securing mortgaged property in order to avoid securing or damaging property that they have no legal right to enter."[60] But, at other times, courts reject there being a relevant duty. In addressing one aggrieved homeowner's negligence claim, the court held that "[a] negligence claim includes as an element a legal duty owed by one person to another … In the mortgage context, there is no special relationship between a mortgagor and a mortgagee, or between a servicer and a borrower, that would impose an independent common-law duty on [the servicer or contractor]."[61]

More broadly instructive of some courts' policy view in this area is the break-in foreclosure case of *Openiano v. Bank of America*. This case involved the entering of a home and the changing of locks, all without permission or notice, to which the court said that the:

> [b]ank's actions did not exceed the scope of its rights in the standard lender-borrower relationship. "'[A]bsent special circumstances … a loan transaction is at arm's length and there is no fiduciary relationship between the borrower and lender.' … A commercial lender pursues its own economic interests in lending money."[62]

Sometimes, in an effort to establish a duty owed to the homeowner by the servicer (or the contractor), homeowner-plaintiffs will look to the obligations imposed on servicers and related contractors in the Fannie Mae or Freddie Mac mortgage servicing guidelines. The idea is that if a servicer is supposed to properly vet, hire, and supervise contractors, and based on a failure to do so injury to the homeowner occurs, then the servicer should be liable for breaching this quasitort/quasicontract duty to the homeowner. However, courts routinely reject such arguments, saying instead that "[borrowers] are not third-party beneficiaries" to servicer guidelines.[63] Rather, the guidelines are meant to protect the GSEs.[64] To the extent some kind of duty is owed, some courts say that there is no breach as the result of the changing of locks, clearing out of the premises, winterizing the property, or any number of other acts because section 9 of the mortgage explicitly authorizes such activity.[65]

Yet other courts dismiss any kind of tort-based negligence claim by using state law doctrines that preclude recovery in tort for injuries that arise from a contractual or commercial relationship. In essence, the idea is that "tort damages are generally not recoverable if the defendant's conduct 'would give rise to liability only because it breaches the parties' agreement.'"[66] In *Warren v. Bank of America*, the court was faced with negligent hiring and supervision allegations against Bank of America, as servicer, for conduct by its contractor Safeguard.[67] The court stated that the negligence claim was barred based on the fact that the claim was essentially related to the contract between Bank of America and Safeguard, to which the homeowner-plaintiff was not a party. Thus, the "economic loss" rule relegated the plaintiff to a contract action, yet she could not bring it because she was not a party to the relevant contract.

Courts are similarly mixed on the invasion of privacy and trespass claims. In the case of *In re Carpenter*, the court upheld the claim in stating that "a person of ordinary sensibilities could have been highly offended, shamed, humiliated or suffered emotionally from having her residence entered unlawfully and all the contents thereof, including those of the most private nature, removed without her knowledge or consent."[68] But the court rejected a trespass claim because "Chase was authorized to enter the house to secure it, which specifically included the right to change the lock on the house."[69] And again, the court in *PNC Bank v. Van Hoornaar* held that the mortgage contract gives the servicer and its agents "consent to entry upon the mortgaged premises when the borrower is in default ... [t]herefore, his trespass claim fails to state a cause of action."[70]

Courts are frequently hesitant to allow any kind of liability to reach up the chain to the servicer or even from a subcontractor to the prime contractor. First, courts often reject such arguments under the theory that the property preservation firm is merely an independent contractor of the servicer or prime contractor.[71] Under American law, if a subordinate is an independent contractor, rather than an employee, then respondeat superior liability does not apply. Thus, the party who hired the independent contractor cannot normally be held liable for the contractor's actions.[72]

At other times, courts take particularly narrow views of agency law to limit the scope of what a master can be liable for when it comes to the acts of its servant. For instance, in *Bittinger v. Wells Fargo* the plaintiff argued that Wells Fargo, as servicer, was liable for the theft of personal property by a subcontractor of Wells Fargo's prime contractor.[73] The theory was based on the fact that the subcontractor was, in the end, an agent of the servicer. The district court judge, however, admonished the plaintiff and stated that:

> It can't be that you can plausibly allege that Wells Fargo hired somebody to steal property for them. Remember, the agent acts for the principal and the principal is bound to the extent that the agent is acting for the principal. So, to hold Wells Fargo in an agency theory for theft or conversion ... you have to allege that that theft or conversion was within the scope of the agency that Wells Fargo set up. You haven't even tried to do that and I can't imagine that you can.[74]

This is not to say that courts never impose liability on servicers for the actions of their contractors or subcontractors. It happens from time to time, but it is rare and far from uniform in application.[75]

This lengthy discussion concerning how homeowners fare in court when they take matters into their own hands (when they can afford to do so) demonstrates that few litigants prevail and when they do it is often for reasons that are not consistent across jurisdictions. Victories are few and far between; in the end, many courts have shown an unwillingness to impose any form of liability – or at least any substantial liability – on servicers and/or their contractors when confronted with break-in foreclosure lawsuits. These cases range from those where the court finds that the parties have failed to allege the necessary facts to meet the elements needed for relief or the courts evidence hostility toward the defaulted homeowner or an unwillingness to make the mortgagee or its agents out to be the wrongdoer.[76] To quote a Connecticut superior court judge in the January 2018 case of *Norboe v. Wells Fargo*:

> This is a lawsuit arising from what defendants call their "property preservation activities," and plaintiff calls defendant's "home break-ins," which took place while plaintiff was in default on his mortgage loan. ...
>
> ... The applicable legal principles and doctrines are not especially complicated in the abstract, but they are numerous, and there is no consensus in the courts as to how many of these various substantive rules (of agency, negligence, trespass, contract, emotional distress, unfair trade practices, etc.) should apply to the particular subject matter at issue.[77]

It is time to recognize that existing law, both statutory and common law, has simply not kept up with the mortgage middleman industry – including as it relates to the use of the mortgage field services industry. To remedy this, I suggest creating a new, more tailored cause of action that homeowners can use to reach servicers and impose liability on them for their wrongful acts and those of their contractors and subcontractors. This would be achieved through the use of uniform or model state law, which I suggest would be developed by the ULC in connection with stakeholders.[78]

First, the statute would impose on mortgage servicers a broad duty to act in good faith toward homeowners in connection with all servicing activities. Servicing activities would include everything from receiving and processing monthly payments, to engaging with the homeowner in connection with loss mitigation, to all forms of foreclosure-related activities. Importantly, servicing activities would encompass the actions undertaken in the servicer's name, such as those by property preservation companies. If the servicer was found to have violated the duty to act in good faith – including in properly supervising its agents and subagents – then this could be used to halt the foreclosure and collect some form of statutory damages. Lastly, the statute would borrow from commercial law regarding the liability of servicers for the acts of their contractors.[79] Specifically, servicers should be held responsible for the actions of others taken on the servicer's behalf, including independent contractors engaged by the servicer in acts of preservation.

This solution achieves a number of important objectives. First, it creates a duty – a sort of contractual privity – between the servicer and the homeowner by virtue of the duty to act in good faith. Courts sometimes reject the imposition of a duty under tort law because of the economic loss doctrine. Yet, they also fail to find a duty under contract law because the homeowner lacks privity with the servicer. This statutory solution, however, creates the needed connection and duty between the two, which can then give rise to liability for the failure of the servicer to hold the contractor accountable for wrongful behavior or else to deal with the homeowner in accordance with servicing guidelines. All these ancillary agreements of the servicer could be used to inform the court's interpretation of whether the servicer has fulfilled its obligation to act in good faith, and thereby give the homeowner a more likely chance of success. Second, it prevents the servicer from being able to disclaim liability in instances in which the court imposes liability on the contractor or a subcontractor. Under current case law, courts are caught in the web of independent contractor and master-servant doctrine that impedes their ability to impose liability on the servicer for the wrongful acts of parties down the chain. Imposing liability up to the servicer for the acts of its vendors will give the mortgage middleman a strong incentive to keep better watch on who they hire.

Creating this duty and imposing this liability helps the law better reflect the realities of the relationship between homeowners and servicers. Although it may not be the servicer that breaks into the home, it is through the authority granted to the servicer under the mortgage contract that this power to enter is being derived. Moreover, in the loss mitigation process it is the servicer that has control over the future of the homeowner, even though technically the homeowner has never entered into a contract giving it such power in the first place. Creating a statutory connection between the servicer and the homeowner brings some level of credit-debtor reciprocity to a relationship that is, from a practical and legal perspective, currently quite one-sided.

TAKING MORTGAGE NOTE REGISTRATION NATIONWIDE

The lack of adequate recordkeeping in the mortgage industry was all too evident as seen through the lens of robo-signing and in light of the convoluted MERS system. But, the way we record information about who has what rights to a mortgage is important. It puts third parties on notice that the property is encumbered and can at least serve as a starting point in figuring out who has rights in that mortgage. But, the "rules-don't-matter" approach taken by many mortgage servicers during the foreclosure crisis created a host of problems for homeowners and courts. The submission of false affidavits whereby servicers – in coordination with MERS – claimed that they had the right to foreclosure on the property even when they had long since lost the homeowner's promissory note or else destroyed it created massive amounts of litigation, loss, and confusion. Sometimes this resulted in the consumer losing his or her home in foreclosure even though the servicer could not show that it had the legal right to foreclose – with the court taking the robo-signed affidavit at face value. At other (less frequent) times it was the servicer who, under direct scrutiny by the judge, saw the homeowner's indebtedness and mortgage eliminated because of the servicer's poor recordkeeping.[80]

The need for better recordkeeping in the securitization of residential notes (and accompanying mortgages) is evident. The current system of numerous county-level recorders with varying requirements and levels of technological sophistication creates unnecessary complexity. A more efficient and less costly system should be created – one that benefits not only actors in the secondary mortgage market but also consumers who desire a clear, reliable, and accessible way to discern who is entitled to seek collection. This particularly benefits homeowners when it comes to knowing precisely who has the authority to treat with the individual when it comes to a foreclosure or a loan modification. And, it is not inconceivable that by reducing the cost of mortgage recordkeeping for those involved in mortgage capital markets and securitization that the cost of residential mortgage credit may be somewhat reduced – again to the benefit of would-be borrowers.

As real estate scholars like Tanya Marsh[81] and Dale Whitman[82] (as well as others)[83] have proposed in the recent past, we need a nationwide electronic registry for mortgage notes. Formulations of such a project are already underway, although none have yet been adopted.[84] First, on March 11, 2015 the Federal Reserve Bank of New York released a draft federal legislative proposal for the creation of a National Mortgage Note Repository Act.[85] The act does a number of noteworthy things in terms of moving toward a better (albeit voluntary) system for mortgage-related paperwork management.

First and foremost, it deals with both paper and electronic promissory notes. This is important because so much of UCC article 3 relies on there being one authoritative paper copy of the original promissory note, while much of modern structured finance has moved toward digital files. Under the proposed system, the borrower would sign a paper copy of the note, but that note would then be scanned into the repository system and the paper copy would be destroyed. But, the note would not lose its legal effect merely because it had been reduced to a digital form. The new electronic version of the note would also be assigned a record locator number that would follow the note for the duration of its life. To give legal effect to this process, in July 2017 the ULC passed a series of prospective changes to articles 1, 3, and 9 of the UCC. These are meant to be enacted by the states if and when the New York Federal Reserve Bank's legislation is adopted by Congress. The switch to a legally validated electronic note system is important and represents an improvement over the paper-based system of UCC article 3. With such large portfolios of loans changing hands in the securitization process, the lugging around of such a massive amount of paper (that can easily get lost or not properly negotiated) creates transaction costs and burdens that do not necessarily serve any legislate purpose in the twenty-first century.

Second, the repository will handle the movement and transfer of rights to the electronic mortgage note as it moves through the securitization system. Whoever is named in the registry in connection with the note will be automatically deemed its holder (and thus have the right to enforce it). This means negotiation is essentially made digital. No transfers are legally effective unless they are conducted through the registry. When it comes to foreclosure, whoever is listed as the registrant for the note is deemed to have the power to foreclose on the mortgaged property connected to that note (regardless of what state law might otherwise provide). The holder in due course concept is maintained but only if the original paper promissory note qualified as a negotiable instrument and the normal UCC requirements are met. The act also makes clear that the mortgage follows the note – the two cannot be separated. This would, I hope, eliminate the use of the "nominee" concept in residential mortgage practices.

Third, the draft legislation sets up a series of promises – warranties – that those submitting a note for registration into the system must make. This includes promising that the person submitting the note is, among other things, a holder of the note under UCC article 3 and, if the note is not negotiable, that the submitter has rights in not only the note but also the accompanying mortgage under relevant state law. The submitter also promises he or she has not double submitted the same note and that all required information in connection with the submission is accurate.

For the benefit of homeowners who may not know who to pay, when the individuals pay the person to whom the note is designated to in the registry then that will discharge the respective amount of the loan. Thus, even if a transfer of servicing rights has occurred and the homeowner pays the "old" servicer (not yet knowing about the transfer), that payment will be credited to the loan as long as the old servicer remains the registered note holder and the borrower has yet to receive notice otherwise. As for the flow of registry information, the borrower on a note has access to all data concerning the loan that is in the possession of the registry system – for free. Various county recording offices also have free access to the system, so they can assure clear chains of title. For consumer privacy, those who wish to purchase a mortgage loan (which would require a registered transfer) may have access to information in the registry system, but such a person would be subject to confidentiality obligations and, importantly, would be prohibited from using any information that was obtained for marketing purposes. And for the public (and mortgage law scholars), data that does not give away personal identifying information would also be available.

Importantly, the act requires that when a consumer and a servicer enter into a loan modification, which might require the promissory note to be amended, the servicer has a certain, limited amount of time to submit that information to the registration system or else suffer monetary penalties until it does so. Thus, while the actual modification does not have to be done within the system and is effective even without registration, there are incentives for the servicer to make sure that the information in the registration system is updated to accurately reflect the economic realities of the homeowner's relationship with the servicer – including the amount that he or she is now required to pay. The registry also bears liability to the homeowner if a delay in registering a modification to the note causes the homeowner damage.

Lastly, the entire system would be regulated by the FHFA – which makes sense considering the significant role that Fannie Mae and Freddie Mac currently play in mortgage securitization, as well as the coordinated relationship between HUD and the FHFA with respect to Ginnie Mae. The FHFA would create rules for how the repository system would operate and would supervise those points of entry (called *gateways*) where notes could be deposited into the system. The CFPB would play a consultative role and would serve on the governing board of the repository.

Now admittedly, the legislation is not perfect. First, the act does require that servicers that submit the note or submit subsequent transfers disclose that they are acting in the position of agents. When they do, they must also disclose the true owner of the note (the securitization trust). However, the explicit nature of the servicer in this respect is left to state substantive law and is not directly addressed in the statute. In other words, the statute hardly addresses the servicer concept at all – which is problematic considering that the mortgage middlemen are the main actors in this process – and instead speaks only of a registrant and what that person may include (such as an agent for the true owner). A more explicit recognition of servicers and a delineation of their role in the process would improve the act. The requirement that the servicer disclose the principal (the owner of the loans) is fine, but it hardly serves any real purpose. As noted in Chapter 3, the trustee of the securitization trust is prohibited from playing an active role in the management of the loans due to various legal and accounting reasons. Thus, it really is the identity of the servicer that matters. MERS has stated that it already does this by keeping contact information for servicers on file, and federal law (RESPA) requires that borrowers be notified when the servicing rights to a federally related mortgage loan are transferred.[86] But as evidenced from the myriad stories of information breakdowns during the foreclosure crisis, homeowners were often left in the dark as to who they should negotiate with to avoid losing their home. Thus, more detailed information should be provided in the registry regarding the servicer and the nature of its obligations – particularly to the extent it has the authority to make modifications to a loan and whether and what powers are allocated between master servicers and subservicers of a loan pool.

The system is also voluntary. While it is certainly true that not all residential mortgage notes are securitized, the vast majority do go through this process. When looking at the total number of first lien mortgage loan originations that took place in the first and second quarter of 2017, GSE securitizations made up 46.4 percent of the market, FHA/VA securitizations made up 25 percent, private-label securitization were 71 percent, and only 27.9 percent of loans were not securitized, but instead held on the books of the issuer.[87] That means more than 72 percent of the mortgage market is comprised of securitized loans. If such is the case, it seems better to require that all residential mortgage notes be registered in the national repository. While it is possible that the advantages of the system would likely provide enough market incentive for the mortgage industry to use the repository in any case, making it required would prevent stray securitizations or transfers outside this well-structured system.

The act also lamentably retains the holder in due course concept. This rule, as noted in Chapter 5, states that a homeowner may have a legal defense to payment (because, for instance, he or she was defrauded by the mortgage lender at the time the loan was made) but may nevertheless be barred from raising that defense against a subsequent purchaser-holder of the note who obtained it in good faith and for value without notice of facts suggesting the fraud. The holder in due course doctrine has been eliminated in many consumer credit transactions by virtue of action by the FTC in 1977, but it has remained alive and well in mortgage credit transactions.[88] Scholars have decried its continued existence, yet neither the FTC nor Dodd-Frank ended its operation in this space.[89] The act being promoted by the New York Federal Reserve Bank should explicitly eliminate the holder in due course doctrine for residential promissory notes. The potential detrimental effects on homeowners are far too great to maintain this relic of the past.

Another weakness is the provision in the act that states that the repository system can be operated by a federally chartered entity or it can be outsourced to a private firm to operate. It does not take much to imagine that MERSCORP will not simply create a new entity, with a different name, and try to obtain that lucrative contract from the FHFA.

One the one hand, this might not be a bad outcome. MERS has significant experience in the area of mortgage information recordkeeping and, to its credit, has made numerous changes to its practices since the crisis. Many of these were the result of a 2011 consent order that was entered into between the company and OCC, the Federal Reserve, the FHFA, the Office of Thrift Supervision (now dissolved), and the FDIC.[90] Under that order, MERS agreed to change a number of its policies and practices, including expanding its staff to create more capacity to handle core functions, developing better methods of communicating with its members, changing its policy on how it appoints certifying officers, and ensuring data integrity. MERS was released from the consent order in January 2018 based on having met the necessary benchmarks.[91]

But, MERSCORP's lack of diligence contributed greatly to the shoddy foreclosure practices of the past, and it is natural to be cautious of allowing them to play the central role when it comes to this new system. In a November 2017 letter, the president of MERSCORP expressed the company's opposition to the project, stating that it is a "solution in search of a problem."[92]

In the end, making some key and significant changes to the nuts and bolts of mortgage law, as well as the procedures and practices that make the wheels of mortgage finance turn, are important in addressing the issues raised by mortgage servicing. Regulating the industry – from both a consumer-facing perspective and a prudential/licensing perspective – is one piece of the puzzle. Creating mechanisms that allow homeowners to defend themselves against foreclosure abuses, as well as reforming how we manage the recordkeeping of the housing finance system, is the second piece. Together, these recommendations can help build a more solid structure for American homeownership to stand upright.

Conclusion

I am finishing this book in 2018 – about a decade after the financial crisis. A great deal has happened since then. We've seen enormous interventions into the private market through government bailouts and public-sector guarantees to the tune of billions. We've also witnessed the decimation of household wealth, with median family net worth shrinking from $139,700 to just under $84,000 between 2007 and 2013.[1] During this same period, many Americans lost their homes. In the second quarter of 2009 alone, nearly 567,000 homeowners entered foreclosure. The jobless rate soared, reaching an historical 10 percent unemployment in October 2009. Since then, the economy has shown slow but steady improvement and the job market is mostly recovered. Despite this encouraging picture, 10 years after the financial crisis, many Americans are still picking up the pieces of shattered lives.

The scars of the financial crisis are often subtle. For instance, the seemingly low unemployment rate at present is somewhat deceiving. Many individuals dropped out of the labor pool after unsuccessfully hunting for employment during the recession years.[2] A 2017 study showed that between 2007 and 2015 the unemployment rate declined 3.6 percent, mostly as a result of millions of adults exiting the labor force. For those that remain in the workforce, so-called middle skill jobs that require a high school degree plus some technical training (but not a college degree) have been hit hard. Jobs like these that usually involve parts manufacturing, delivery services, and telemarketing have been replaced by newer technologies.[3] This means that lower-skilled workers have found themselves frozen out of the postrecession economy altogether.

More broadly, the middle class has been shrinking as upper and lower tiers of the income spectrum are expanding. In a Pew Research Center study of 229 American metropolitan areas such as Boston, Dallas, and Seattle, the share of middle-class families in 203 of these urban areas saw a decrease of 6 percent or more.[4] This represents a tremendous number of people as these metropolitan areas account for 76 percent of the American population as of 2014. The middle class is losing footing as it sees the continued decline of its share of U.S. household wealth.[5]

The recovery has also been lopsided. While many white families have rebounded, communities of color continue to struggle. Black and Latino families have a disproportionate amount of their household wealth tied up in their homes.[6] Therefore, the forfeiture of the home in foreclosure represents a tremendous financial loss. White families, however, are more likely to have investments in stocks and equity markets, which eventually recovered their value after the crisis.[7] Homeownership rates for black and Latino Americans lag behind white residents.[8] In the fourth quarter of 2017, nearly 78 percent of white households owned their homes while the homeownership rate for black families was only 42 percent and about 47 percent for Latino families.[9] People of color are less likely to purchase a home and when they do their homes are less likely to increase in value over time.[10] Even getting a loan has been difficult for people of color since the Great Recession. In a study conducted by the *Wall Street Journal* that analyzed 38 million mortgage applications between 2007 and 2014, the share of home loans extended to white families increased by 5 percent.[11] The share of mortgage loans made to black borrowers, however, dropped nationwide from 8 percent to 5 percent and from 11 percent to 9 percent for Latino families.

Additionally, many of the individuals who managed to make it through the crisis and rebuild their lives are still haunted by the aftereffects of 2008. For example, a foreclosure listed on someone's credit score can severely impact whether that person can get a loan in the future. A foreclosure can also cause someone to be denied a job, be rejected on a rental application, or pay more in auto insurance.[12]

Against this backdrop, one sees a picture of two Americas: one that has reaped the benefits of the recovery and one that is still struggling to recover. Yet, the prevailing narrative is one of prosperity, reform, and revival. In 2016, President Obama said that the United States "probably managed [the recovery from financial crisis] better than any large economy on Earth in modern history."[13] In a June 2016 weekly address, he asserted that "America's businesses have created 14.5 million new jobs over 75 straight months . . . . We've cut unemployment by more than half . . . . And we've cut our deficits by nearly 75 percent."[14] Similarly, at the Davos summit in 2018, President Trump noted that "after years of stagnation, the United States is once again experiencing strong economic growth."[15] He stated that "the stock market is smashing one record after another . . . . Consumer confidence, business confidence, and manufacturing confidence are the highest they have been in many decades."[16]

Based on these confident statements, one might think that the necessary reforms have been put into place to ensure a financial crisis never happens again. Since the passage of the Dodd-Frank Act, the financial services landscape has been reshaped in a number of important ways. Those who originate mortgage loans must now make a good faith determination that borrowers have the ability to repay. Risky swap contracts that were used by Wall Street to gamble on mortgage loans are now regulated.[17] And the consumer-facing rules for how the mortgage middlemen interface with homeowners have been improved. The private-label market, which was ground zero for residential subprime lending, is practically dead.[18]

In essence, America is great again.[19]

The hardships of people like Barry Tatum, Ceith and Louise Sinclair, Jeremy Fletcher, and the 70-year-old parents of Alisa may seem like remnants of a time that is behind us. The lessons seem to have been learned and the country is now more aware of financial risk and how greed can fuel an economic disaster. We have created a regulatory structure that will prevent the kind of collapse that happened in 2008.

But to adopt this view would be to embrace a false sense of security. Post-2008 financial regulation has not cured all ills and prevented all problems. Many Americans are still financial weak and economically vulnerable. We face fresh evidence of predatory lending activities and risky financial practices. Consider some fairly recent stories. In November 2015, a jury in Houston, Texas awarded homeowners Mary Ellen and David Wolf $5.38 million in connection with their mortgage servicer's fraudulent foreclosure activities.[20] In September 2016, local government officials in Seattle, Washington, found that mortgage servicers and their giant electronic database partner, MERS, had attempted to sell mortgage loans that they did not own, frequently forging documents and filing them into the King County public records.[21] A comprehensive audit found a "flooding of void title documents [filed] into the public land recording offices throughout Washington."[22]

And in 2017, the CFPB, the Florida Attorney General, and Florida's banking regulator sued the major shadow bank mortgage servicer Ocwen Financial for sundry wrongdoing, including failing to send accurate monthly statements to borrowers, correctly credit customers' accounts for payments, and properly handle homeowners' property insurance and tax obligations.[23] The complaint also accused Ocwen of illegally foreclosing on homeowners in distress and failing to answer homeowner complaints.

Also in 2017, Wells Fargo was sued for damage to property when it sent a contractor to a home that the servicer had already approved for a short sale and knew was not abandoned by the owners.[24] The homeowner claims, like so many before him, that Wells Fargo failed to "'properly supervise and monitor'" its contractors and subcontractors, which resulted in the home being broken into, the locks changed, the property ransacked, and "a large quantity of personal property belonging to him" having gone missing.[25]

If you think these accounts are troubling, consider that the preceding reports merely deal with the mortgage servicing industry. There's more to shock the conscience when we look to the broader consumer financial sector, which has seen its share of fraudulent and bad faith practices of late. As recently as 2016, it was discovered that Wells Fargo created roughly 3.5 million fake bank and credit card accounts for its customers.[26] Under the company's personnel incentive program,

Wells Fargo employees were basically encouraged to create these fraudulent accounts. To keep the customer from finding out about the new product in his or her name, bank staffers would often use their individual contact information so as to direct disclosures and related mail away from the customer's notice.[27] These practices resulted in consumers being hit with numerous illegal fees and charges.

At this same time, Wells Fargo was also issuing unnecessary and unauthorized insurance policies – both life insurance and auto insurance – in the names of its customers who had car loans with the bank.[28] This had significant effects on the lives of many Americans. For instance, the unwanted (and unwarranted) auto insurance policies caused nearly 275,000 Wells Fargo customers to default on their car loans when they failed to pay the amount necessary to cover the additional (but secret) insurance premium that was added on to their monthly payments.[29] According to one report, this resulted in 25,000 cases of wrongful vehicle repossession.[30]

There are real people behind these stories, such as Allan Dunlap, a 55-year-old man who took out an auto loan with Wells Fargo for $21,000 so he could purchase a used truck.[31] At the time of the purchase and loan, documentation showed that Dunlap had auto insurance with State Farm. His monthly loan amount was $410, which he promptly paid without issue. But then, Wells Fargo started contacting Dunlap to tell him that the bank lacked evidence that his vehicle was properly insured. He tried to call the bank and explain that he already had insurance but noted that he would eventually hang up due to the long wait times before a customer service representative would answer. When July rolled around, Dunlap's auto loan statement showed that Wells Fargo assessed him $1,079 for auto insurance – an annual premium charge going back to March when he first acquired the truck. Not noticing or having reason to know about the additional charge, he failed to pay the increased amount. His loan thus went into default, which caused both late fees to accrue and a report to be sent to the credit bureaus. What followed were endless attempts by Mr. Dunlap to work his way through the labyrinth of the bank's corporate structure before finally receiving help – more than a year later.

The same sort of story can be seen in the life insurance portion of the scandal.[32] Policies were opened by Wells Fargo employees, unbeknownst to the bank's customers, whereby monthly premiums would be quietly debited from individual accounts. Some lawsuits related to these illegal practices assert that Wells Fargo employees would have the policies issued, cancel them, and then reissue them to artificially drive up their sales numbers.[33]

So, do not believe anyone who claims that things are materially better and that systems have been put in place to prevent the harms of 2008 from happening again. They are wrong. Being led into such a false sense of security is what allows the most insidious practices to fester. In this era of deregulation, many of the gains – imperfect as they might be – that were achieved in the years that followed 2008 may soon be lost. The financial services industry is spending big money to promote a robust regulatory rollback. During the cycle that saw the election of President Donald

Trump, banks and other financial institutions (including shadow banks) spent record amounts to influence elections.[34] From 2015 through the end of 2016, the financial industry shelled out $2 billion worth of political expenditures (with a little more than half of that going to campaign contributions). In the highest amount per head going back to 1990, that amounts to about $3.7 million for each member of Congress. That's to say nothing of the money that went to political action committees (PACs) and other nonprofit political fundraising entities. The Republican chairperson of the Financial Services Committee in the U.S. House of Representatives received $1.9 million while his Republican counterpart on the Senate Banking Committee enjoyed $2.1 million in donations.[35]

The financial sector is an equal opportunity donor when it comes to keeping regulation of the industry under its influence. Both Democrats and Republicans benefited from large political gifts from this sector. Senator Chuck Schumer of New York, the Democratic minority leader in the U.S. Senate, received $5.3 million from the finance industry.[36] Democratic presidential candidate Hillary Clinton received around $47.6 million from a number of financial services firms.[37] During his first election to the presidency, Wall Street firms put enormous amounts of money behind Democratic candidate Barack Obama.[38] Even Senator Chris Dodd who was the House committee chairman responsible for drafting the Dodd-Frank Act took $442,000 in campaign contributions from the financial sector in his last year in office.[39]

The lobbying efforts of the financial services industry are not, however, merely relegating to Washington, D.C. The subprime mortgage mill and servicer Ameriquest spent $20 million in the years before the housing crisis to kill lending reform in the state of New Jersey.[40] These lobbyists, both at the state and federal level, control the narrative and urge lawmakers to "trust us" in understanding the system and making the best decisions for what is good for borrowers.

This policy of deregulation has made major strides of late. First, President Trump has led the charge in setting an agenda for deregulation. In January 2017, he issued an executive order stating arbitrarily that "for every one new regulation issued, at least two prior regulations [must] be identified for elimination."[41] He promised business leaders later that month that he would cut all federal regulation by 75 percent.[42] This was all followed by a February 2017 executive order that focused specifically on financial deregulation, calling for Americans to be given the power "to make independent financial decisions and informed choices in the marketplace" through, as the document not so subtly suggests, deregulation.[43]

But it's not just through broad policy statements that the deregulatory agenda has been set. New heads of federal financial regulators are also committed to the cause. President Trump's new vice chair of supervision at the Federal Reserve has promised a scaling back of capital and liquidity requirements for banks.[44] New leadership at the FTC, which performs a number of important functions including serving as the country's chief antitrust watchdog, has promised to promote "economic liberty" by removing regulations that are said to drive up costs for consumers.[45] Trump SEC chief pledged to loosen regulations on corporations seeking to raise capital.[46] New Comptroller of the Currency Joseph Otting stated that he would roll back "unnecessary burden[s]" on banks.[47] HUD secretary and one-time presidential contender Ben Carson described fair housing laws (which include fair lending) as a form of "social engineering."[48] And importantly, Trump's head of the treasury, Steven Mnuchin, has specifically recommended rolling back mortgage lending restrictions.[49]

Perhaps nowhere, however, have the gains of post-2008 reform seen the most pull back than at the CFPB. At the time of this writing, President Trump has appointed an acting director to head the consumer watchdog agency, Mick Mulvaney.[50] Mulvaney is a former congressman and fervent opponent of the CFPB, and he once described the agency as "a sad, sick joke."[51] Since taking the helm, Mulvaney has set about on a mission to significantly scale back the CFPB's activities, stating that the bureau would no longer "push the envelope"[52] in its enforcement and regulatory activities and asserting that the agency not only represents consumers but also financial service providers.[53]

Mulvaney's perspective has been implemented in tangible ways. For example, prior to the election of Donald Trump, the CFPB had been building a case against a predatory lender named Golden Valley Financial and three other similar finance companies that were alleged to have charged interest rates of between 440 percent and 900 percent.[54] The companies marketed loan products in several states, all of which prohibited interest rates of such levels. However, the lenders incorporated on Native American reservations and, in doing so, used the tribe's legal sovereignty to exempt themselves from state law usury limits.[55] This process, known as "rent-a-tribe," and the accompanying loans were viewed by the CFPB as abusive, and the agency filed suit against the companies in April 2017.[56] Once Mulvaney took over, however, things changed. In January 2018, without explanation, the CFPB dropped the lawsuits.[57] As of this writing, Mulvaney also put on hold payday lending regulations that recently went into effect at the beginning of 2018[58] and he even urged Congress to use its authority under the Congressional Review Act to overturn the rules altogether.[59] Mulvaney has been heavily criticized for these actions not only because the rules are said to provide much needed protection for consumers but also because he received almost $63,000 in campaign contributions from the payday lending industry over his time in Congress.[60]

Importantly, this is not to say that all regulation is good. As I have pointed out in various chapters of this book, sometimes well-intentioned rules can create just as many problems that they seek to solve when layered on top of preexisting regulatory labyrinths. But the financial services industry is complex and ever-evolving. This means that detailed and ever-evolving rules are needed to protect consumers who are rarely poised to fully protect themselves from being taken advantage of by institutions with greater knowledge, power, and resources at their disposal.

There are few places in the American economy, however, that merit as much thoughtful oversight and careful regulation than in the way we finance the purchase of our home and how we deal with those firms that manage the life cycle of that process. In the end, we all recognize that there is something special about the home. There's no place like home.[61] The dream of homeownership has been and continues to be a cornerstone of American law and policy making.[62] The law accords homeowners a host of rights when it comes to criminal liability, damages in tort, tax treatment, property law–based protections, and constitutional guarantees. Policy makers focus on homeownership as a way to advance social and economic goals.[63] Purchasing a home is encouraged by public spending and federal and state programs that seek to open credit markets to would-be borrowers.[64] Legal scholars speak of the "inherent dignity of homeownership."[65] Municipal planning exercises are focused on engineering livable spaces and creating strategically zoned buffers to ensure residential areas are protected from other uses.[66] Large enterprises backed by the credit of the U.S. government exist for the sole purpose of promoting homeownership.[67] And, in the wake of natural disasters, governmental spending and political rhetoric focus on rebuilding and bringing people back "home."[68] In fact, American's entire economic and political history is rife with examples of "[p]ublic interventions in the housing market" based all on the notion that good housing policy makes for good public policy overall.[69]

It's not only law and policy, however, that favor homeownership. Society and popular culture do as well. Notions of success and images of independence and achievement are acutely focused on ownership of one's home. Proponents assert that those who own their homes have a propensity to be more invested in their communities, and thus be better citizens.[70] From an economic perspective, equity in one's home is espoused as being the safest and most certain way to transmit wealth from one generation to the next.[71] The purchase of a home is viewed as a good investment, and as a corollary to income success.[72] Ownership of one's home is lauded as being the best adjunct to the successful rearing of children, the maintenance of good health, and for building a secure social network.[73] Indeed, society often cites the proverb of a man and his castle to harken to mind a sense of dignity, autonomy, and strength.[74]

Yet, our rights in the home are less secure than we might think. In fact, tenants may have more security than do homeowners. The crux of this insecurity comes chiefly from the power and position of mortgage servicers. Servicers hold tremendous sway over the home and usually in ways that go beyond the limits of how most Americans imagine the typical creditor-debtor relationship. Despite this authority and the important task assigned to them, servicers have not always been well suited to the job. In the years after the financial crisis, mortgage servicing suffered from a lack of direction from loan investors, misaligned incentives in dealing with homeowners in distress, and a lack of resources and capacity to handle market downturns. All these elements combined to create an environment in which many homeowners were left feeling powerless and vulnerable.

Now, a decade after the crisis, much of the work of law and policy makers – from both parties – in creating safeguards and building institutions that can help prevent a future crisis are under attack. For servicing, this shift in regulatory dynamic comes at a most important time because these firms are moving more aggressively into the nonbanking arena – one in which there is less oversight and fewer restrictions. The recommendations provided in this book are meant to serve as a starting point for fortifying the mortgage middleman industry. I value and agree with the points made by mortgage servicing industry advocates who say that the mortgage middlemen deserve a seat at the table when rules governing servicing are crafted. Understanding how overlapping agencies and shifting regulations impact servicer cost and performance is important for public policy making. But servicers must also understand that because of the important role they play in holding up the architecture of American housing finance, the public has an interest – a bipartisan interest – in ensuring they operate in a way that is financially healthy and that keeps consumers safe.

Effective and suitable financial regulation aimed at protecting homeowners needs no defense. It is imperative that we have a system of laws that gives Americans a chance to stay in their homes when life gets unexpectedly rough and that makes sure servicers don't abuse their considerable powers when people are most vulnerable. A strong, competitive, and safe mortgage servicing sector – including the shadow-banking portion of the industry – is at the heart of achieving these goals. Through a better understanding of servicing, through an appreciation of the vital role it plays in our housing lives, and by implementing thoughtful reform – goals that I hope this book has advanced – we can collectively strengthen and fortify the buttresses, beams, and bridges of America's housing architecture.

Notes

Introduction

1. *See* James E. McNulty, *Subprime-Mortgage Servicing Regulation and the Financial Crisis*, CLS BLUE SKY BLOG (Nov. 6, 2017), http://clsbluesky.law.columbia.edu/2017/11/06/subprime-mortgage-servicing-regulation-and-the-financial-crisis/ ("Scholars are attempting to fully understand all the causes of the 2007–09 US financial crisis, hoping their efforts will ensure that something like this will not happen again. Nonetheless, in this research, weaknesses in mortgage servicing regulation have been largely ignored."); Adam J. Levitin & Tara Twomey, *Mortgage Servicing*, 28 YALE J. ON REG. 1, 5 (2011) ("The business model and economics of servicing remain largely unexplored, and there has been almost no theorizing of the industry."); James E. McNulty, Luis Garcia-Feijoo, & Ariel Viale, *The Regulation of Mortgage Servicing: Lesson from the Financial Crisis*, CONTEMP. ECON. POL'Y (Dec. 20, 2017), https://onlinelibrary.wiley.com/doi/abs/10.1111/coep.12272 (using subscription) ("Literature on the appropriate regulation of mortgage servicers is scant, even though the aftermath of the 2007 to 2009 US financial crisis revealed serious issues with US servicers."); Maurna Desmond, *The Next Mortgage Mess: Loan Servicing?*, FORBES (Mar. 20, 2009), www.forbes.com/2009/03/20/subprime-mortgages-carrington-capital-business-wall-street-servicers.html#1b4ba6465b03 (noting the lack of attention and regulation over mortgage servicing firms).
2. The majority of residential mortgage loans are securitized (almost 65 percent as of December 2017), therefore most American homeowners must contend with a servicer. *See* HOUS. FIN. POL'Y CTR., URBAN INST., HOUSING FINANCE AT A GLANCE: A MONTHLY CHARTBOOK 6 (Feb. 2018).
3. Unless stated otherwise, the terms *lender* and *mortgage lender* as they appear in this book refer to either the financial institution that originates the loan or the broker who facilitates the origination of the loan between the borrower and the financial institution. From the borrower's perspective, both facilitate the "lending" of the money and thus, from a layman's perspective, are both lenders.

4. There are some instances where the loan originator also serves as the servicer of that loan. *See* Steven L. Schwarcz, *The Conundrum of Covered Bonds*, 66 BUS. LAW. 561, 576 (2011).
5. Denise Richardson, *Disabled FL Woman Fears Wrongful Foreclosure May Leave Her Homeless!*, DENISE RICHARDSON (BLOG) (Oct. 5, 2011, 3:08 PM), www.givemebackmycredit.com/blog/2011/10/disabled-fl-woman-fears-wrongful-foreclosure-may-leave-her-homeless.html#more.
6. Jessica Silver-Greenberg, *Invasive Tactic in Foreclosures Draws Scrutiny*, N.Y. TIMES: DEALBOOK (Sept. 9, 2013, 8:23 PM), https://dealbook.nytimes.com/2013/09/09/invasive-tactic-in-foreclosures-draws-scrutiny/.
7. David Dayen, *Banks Find Appalling New Way to Cheat Homeowners*, SALON (Sept. 24, 2013), www.salon.com/2013/09/24/banks_find_appalling_new_way_to_cheat_homeowners_partner/.
8. Rudabeh Shahbazi, *Foreclosure Nightmare: Family's Home Sold, but It Wasn't for Sale*, ABC7 (KABC-TV, LOS ANGELES), (Sept. 12, 2013), http://abc7.com/archive/9246636/.
9. Joshua Coval et al., *The Economics of Structured Finance*, J. ECON. PERSP., Winter 2009, at 3, 17–19 (describing how investors purchase mortgage-backed securities without necessarily appreciating the risk involved in holding these assets).
10. ADAM B. ASHCRAFT & TIL SCHUERMANN, FED. RESERVE BANK OF N.Y., STAFF REPORT NO. 318, UNDERSTANDING THE SECURITIZATION OF SUBPRIME MORTGAGE CREDIT 4 (2008).
11. *Dual-Tracking and Loss Mitigation Runarounds Are among Servicing Problems Found by CFPB*, DSNEWS (June 23, 2015), http://dsnews.com/news/06-23-2015/dual-tracking-and-loss-mitigation-runarounds-are-among-servicing-problems-found-by-cfpb; Press Release, Consumer Fin. Prot. Bureau, CFPB Takes Action against Mortgage Company for Blocking Consumers' Attempts to Save Their Homes (July 30, 2015).
12. 78 Fed. Reg. 10,695 (2013).
13. David Dayen, *Portrait of HAMP Failure: The Mother of All HAMP Nightmares*, SHADOWPROOF (Feb. 9, 2011), https://shadowproof.com/2011/02/09/portrait-of-hamp-failure-the-mother-of-all-hamp-nightmares/ (describing his drop in sales from $250,000 in 2007 down to $40,000 in 2008).
14. *Id.* (Jeremy Fletcher quoting the CitiMortgage loan specialist).
15. *See* Denise Richardson, *Daughter Fights Wrongful Foreclosure, While Mom Fights Cancer*, DENISE RICHARDSON (BLOG) (June 25, 2013, 6:01 PM), www.givemebackmycredit.com/blog/2013/06/daughter-fights-wrongful-foreclosure-while-mom-fights-cancer.html. By equity, I mean that the amount of money they owed on their home loan represented as a percentage of the value of the home was rather low.
16. IT'S A WONDERFUL LIFE (Liberty Films 1946). *Portfolio-held* means that the bank does not sell the loan to another financial institution after it is made. Rather, the bank keeps the loan on its own books and manages it until the debt is paid off by the homeowner.

17. Pub. L. No. 111–203, 124 Stat. 1376 (2010) (codified as amended in scattered sections of 7, 12, 15, and 31 U.S.C); *see also* Damian Paletta, *It Has a Name: The Dodd/Frank Act*, WALL ST. J.: WASH. WIRE (June 25, 2010, 6:06 AM ET), https://blogs.wsj.com/washwire/2010/06/25/it-has-a-name-the-doddfrank-act/ (using subscription).
18. *See, e.g.*, Stacy Cowley & Jessica Silver-Greenberg, *Regulators Accuse Subprime Mortgage Servicer of Years of Abuses*, N.Y. TIMES: DEALBOOK (Apr. 20, 2017), www.nytimes.com/2017/04/20/business/dealbook/subprime-mortgage-servicer-is-accused-of-years-of-abuses.html.
19. BD. OF GOVERNORS OF THE FED. RESERVE SYS. ET AL., REPORT TO THE CONGRESS ON THE EFFECT OF CAPITAL RULES ON MORTGAGE SERVICING ASSETS 19 (2016) (hereinafter MSA FED. REPORT). The right to service loans is considered to be an asset. The more servicing rights you have, the higher your "mortgage servicing assets" become.
20. FIN. STABILITY BD., STRENGTHENING THE OVERSIGHT AND REGULATION OF SHADOW BANKING: PROGRESS REPORT TO G20 MINISTERS AND GOVERNORS 1 n. 2 (Apr. 2012) ("It is important to note the use of the term 'shadow banking' is not intended to cast a pejorative tone on this system of credit intermediation."). Also, the term *shadowing bank*, coined by economist Paul McCalley in 2007, originally referred to financial institutions that engaged in maturity transformation in that they took short-term borrowed funds (rather than bank deposits, like banks) and make long-term loans. Laura E. Kodres, *What Is Shadow Banking?*, FIN. & DEV., June 2013, at 42, 42, www.imf.org/external/pubs/ft/fandd/2013/06/pdf/basics.pdf. However, the term has grown significantly since then. In this work, I use the term as an activity – "shadow banking" – in the vein described by Steven Schwarcz. See Steven L. Schwarcz, *Regulating Shadow Banking: Inaugural Address for the Inaugural Symposium of the Review of Banking & Financial Law*, 31 REV. BANKING & FIN. L. 619, 621 (2012). This includes, as it appears in this book, the provision of financial products or services that are ordinarily provided by traditional financial institution, like regulated banks. *See* ZOLTAN POZSAR ET AL., FED. RESERVE BANK OF N.Y., STAFF REPORT NO. 458, SHADOW BANKING 23 (rev. Feb. 2012) ("[Shadow banks] include non-bank finance companies, which can be more efficient than traditional banks through specialization and economics of scale in the origination, *servicing*, structuring, trading and funding of loans."; emphasis added).
21. *US Regulatory Fog*, FIN. TIMES (June 15, 2012), www.ft.com/content/a45fadb4-b628-11e1-a511-00144feabdco (using subscription); *see also* Schwarcz, *supra* note 20. The use of the term *shadow bank* to describe mortgage loan servicing by nonbank financial institutions has been used by others as well. See Greg Buchak et al., *Fintech, Regulatory Arbitrage, and the Rise of Shadow Banks* 3 (Columbia Bus. Sch., Research Paper No. 17-39, Sept. 2017); Rachel Witkowski, *Mortgage Servicing Shrinks at Biggest U.S. Banks*, WALL ST. J. (July 1, 2016), www.wsj.com/articles/mortgage-servicing-shrinks-at-biggest-u-s-banks-1467384050 (using subscription); RYAN M. NASH & ERIC BEARDSLEY, GOLDMAN SACHS, THE FUTURE OF FINANCE PART 1: THE RISE OF THE NEW SHADOW BANK 3 (2015); *CFP Conference Highlights: The Financial Industry in a Post-Crisis World*, UNIV. OF MD.: CTR.

FOR FIN. POL'Y (BLOG) (July 16, 2014), https://blogs.rhsmith.umd.edu/financial policy/commentary/regulation-oversight/cfp-conference-highlights-the-financial-industry-in-a-post-crisis-world/ (keynote remarks by Office of Financial Research [OFR] Director Richard Berner).

22. Daniel Sanches, *Shadow Banking and the Crisis of 2007–08*, BUS. REV., Second Quarter 2014, at 7, www.philadelphiafed.org/-/media/research-and-data/publications/business-review/2014/q2/brq214_shadow_banking.pdf?la=en.
23. Milan Markovic, *The Sophisticates: Conflicted Representation and the Lehman Bankruptcy*, 2012 UTAH L. REV. 903.
24. Larry Light, *Shadow Banking Is Growing Fast – Is That a Threat?*, CBS NEWS MONEYWATCH (Mar. 9, 2017), www.cbsnews.com/news/shadow-banking-fast-growth-threat/.
25. MSA FED. REPORT, *supra* note 19, at 20.
26. Brena Swanson, *CFPB Fines CitiFinancial Servicing and CitiMortgage $29 Million*, HOUSINGWIRE (Jan. 23, 2017), www.housingwire.com/articles/39012-cfpb-fines-citifinancial-servicing-and-citimortgage-29-million.
27. Press Release, Citigroup Inc., CitiMortgage Inc. Announces Strategic Exit of Mortgage Servicing Operations by End of 2018 (Jan. 30, 2017).
28. David Benoit, *Bank of America Sells More Mortgage Servicing Rights*, WALL ST. J.: DEAL J. (June 5, 2012, 8:52 AM ET), https://blogs.wsj.com/deals/2012/06/05/bank-of-america-sells-more-mortgage-servicing-rights/ (using subscription).
29. US GOV'T ACCOUNTABILITY OFFICE, NONBANK MORTGAGE SERVICERS: EXISTING REGULATORY OVERSIGHT COULD BE STRENGTHENED 9 (Mar. 2016) (hereinafter GAO, NONBANK SERVICERS) (stating 24.2 percent based on data from the various federal government agencies); *see also* KARAN KAUL & LAURIE GOODMAN, URBAN INST., NONBANK SERVICER REGULATION: NEW CAPITAL AND LIQUIDITY REQUIREMENTS DON'T OFFER ENOUGH LOSS PROTECTION 2 fig. 1 (Feb. 2016) (stating 31 percent based on Inside Mortgage Finance data).
30. Buchak et al., *supra* note 21, at 20; ROY J. GIRASA, SHADOW BANKING: THE RISE, RISKS, AND REWARDS OF NON-BANK FINANCIAL SERVICES (2016); Edmund L. Andrews, *Shadow Banking: The Big Winner from the Financial Crisis*, STANFORD GRADUATE SCH. BUS. (Apr. 13, 2017), www.gsb.stanford.edu/insights/shadow-banking-big-winner-financial-crisis; Malgorzata Solarz, *The Importance of Shadow Banking Sector Entities for Population Affected by Credit Exclusion*, COPERNICAN J. FIN. & ACCT., vol. 2, no. 2 (2013), at 189.
31. GAO, NONBANK SERVICERS, *supra* note 29, at 14.
32. *Paths to Homeownership for Low-Income and Minority Households*, EVIDENCE MATTERS (US Dep't of Housing & Urban Dev., Wash. D.C.), Fall 2012, at 1, 7–8 ("One source of help for these households is the Federal Housing Administration [FHA], which facilitates first-time homeownership for low-wealth buyers."); US DEP'T OF THE TREASURY & US DEP'T OF HOUS. & URBAN DEV., REFORMING AMERICA'S HOUSING FINANCE MARKET: A REPORT TO CONGRESS 14 (Feb. 2011) (describing Fannie and Freddie's historic role as "provider[s] of mortgage credit access for low- and moderate-income Americans and first-time homebuyers").

33. *Ginnie Servicers Shudder at Hurricane Losses; Some Plan HUD Appeal*, DEBTWIRE (Sept. 14, 2017), www.debtwire.com/info/ginnie-servicers-shudder-hurricane-losses-some-plan-hud-appeal; Buchak et al., *supra* note 21, at 3.
34. Deon Roberts, *Wells Fargo: No. 4 in Assets, No. 1 in Lobbying*, CHARLOTTE OBSERVER (May 8, 2015), www.charlotteobserver.com/news/business/banking/article20589309.html.
35. Peter Schroeder, *Behind the Scenes, Bank Lobbyists Temper Expectations for Dodd-Frank Overhaul*, REUTERS (Mar. 22, 2017), www.reuters.com/article/us-usa-banks-lobbyists/behind-the-scenes-bank-lobbyists-temper-expectations-for-dodd-frank-overhaul-idUSKBN16T19G ("'This year poses the biggest opportunity that we have seen in a long time to see some action on much-needed regulatory relief,' Rob Nichols, the [American Bankers Association] president and chief executive officer, said at the [group's DC] conference.").
36. Press Release, Chase, Chase to Purchase $45 Billion in Mortgage Servicing Rights from Ocwen (May 14, 2015).
37. Alex Morell, *Jamie Dimon Says Something Shameful Is Going on with the Mortgage Market*, BUS. INSIDER (Apr. 13, 2017), www.businessinsider.com/jamie-dimon-on-mortgage-market-2017-4.
38. Editorial, *Will Gov't Regulation Kill the Housing Market – Again?*, INV. BUS. DAILY (May 19, 2016), www.investors.com/politics/editorials/will-these-new-rules-kill-the-housing-market/.
39. Carrie Sheffield, *Dodd-Frank Is Killing Community Banks*, FORBES (Feb. 9, 2015), www.forbes.com/sites/carriesheffield/2015/02/09/dodd-frank-is-killing-community-banks/#1b1b34b873a7. For a full discussion of how post-2008 financial regulation has driven many community banks to merge or be eaten up by larger banks, see Tanya D. Marsh, *Reforming the Regulation of Community Banks After Dodd-Frank*, 90 IND. L.J. 179 (2015).
40. Stephen Gandel, *Jamie Dimon Calls Regulation Un-American, Once Again*, FORTUNE (Jan. 14, 2015), http://fortune.com/2015/01/14/jamie-dimon-financial-regulation/.
41. Diane Katz, *A Better Path for Mortgage Regulation*, *in* Heritage Found., Prosperity Unleashed: Smarter Financial Regulation 37 (Norbert J. Michel ed., 2017).
42. *Id*. at 44.
43. *Id*.
44. Donna Borak, *Trump Gives Banks (a Lot of) What They Want*, CNN MONEY (June 13, 2017), http://money.cnn.com/2017/06/12/news/economy/treasury-dodd-frank-trump/index.html.
45. Gary Rivlin, *How Wall Street Defanged Dodd-Frank*, NATION (Apr. 30, 2013), www.thenation.com/article/how-wall-street-defanged-dodd-frank/.
46. *Id*.
47. Ailsa Chang, *All Things Considered: When Lobbyists Literally Write the Bill* (National Public Radio broadcast, Nov. 11, 2013).

48. Erika Eichelberger, *House Passes Bill Written by Citigroup Lobbyists*, MOTHER JONES (Oct. 31, 2013), www.motherjones.com/politics/2013/10/citigroup-bill-passes-house/.
49. Gabby Morrongiello, *Mick Mulvaney Promises "Structural Change" to CFPB, So Long As He Remains in Charge*, WASH. EXAMINER (Nov. 27, 2017), www.washingtonexaminer.com/mick-mulvaney-promises-structural-change-to-cfpb-so-long-as-he-remains-in-charge; Caroline Basile, *Leaked Mulvaney Memo: CFPB Must End Regulation by Enforcement*, HOUSINGWIRE (Jan. 23, 2018), www.housingwire.com/articles/42357-mulvaney-memo-cfpb-to-end-regulation-by-enforcement; Michael C. Bender & Damian Paletta, *Donald Trump Plans to Undo Dodd-Frank Law, Fiduciary Rule*, WALL ST. J. (Feb. 3, 2017), www.wsj.com/articles/trump-moves-to-undo-dodd-frank-law-1486101602 (using subscription); Gillian B. White, *Trump Begins to Chip Away at Banking Regulations*, ATLANTIC (Feb. 3, 2017), www.theatlantic.com/business/archive/2017/02/trump-dodd-frank/515646/; Kathy Kristof, *Watchdog Groups Decry "Attack" on Consumer Protections*, CBS NEWS MONEYWATCH (May 9, 2017), www.cbsnews.com/news/cfpb-consumer-financial-protection-bureau-choice-act/.

1 The Lead-Up to the Crisis

1. These statistics come from the National Suburban Poll. It covers not only traditional foreclosures but also shorts sales where the property is sold for less than what is owed on the loan and deeds in lieu of foreclosure where the property is voluntarily transferred to the lender by the homeowner. *See* ISAAC WILLIAM MARTIN & CHRISTOPHER NIEDT, FORECLOSED AMERICA 83 (2015).
2. Justin Lahart, *Egg Cracks Differ in Housing, Finance Shells*, WALL ST. J.: AHEAD OF THE TAPE (Dec. 24, 2007), www.wsj.com/articles/SB119845906460548071.
3. FIN. CRISIS INQUIRY COMM'N, THE FINANCIAL CRISIS INQUIRY REPORT 85–86 (2011) (hereinafter FINANCIAL CRISIS INQUIRY REPORT).
4. *Id.* at 85.
5. *CSI: Credit Crunch*, ECONOMIST (Oct. 18, 2007), www.economist.com/node/9972489.
6. FINANCIAL CRISIS INQUIRY REPORT, *supra* note 3, at 86.
7. *Id.* at 87.
8. By a junior mortgage on the home, I mean that the debt that the homeowner owed to the first lender was senior to the debt owed to the second lender (the lender that gave the "home equity line of credit" loan). Thus, if the homeowner defaulted on both the loans, the money that resulted from the seizure and sale of the home in foreclosure would go first to pay off the first lender and then, if anything was left, would go to pay off the second lender. *See* 59A C.J.S. *Mortgages* § 1404 (2018); IRS, INTERNAL REVENUE MANUAL § 5.17.2.7.1.7 (Mar. 27, 2012) ("Home Equity Line of Credit or Open-end Mortgage").
9. FINANCIAL CRISIS INQUIRY REPORT, *supra* note 3, at 87.

10. *Id.* The percentage is more than 100 because this figure compares a new, larger quantity of consumer spending as a share of GDP to an old, smaller quantity.
11. U.S. Dep't of Housing & Urban Dev., The National Homeownership Strategy: Partners in the American Dream (May 1995).
12. Carol D. Leonnig, *How HUD Mortgage Policy Fed the Crisis*, Wash. Post (June 10, 2008), www.washingtonpost.com/wp-dyn/content/article/2008/06/09/AR2008060902626.html.
13. *Fact Sheet: America's Ownership Society: Expanding Opportunities*, White House: President George W. Bush (Aug. 9, 2004), https://georgewbush-whitehouse.archives.gov/news/releases/2004/08/20040809-9.html. "[W]e can put light where there's darkness, and hope where there's despondency in this country, and part of it is working together as a nation to encourage folks to own their own home." Remarks at the White House Conference on Minority Homeownership, 2 Pub. Papers 1807, 1811 (Oct. 15, 2002).
14. Remarks in a Discussion on Homeownership in Phoenix, Arizona, 1 Pub. Papers 468, 470 (Mar. 26, 2004).
15. Financial Crisis Inquiry Report, *supra* note 3, at 84.
16. *Id.*
17. *Id.*
18. *Id.* at 85.
19. Press Release, U.S. Census Bureau, Quarterly Residential Vacancies and Homeownership, Fourth Quarter 2016, at tbl. 4SA (Jan. 31, 2017).
20. *See* Gerald Korngold, *Legal and Policy Choices in the Aftermath of the Subprime and Mortgage Financing Crisis*, 60 S.C. L. Rev. 727 (2009).
21. Nontraditional financial institutions (i.e., shadow banks) had long desired to break into the subprime lending market, but it was not until private-label securitization took off that doing so became so possible and profitable.
22. Kathleen C. Engel & Patricia A. McCoy, The Subprime Virus: Reckless Credit, Regulatory Failure, and Next Steps 34 (2011).
23. Financial Crisis Inquiry Report, *supra* note 3, at 85; Sheila Bair, Bull by the Horns: Fighting to Save Main Street from Wall Street and Wall Street from Itself 43 (2012).
24. Banks were not always allowed to make mortgage loans subject to adjustable rates. The authority was not granted until the early 1980s under title VIII of the Garn-St. Germain Depository Institutions Act of 1982. *See* Pub. L. No. 97-320, 96 Stat. 1469.
25. Engel & McCoy, *supra* note 22, at 23.
26. *Id.* at 16, 34; Bair, *supra* note 23, at 43.
27. Mortgage lenders, as used here, includes both brokers who earn commissions and actual originators who earn fees. In either case, both get paid something at the time the loan is made.
28. John W. Schoen, *"Pay Option" Mortgages Could Swell Foreclosures*, NBCNews.com (Dec. 10, 2008), www.nbcnews.com/id/28035238/ns/business-real_estate/t/pay-option-mortgages-could-swell-foreclosures/#.WsVvcPnwbGh.
29. *Id.*

30. ENGEL & MCCOY, *supra* note 22, at 21.
31. Gretchen Morgenson, *Inside the Countrywide Lending Spree*, N.Y. TIMES (Aug. 26, 2007), www.nytimes.com/2007/08/26/business/yourmoney/26country.html.
32. *All Things Considered: Economists Brace for Worsening Subprime Crisis* (National Public Radio broadcast, Aug. 7, 2007).
33. *Id.*
34. *Surge in No-Money Down Loans Could Bite*, CNN MONEY (Jan. 18, 2006), http://money.cnn.com/2006/01/18/real_estate/downpayments/.
35. ENGEL & MCCOY, *supra* note 22, at 30.
36. FINANCIAL CRISIS INQUIRY REPORT, *supra* note 3, at 91.
37. ENGEL & MCCOY, *supra* note 22, at 30.
38. David Heath, *At Top Subprime Mortgage Lender, Policies Were an Invitation to Fraud*, HUFFINGTON POST (Mar. 18, 2010), www.huffingtonpost.com/2009/12/21/at-long-beach-mortgage-a_n_399295.html.
39. *See id.*
40. Julie Creswell, *Web Help for Getting Mortgage the Criminal Way*, N.Y. TIMES (June 16, 2007), www.nytimes.com/2007/06/16/technology/16fraud.html.
41. *Id.*
42. *Id.*
43. FINANCIAL CRISIS INQUIRY REPORT, *supra* note 3, at 89.
44. Michael Powell, *Bank Accused of Pushing Mortgage Deals on Blacks*, N.Y. TIMES (June 6, 2009), www.nytimes.com/2009/06/07/us/07baltimore.html.
45. *See id. See also* Fowler v. Wells Fargo Home Mortg., No. GJH–15–1084, 2015 WL 2342377, at *1-2 (Bankr. S.D. Md. May 13, 2015).
46. *See* ENGEL & MCCOY, *supra* note 22, at 22.
47. MECHELE DICKERSON, HOMEOWNERSHIP AND AMERICA'S FINANCIAL UNDERCLASS: FLAWED PREMISES, BROKEN PROMISES, NEW PRESCRIPTIONS 171–72 (2014).
48. *Id. See also* Pamela Foohey, *Lender Discrimination, Black Churches, and Bankruptcy*, 54 HOUS. L. REV. 1079 (2017) (describing discrimination against black churches by creditors in the bankruptcy context).
49. Richard Williams, Reynold Nesiba, & Eileen Diaz McConnell, *The Changing Face of Inequality in Home Mortgage Lending*, 52 SOC. PROBS. 181 (2005).
50. DICKERSON, *supra* note 47, at 166.
51. Am. Sociological Ass'n, *Wealthier Minorities More Likely Than White Counterparts to Receive Subprime Loans, Study Finds*, PHYS.ORG (Aug. 11, 2013), https://phys.org/news/2013-08-wealthier-minorities-white-counterparts-subprime.html.
52. ALLEN J. FISHBEIN & PATRICK WOODALL, CONSUMER FED'N OF AM., WOMEN ARE PRIME TARGETS FOR SUBPRIME LENDING: WOMEN ARE DISPROPORTIONATELY REPRESENTED IN HIGH-COST MORTGAGE MARKET (2006).
53. Rick Brooks & Ruth Simon, *Subprime Debacle Traps Even Very Credit-Worthy*, WALL ST. J. (Dec. 3, 2007), www.wsj.com/articles/SB119662974358911035 (using subscription).
54. Real Estate Lending by National Banks, 48 Fed. Reg. 40,699 (Sept. 9, 1983).

55. John Pottow, *Ability to Repay*, 8 BERKELEY BUS. L.J. 175, 185 (2011); John A. E. Pottow, *Private Liability for Reckless Consumer Lending*, 2007 U. ILL. L. REV. 405, 439.
56. *See* Saule T. Omarova, *From Gramm-Leach-Bliley to Dodd-Frank: The Unfulfilled Promise of Section 23A of the Federal Reserve Act*, 89 N.C. L. REV. 1683 (2011) (explaining the ways banks indirectly used their governmental subsidies to gamble in the subprime mortgage market).
57. ANDREW JAKABOVICS & JEFF CHAPMAN, CTR. FOR AM. PROGRESS, UNEQUAL OPPORTUNITY LENDERS? ANALYZING RACIAL DISPARITIES IN BIG BANKS' HIGHER-PRICED LENDING (Sept. 2009).
58. BD. OF GOVERNORS OF THE FED. RESERVE SYS. & DEP'T OF HOUS. & URBAN DEV., JOINT REPORT CONCERNING REFORM TO THE TRUTH IN LENDING ACT AND THE REAL ESTATE SETTLEMENT PROCEDURES ACT (1998).
59. U.S. DEP'T OF THE TREASURY & U.S. DEP'T OF HOUS. & URBAN DEV., CURBING PREDATORY HOME LENDING (2000).
60. FINANCIAL CRISIS INQUIRY REPORT, *supra* note 3, at 79.
61. Rebecca Ungarino & Alex Rosenberg, *Growth of Shadow Banking Spurs Warnings of a New Credit Crisis*, CNBC (Oct. 14, 2016), www.cnbc.com/2016/10/14/growth-of-shadow-banking-spurs-warnings-of-a-new-credit-crisis.html.
62. FINANCIAL CRISIS INQUIRY REPORT, *supra* note 3, at 79; *see also* Edmund L. Andrews, GREENSPAN CONCEDES ERROR ON REGULATION, N.Y. Times (Oct. 23, 2008), www.nytimes.com/2008/10/24/business/economy/24panel.html. Alan Greenspan was chairman of the Federal Reserve from 1987 until 2006.
63. FINANCIAL CRISIS INQUIRY REPORT, *supra* note 3, at 93 (quoting Greenspan's written testimony to the Financial Crisis Inquiry Commission on April 7, 2010).
64. *Id.* at 95.
65. SOUPHALA CHOMSISENGPHET & ANTHONY PENNINGTON-CROSS, *The Evolution of the Subprime Mortgage Market*, FED. RESERVE BANK OF ST. LOUIS REV., Jan./Feb. 2006, at 31, https://files.stlouisfed.org/research/publications/review/06/01/ChomPennCross.pdf.
66. FINANCIAL CRISIS INQUIRY REPORT, *supra* note 3, at 80.
67. *Id.* at 70 fig. 5.2.
68. Associated Press, *Will Subprime Mess Ripple through Economy?*, NBCNews.com (Mar. 13, 2007), www.nbcnews.com/id/17584725#.
69. *The 4 Cs of Qualifying for a Mortgage*, FREDDIE MAC (Dec. 4, 2017), www.freddiemac.com/blog/homeownership/20171204_4Cs_qualifying_mortgage.html; *see also* FINANCIAL CRISIS INQUIRY REPORT, *supra* note 3, at 67.
70. Adam J. Levitin & Tara Twomey, *Mortgage Servicing*, 28 YALE J. ON REG. 1, 12 (2011).
71. Diane E. Thompson, *Foreclosing Modifications: How Servicer Incentives Discourage Loan Modifications*, 86 WASH. L. REV. 755, 764–65 (2011).
72. MARVIN M. SMITH & CHRISTY CHUNG HEVENER, FED. RESERVE BANK OF PHILA., SUBPRIME LENDING OVER TIME: THE ROLE OF RACE 7 (Oct. 2010).
73. *See* Joseph William Singer, *Foreclosure and the Failures of Formality, or Subprime Mortgage Conundrums and How to Fix Them*, 46 CONN. L. REV. 497

(2013); *see also* JOSEPH WILLIAM SINGER, NO FREEDOM WITHOUT REGULATION: THE HIDDEN LESSON OF THE SUBPRIME CRISIS (2015).

74. For empirical studies connecting securitization to a decline in underwriting standards, see Benjamin J. Keys et al., *Did Securitization Lead to Lax Screening? Evidence from Subprime Loans*, 125 Q.J. Econ. 307, 354 (2010); *see also* Giovanni Dell'Ariccia et al., *Credit Booms and Lending Standards: Evidence from the Subprime Mortgage Market* 31 (Int'l Monetary Fund, Working Paper WP/08/106, 2008).

75. For a discussion of the private-label market, see David Reiss, *The Federal Government's Implied Guarantee of Fannie Mae and Freddie Mac's Obligations: Uncle Sam Will Pick Up the Tab*, 42 GA. L. Rev. 1019, 1030–33 (2008).

76. Banks were not always allowed to purchase mortgage-backed securities. However, Congress gradually loosened those restrictions to help increase homeownership rates. Erik F. Gerding, *Bank Regulation and Securitization: How the Law Improved Transmission Lines between Real Estate and Banking Crises*, 50 GA. L. REV. 89, 101 (2015). Also, mortgage-backed securities were given favorable treatment under bank capital hold requirements, which made them all the more attractive for banks to purchase. *See id.* at 106.

77. Ginnie Mae is a corporation that is wholly owned by the U.S. Department of Housing and Urban Development. It provides guarantees on mortgage-backed securities that are derived from loans that carry government-backed guarantees (like under the FHA or Veterans' Administration's insurance programs). Ginnie Mae does not purchase or securitize loans itself.

78. Levitin & Twomey, *supra* note 70, at 12.
79. FINANCIAL CRISIS INQUIRY REPORT, *supra* note 3, at 102.
80. *Id.* at 105.
81. *Id.* at 71–72.
82. Thompson, *supra* note 71, at 768–69.
83. *Id.* at 774.
84. BAIR, *supra* note 23, at 54.
85. David Reiss, *Subprime Standardization: How Rating Agencies Allow Predatory Lending to Flourish in the Secondary Mortgage Market*, 33 FLA. ST. U. L. REV. 985 (2006).

2 The Crisis Hits

1. Adam J. Levitin & Susan M. Wachter, *Explaining the Housing Bubble*, 100 Geo. L.J. 1177 (2012) (describing the causes of the housing bubble).
2. FIN. CRISIS INQUIRY COMM'N, THE FINANCIAL CRISIS INQUIRY REPORT 214 (2011) (hereinafter FINANCIAL CRISIS INQUIRY REPORT).
3. *Id.* at 215 (quoting MARK ZANDI, CELIA CHEN, & BRIAN CAREY, MOODY'S ECONOMY.COM, HOUSING AT THE TIPPING POINT 7 [Oct. 2006]).
4. WILLIAM BOYES & MICHAEL MELVIN, THE FUNDAMENTALS OF ECONOMICS 137 (2012).

5. WELLS Fargo Econ. Grp., Weekly Economic & Financial Commentary 7 (Sept. 7, 2010).
6. See Joseph William Singer, *Foreclosure and the Failures of Formality, or Subprime Mortgage Conundrums and How to Fix Them*, 46 CONN. L. REV. 497, 507 (2013).
7. See David R. Greenberg, Neglected Formalities in the Mortgage Assignment Process and the Resulting Effects on Residential Foreclosures, 83 TEMP. L. REV. 253, 260–63 (2010) (citations omitted).
8. FINANCIAL CRISIS INQUIRY REPORT, *supra* note 2, at 215–16.
9. Ivan Vidangos, *Deleveraging and Recent Trends in Household Debt*, FEDS NOTES: BD. OF GOVERNORS OF THE FED. RESERVE SYS. (Apr. 6, 2015), www.federalreserve.gov/econresdata/notes/feds-notes/2015/deleveraging-and-recent-trends-in-household-debt-20150406.html.
10. Richard H. Thaler, *Underwater, but Will They Leave the Pool?*, N.Y. TIMES, Jan. 24, 2010, at BU3; see also Singer, *supra* note 6, at 534 (citing Robert C. Hockett, *Paying Paul and Robbing No One: An Eminent Domain Solution for Underwater Mortgage Debt*, 19 CURRENT ISSUES ECON. & FIN. 1, 6–7 [2013]).
11. Jenny Anderson & Heather Timmons, *Why a U.S. Subprime Mortgage Crisis Is Felt Around the World*, N.Y. TIMES (Aug. 31, 2007), www.nytimes.com/2007/08/31/business/worldbusiness/31derivatives.html; Gregorio Impavido & Ian Tower, *How the Financial Crisis Affects Pensions and Insurance and Why the Impacts Matter*, Int'l Monetary Fund, Working Paper No. WP/09/151, 2009).
12. Greenberg, *supra* note 7, at 260; see also TAMIM BAYOUMI, UNFINISHED BUSINESS: THE UNEXPLORED CAUSES OF THE FINANCIAL CRISIS AND THE LESSONS YET TO BE LEARNED (2017) (describing the linkages between the American financial crisis and the collapse of the European financial system in 2008).
13. FINANCIAL CRISIS INQUIRY REPORT, *supra* note 2, at 214.
14. *Id.* at 302.
15. Essentially, the federal government agreed to buy the toxic assets held on the books of Bear Stearns so that it would be much healthier for JPMorgan Chase to then buy. It was, in essence, an indirect bailout. Robin Sidel, Dennis K. Berman, & Kate Kelly, *J.P. Morgan Buys Bear in Fire Sale, as Fed Widens Credit to Avert Crisis*, WALL ST. J. (Mar. 17, 2007), www.wsj.com/articles/SB120569598608739825 (using subscription).
16. Erik F. Gerding, *Deregulation Pas de Deux: Dual Regulatory Causes of Financial Institutions and the Path to Financial Crisis in Sweden and the United States*, 15 NEXUS: CHAPMAN'S J.L. & POL'Y 135, 153–54 (2010).
17. SHEILA BAIR, BULL BY THE HORNS: FIGHTING TO SAVE MAIN STREET FROM WALL STREET AND WALL STREET FROM ITSELF 56 (2012); see also Andrea J. Boyack, *Laudable Goals and Unintended Consequences: The Role and Control of Fannie Mae and Freddie Mac*, 60 AM. U. L. REV. 1489, 1509 (2011).
18. FINANCIAL CRISIS INQUIRY REPORT, *supra* note 2, at 312.
19. *Id.*
20. *Id.* at 325.
21. *Id.* at 334.

22. *Id.* at 346.
23. *Id.* at 381.
24. Eamon Javers, *Citigroup Tops List of Banks Who Received Federal Aid*, CNBC (Mar. 16, 2011), www.cnbc.com/id/42099554.
25. Quizzically, the shares that the government took in Citigroup were different than those it took when it bailed out several other financial institutions. These shares came with the right of the government to receive special dividend payments, but they did not carry with them any voting rights. Thus, the government was entitled to money from the company in exchange for providing the infusion of cash, but it could not exercise any control over the company's decisions. David Ellis, *Citi Dodges Bullet*, CNN MONEY (Nov. 24, 2008), http://money.cnn.com/2008/11/23/news/companies/citigroup/index.htm.
26. Phillip Inman, *Wall Street Crisis: Bank of America Buys Merrill Lynch*, GUARDIAN (Sept. 15, 2008), www.theguardian.com/business/2008/sep/15/merrill lynch.wallstreet.
27. By October 2016, the government had spent 22.6 billion on homeowner relief. *See* U.S. GOV'T ACCOUNTABILITY OFFICE, TROUBLED ASSET RELIEF PROGRAM: STATUS OF HOUSING PROGRAMS 5 (Jan. 2017). This is compared to the $4.6 trillion that was paid out by the government as of 2015 to bailout banks and Wall Street firms. *See* Mike Collins, *The Big Bank Bailout*, FORBES (July 14, 2015), www.forbes.com/sites/mikecollins/2015/07/14/the-big-bank-bailout/#7f360d072d83.
28. FINANCIAL CRISIS INQUIRY REPORT, *supra* note 2, at 381.
29. *Id.* at 393.
30. MATTHEW DESMOND, EVICTED: POVERTY AND PROFIT IN THE AMERICAN CITY 124 (2016).
31. Researchers note that a significant reason for this disparity is the fact that equity in real estate comprises a disproportionate share of the total household wealth of communities of color compared to that of white families. This disparity existed at the time of the crisis and persists today. In 2017, real estate accounts for 46 percent of the wealth in black families and 43 percent in Latino families. Conversely, it is only 27 percent in white households. *See Why Did the Housing Bust Hit Black and Latino Families Harder?*, FED. RESERVE BANK OF ST. LOUIS: ON THE ECON. BLOG (Aug. 10, 2017), www.stlouisfed.org/on-the-economy/2017/august/why-housing-bust-hit-black-latino-families-harder; *see also* Thomas W. Mitchell, *From Reconstruction to Deconstruction: Undermining Black Landownership, Political Independence, and Community through Partition Sales of Tenancies in Common*, 95 NW. U. L. REV. 505 (2001) (discussing the importance of land as an principal asset in the household wealth of black American families).
32. FINANCIAL CRISIS INQUIRY REPORT, *supra* note 2, at 390.
33. *See* DESMOND, *supra* note 30, at 150.
34. Because of their many beaches and deserts, Arizona, California, Florida, Nevada, and Texas are often collectively referred to as the sand states. Many of them were the hardest hit by the bursting of the housing bubble. *See* Jon Prior, Spreading Foreclosures Still Concentrated in Sand States: RealtyTrac,

HOUSINGWIRE (Jan. 28, 2010), www.housingwire.com/articles/spreading-foreclo sures-still-concentrated-sand-states-realtytrac.
35. Timothy Williams, *Blighted Cities Prefer Razing to Rebuilding*, N.Y. TIMES (Nov. 12, 2013), www.nytimes.com/2013/11/12/us/blighted-cities-prefer-razing-to -rebuilding.html.
36. In some parts of the valley, whole neighborhoods seemed to return to nature as bobcats took up residence in homes and deer and other wildlife drank from swimming pools. See David Kelly, *With Homeowner in Doghouse, Bobcats Move In*, L.A. TIMES (Sept. 5, 2008), www.latimes.com/local/la-me-bobcats5-2008sep05 -story.html.
37. Laura Kusisto, *Many Who Lost Homes to Foreclosure in Last Decade Won't Return – NAR*, WALL ST. J. (Apr. 20, 2015), www.wsj.com/articles/many-who-lost-homes-to -foreclosure-in-last-decade-wont-return-nar-1429548640 (using subscription).
38. FINANCIAL CRISIS INQUIRY REPORT, *supra* note 2, at 403.
39. BAIR, *supra* note 17, at 134 (citing RealtyTrac data).
40. *Id.* at 135.
41. *Id.* at 131.
42. Renae Merle, *After Helping a Fraction of Homeowners Expected, Obama's Foreclosure Prevention Program Is Finally Ending*, WASH. POST (Dec. 30, 2016), www.washingtonpost.com/news/business/wp/2016/12/30/after-helping-a-fraction -of-homeowners-expected-obamas-foreclosure-prevention-program-is-finally-end ing/?utm_term=.65f7f0e0822c.
43. BAIR, *supra* note 17, at 151.
44. SIGTARP: OFFICE OF THE SPECIAL INSPECTOR GENERAL FOR THE TROUBLED ASSET RELIEF PROGRAM, QUARTERLY REPORT TO CONGRESS 112 (Oct. 2016).
45. Merle, *supra* note 42.

3 At Your (Mortgage) Service

1. *See* Joel Goldberg, *It Takes a Village to Determine the Origins of an African Proverb*, NPR: GOATS & SODA (July 30, 2016), www.npr.org/sections/goatsand soda/2016/07/30/487925796/it-takes-a-village-to-determine-the-origins-of-an-afri can-proverb.
2. MORTG. BANKERS ASS'N & PwC, THE CHANGING DYNAMICS OF THE MORTGAGE SERVICING LANDSCAPE 5 (June 2015) (hereinafter CHANGING DYNAMICS).
3. You Suk Kim et al., *Liquidity Crisis in the Mortgage Market* 7 (Brookings Papers on Economic Activity Conference Draft, Feb. 27, 2018), www.brookings.edu/ wp-content/uploads/2018/03/5_kimetal.pdf (hereinafter Brookings, Mortgage).
4. Savings and loan associations (S&Ls), first created in the 1800s and also known as thrifts, are financial institutions designed to promote affordable homeowner ship. They were created at a time when traditional banks were not heavily involved in the residential mortgage lending business. *See* Richard K. Green & Susan M. Wachter, *The American Mortgage in Historical and International Context*, J. ECON. PERSP., Fall 2005, at 93, 97. One of the most infamous S&Ls of the financial crisis was Washington Mutual, which collapsed and was eventually

sold off to JPMorgan Chase. There are not many S&Ls in operation today. *See* Timothy Curry & Lynn Shibut, *The Cost of the Savings and Loan Crisis: Truth and Consequences*, FDIC BANKING REV., vol. 13, no. 2 (2000), at 26, www.fdic.gov/bank/analytical/banking/2000dec/brv13n2_2.pdf; Kimberly Amadeo, *What Are Savings and Loans? History and Today*, BALANCE (Oct. 25, 2016), www.thebalance.com/what-are-savings-and-loans-history-and-today-3305959.

5. Brookings, Mortgage, *supra* note 3, at 7.
6. FRANK J. FABOZZI & VINOD KOTHARI, INTRODUCTION TO SECURITIZATION 124 (2008).
7. CHANGING DYNAMICS, *supra* note 2, at 6. The constellation of servicers can become even more complex in the case of a securitization of commercial (as opposed to residential) mortgage-backed securities. *See* MORTG. BANKERS ASS'N, STANDARD ROLES AND RESPONSIBILITIES OF THE MASTER AND SUB-SERVICERS IN CMBS Transactions (2000).
8. As noted in prior parts of this book, little to no academic writing has been done on mortgage servicing. I am indebted to Adam Levitin, Tara Twomey, Diane Thompson, Larry Cordell, Karen Dynan, Andreas Lehnert, Nellie Liang, and Eileen Mauskopf for their tremendous work in this area, much of which helped build the foundations of this chapter.
9. Connie Bruck, *Angelo's Ashes: The Man Who Became the Face of the Financial Crisis*, NEW YORKER, June 29, 2009, at 49; *see also* Reuters, *Fed Fines 5 Big Banks $35M over Mortgage Servicing*, N.Y. POST (Jan. 12, 2018), https://nypost.com/2018/01/12/fed-fines-5-big-banks-35m-over-mortgage-servicing/ (naming Goldman Sachs, Morgan Stanley, CIT Group, U.S. Bancorp, and PNC Financial, many of which also originated or worked with other firms to originate subprime loans). At other times, these financial giants would sponsor the securitization of loans that they knew were (or even had encouraged to be) subprime and then acted as trustee thereafter.
10. Since 2009, federal regulations require that homeowners be advised when ownership of their loan has been transferred. However, the notice document typically says "your loan is now owned by ABC14589W34 Asset-Backed Security Trust" or something equally unhelpful.
11. Adam J. Levitin & Tara Twomey, *Mortgage Servicing*, 28 YALE J. ON REG. 1, 24 (2011); *see also* CHANGING DYNAMICS, *supra* note 2, at 11.
12. *See* Levitin & Twomey, *supra* note 11, at 31; Diane E. Thompson, *Foreclosing Modifications: How Servicer Incentives Discourage Loan Modifications*, 86 WASH. L. REV. 755, 766 (2011); Larry Cordell et al., *The Incentives of Mortgage Servicers: Myths and Realities* 3 (Fed. Reserve Bd., Fin. & Econ. Discussion Series, Working Paper No. 2008-46, 2008). For examples, see Salomon Brothers, Mortgage Securities VII, Inc., Asset-Backed Certificate Series 1997-LB6, Pooling and Servicing Agreement, Form 8-K, Exhibit 4.1 (Nov. 1, 1997), www.sec.gov/Archives/edgar/data/1050361/0000882377-97-000420.txt; Option One Mortg. Acceptance Corp., Asset-Backed Certificates, Series 2003-5, Pooling and Servicing Agreement, Form 8-K, Exhibit 4.1 (July 1, 2003), www.sec.gov/Archives/edgar/data/1256334/000088237703001311/d159895.txt; EMC Mortg. Corp., Bear Stearns Asset-Backed Certificates, Series 2005-HE11, Pooling and Servicing Agreement, Form 8-K,

Exhibit 4.1 (Nov. 1, 2005), www.sec.gov/Archives/edgar/data/1345748/000088237705003545/d401170_exh4-1.htm.
13. Ameriquest Mortg. Sec. Inc., Asset-Backed Pass-Through Certificates Series 2005-R2, Pooling and Servicing Agreement § 3.01 (Mar. 1, 2005), www.sec.gov/Archives/edgar/data/1321383/000088237705000777/d315156.txt ("The Master Servicer shall service and administer the Mortgage Loans on behalf of the Trustee and in the best interests of and for the benefit of the Certificate holders [as determined by the Master Servicer in its reasonable judgment].").
14. Special Inspector Gen. for the Troubled Asset Relief Program, SIGTARP 12-003, The Net Present Value Test's Impact on the Home Affordable Modification Program (2012).
15. Thompson, *supra* note 12, at 766.
16. *Id.*
17. Importantly, this requirement has not historically been a part of the servicing agreement. Rather, this was mandated by Fannie/Freddie servicing guidelines and the CFPB as recently as 2014.
18. Cordell et al., *supra* note 12, at 21.
19. Sheila Bair, Bull by the Horns: Fighting to Save Main Street from Wall Street and Wall Street from Itself 151 (2012).
20. Levitin & Twomey, *supra* note 11, at 28.
21. Thompson, *supra* note 12, at 776.
22. Furman Ctr. for Real Estate & Urban Pol'y, N.Y. Univ., Foreclosed Properties in NYC: A Look at the Last 15 Years (Jan. 2, 2010).
23. Family Hous. Fund, Cost Effectiveness of Mortgage Foreclosure Prevention 6 (1995).
24. Thompson, *supra* note 12, at 759.
25. Cordell et al., *supra* note 12, at 7.
26. Not all loan modification resulted in a principal write-down. Many modifications did not extend the term, but rather the amortization period. This meant that many homeowners faced balloon principal payments in 15 to 30 years.
27. Cordell et al., *supra* note 12, at 10–11.
28. Francie Cohen Spahn, *Deeds in Lieu of Foreclosure*, Prac. Real Est. Law, July 2010, at 47.
29. Alan Zibel, *"Short Sales" to Get a Boost*, Wall St. J. (Aug. 21, 2012), www.wsj.com/articles/SB10000872396390444443504577603552056318314 (using subscription).
30. This scenario assumes, however, that the ability to go after the homeowners for the deficiency has been waived.
31. Bair, *supra* note 19, at 244; Cordell et al., *supra* note 12, at 12–13. In a rising real estate market, the loss on a foreclosure can be much less. The value of the collateral is one of the major drivers of the net present value analysis.
32. Fin. Crisis Inquiry Comm'n, The Financial Crisis Inquiry Report 70 (2011). Generally, Fannie Mae and Freddie Mac did not use tranching like this in issuing their mortgage-backed securities. Levitin & Twomey, *supra* note 11, at 21. However, there were some instances where payment slicing did take place with GSE securities. *See* Fed. Hous. Fin. Agency, Examination Manual – Public:

Securitizations 19 (July 2013) (Version 1.0), www.fhfa.gov/SupervisionRegulation/Documents/Securitizations_Module_Final_Version_1.0_508.pdf.
33. Cordell et al., *supra* note 12, at 4.
34. *Id.* at 22–23.
35. BAIR, *supra* note 19, at 52.
36. Thompson, *supra* note 12, at 769.
37. Cordell et al., *supra* note 12, at 19.
38. Thompson, *supra* note 12, at 785.
39. KATHLEEN C. ENGEL & PATRICIA A. MCCOY, THE SUBPRIME VIRUS: RECKLESS CREDIT, REGULATORY FAILURE, AND NEXT STEPS 132 (2011); *see also* Manuel Adelino, Kristopher Gerardi, & Paul S. Willen, Fed. Reserve Bank of Bos., *Why Don't Lenders Renegotiate More Home Mortgages? Redefaults, Self-Cures, and Securitization* (Public Policy Discussion Paper No. 2009-425, July 2009).
40. *See* HOPE for Homeowners Act of 2008, Pub. L. No. 110-289, 122 Stat. 2654; *see also* Helping Families Save Their Homes Act of 2009, Pub. L. No. 111-22, 123 Stat. 1632 (codified at 15 U.S.C. 1639a).
41. Cordell et al., *supra* note 12, at 21–22; *see also* CREDIT SUISSE, THE DAY AFTER TOMORROW: PAYMENT SHOCK AND LOAN MODIFICATIONS (2007).
42. Cordell et al., *supra* note 12.
43. Thompson, *supra* note 12, at 784.
44. Cordell et al., *supra* note 12, at 22.
45. Thompson, *supra* note 12, at 768.
46. Cordell et al., *supra* note 12, at 23.
47. Levitin & Twomey, *supra* note 11, at 61 n. 228; Lorraine Woellert & Meera Louis, *Fannie, Freddie Defend Foreclosures Amid Criticism*, BLOOMBERG (Dec. 1, 2010), www.bloomberg.com/news/articles/2010-12-01/foreclosures-should-not-pause-during-loan-workouts-freddie-mac-aide-says (using subscription); Alan Zibel, *Banks Told to Stop Foreclosures during Mortgage Modification*, WALL ST. J. (Dec. 1, 2010, 1:15 PM ET), https://blogs.wsj.com/developments/2010/12/01/banks-told-to-stop-foreclosures-during-mortgage-modification/ (using subscription).
48. Cordell et al., *supra* note 12, at 9.
49. *Id.*
50. Thompson, *supra* note 12, at 772–73.
51. Levitin & Twomey, *supra* note 11, at 21; Thompson, *supra* note 12, at 779.
52. Thompson, *supra* note 12, at 772.
53. Cordell et al., *supra* note 12, at 32.
54. Nelson D. Schwartz, *Voices of Foreclosure Speak Daily About Desperation and Misery*, N.Y. TIMES (Nov. 16, 2010), www.cnbc.com/id/40213535; *see also* Thompson, *supra* note 12, at 794.
55. Fannie Mae, Foreclosure Time Frames and Compensatory Fee Allowable Delays Exhibit (Sept. 29, 2016), www.fanniemae.com/content/guide_exhibit/foreclosure-timeframes-compensatory-fees-allowable-delays.pdf; Freddie Mac, Bulletin No. 2017-1, Exhibit 83A: Determining State Foreclosure Timeline Performance Compensatory Fees (Feb. 15, 2017), www.freddiemac.com/singlefamily/service/pdf/exh83A.pdf.

56. Fannie Mae, *supra* note 55, at 1–2.
57. Margaret R. T. Deware, Comment, *Regulation X: A New Direction for the Regulation of Mortgage Servicers*, 63 Emory L.J. 175, 187 (2013).
58. Alexandra Andrews & Emily Witt, *The Secret Test That Ensures Lenders Win on Loan Mods*, ProPublica (Sept. 15, 2009), www.propublica.org/article/the-secret-test-that-ensures-lenders-win-on-loan-mods-915 (noting congressional testimony by national consumer advocates, such as Diane Thompson with the National Consumer Law Center); Holden Lewis, *Want a Loan Modification? Pass the NPV Test*, BankRate (Dec. 17, 2009), www.bankrate.com/finance/mortgages/want-a-loan-modification-pass-the-npv-test-1.aspx.
59. Andrews & Witt, *supra* note 58.
60. *Id.* (describing a situation involving Wells Fargo).
61. Cordell et al., *supra* note 12, at 18.
62. *Id.*
63. Shahien Nasiripour, *Foreclosures Are More Profitable Than Loan Modifications, According to New Report*, Huffington Post (Mar. 18, 2010), www.huffingtonpost.com/2009/10/21/perverse-incentives-lead_n_328378.html.
64. Cordell et al., *supra* note 12, at 19.
65. The Obama-era HAMP program did provide a base level analysis for how the NPV calculation should work, but servicers were allowed to deviate from it if they notified the Department of the Treasury. Those servicer modifications were not, however, made public by the government despite repeated requests.
66. *See* Thompson, *supra* note 12, at 779, for the competing servicer incentives between foreclosure and a loan modification.
67. In a study done by ProPublica of 300,000 subprime, securitized loans, JPMorgan Chase's servicer took, on average, 11 months to complete a modification and Ocwen Financial took seven. Paul Kiel & Olga Pierce, *Homeowner Questionnaire Shows Banks Violating Gov't Program Rules*, ProPublica (Aug. 16, 2010), www.propublica.org/article/homeowner-questionnaire-shows-banks-violating-govt-program-rules.
68. *Id.* (studying subprime loan data provided by Moody's rating agency).
69. State Foreclosure Prevention Working Grp., Conference of State Bank Supervisors, Data Report No. 2, Analysis of Subprime Mortgage Servicing Performance (Apr. 2008).
70. Consumer Prot. Fin. Bureau, Supervisory Highlights Mortgage Servicing Special Edition 7 (Issue 11, June 2016).
71. Cordell et al., *supra* note 12, at 9.
72. *Id.* at 9.
73. *Id.*
74. Levitin & Twomey, *supra* note 11, at 4.
75. *Id.*; Kiel & Pierce, *supra* note 67.
76. Changing Dynamics, *supra* note 2, at 6. For a description of Fannie Mae's servicing fee structure, see Fannie Mae, Fannie Mae Investor Reporting Manual 38 (Feb. 14, 2018) ("All mortgage loans have a servicing fee that is specified at the time the mortgage loan is purchased or securitized and that

generally remains constant over the life of the mortgage loan [although it may change when an ARM is converted to a fixed-rate mortgage loan].").
77. Cordell et al., *supra* note 12, at 15.
78. Levitin & Twomey, *supra* note 11, at 38. For a similar example using a different principal amount, see Cordell et al., *supra* note 12, at 15.
79. Thompson, *supra* note 12, at 769.
80. *Id.* at 777.
81. CHANGING DYNAMICS, *supra* note 2, at 6.
82. Levitin & Twomey, *supra* note 11, at 39–40.
83. TWO HARBORS INV. CORP., MORTGAGE SERVICING RIGHTS (MSR) PRIMER 12 (Dec. 16, 2010).
84. Levitin & Twomey, *supra* note 11, at 39; Thompson, *supra* note 12, at 807.
85. Thompson, *supra* note 12, at 803 n. 237.
86. Levitin & Twomey, *supra* note 11, at 42–43.
87. Gretchen Morgenson, *Dubious Fees Hit Borrowers in Foreclosures*, N.Y. TIMES (Nov. 6, 2007), www.nytimes.com/2007/11/06/business/06mortgage.html.
88. *Id.*
89. Levitin & Twomey, *supra* note 11, at 43.
90. Cordell et al., *supra* note 12, at 16.
91. For a discussion of the lack of loan modifications after 2008, see Paul Kiel, *Bank of America Lied to Homeowners and Rewarded Foreclosures, Former Employees Say*, PROPUBLICA (June 14, 2013), www.propublica.org/article/bank-of-america-lied-to-homeowners-and-rewarded-foreclosures.
92. Ben Lane, *How Much Offshore Staff Do the Top Mortgage Servicers Use?*, HOUSINGWIRE (Oct. 30, 2014), www.housingwire.com/articles/31905-how-much-offshore-staff-do-the-top-mortgage-servicers-use.
93. FITCH RATINGS, OUTSOURCING TRENDS IN RMBS MORTGAGE SERVICING (Jan. 2009).
94. Thompson, *supra* note 12, at 814.
95. Maurna Desmond, *How Dodd Helped a Troubled Hedge Fund Fight for Help*, FORBES (Aug. 28, 2009), www.forbes.com/2009/08/28/dodd-carrington-capital-business-wall-street-dodd.html#53278ae72d8a (discussing this liquidity problem for the nonbank servicer Carrington Mortgage).
96. Thompson, *supra* note 12, at 777.
97. Some have seriously criticized this structure because it can cause servicers to rush to foreclosure. See Brookings, Mortgage, *supra* note 3, at 33–34; Darren Aiello, Value Destruction and Aggressive Foreclosures: The Behavior of Financially Constrained Mortgage Servicers (Jan. 16, 2018), https://papers.ssrn.com/sol3/papers.cfm?abstract_id=3063513. The liquidity problems associated with nonbank servicers in making these advances to investors when homeowners stop paying s more fully discussed in Chapter 7.
98. Levitin & Twomey, *supra* note 11, at 48.
99. Thompson, *supra* note 12, at 770.
100. Cordell et al., *supra* note 12, at 17–19.

101. Levitin & Twomey, *supra* note 11, at 21 (noting that private-label market pooling and servicing contracts are heterogeneous).
102. Jumbo loans refer to those that are in amounts that exceed what is for purposes of being considered "conforming." The GSEs can only purchase conforming loans and because of this jumbo loans became the domain of the private-label market. At the time of this writing the private-label market is nearly nonexistent. To the extent it does exist, it consists predominately of jumbo loans.
103. Cordell et al., *supra* note 12, at 19.
104. *Id.*
105. For instance, the value of the mortgage property was a principal driver of the analysis. To determine this number, many servicers used something called an *automated valuation model* (AVM), which is computer service that uses mathematical models to calculate the value of property. However, the AVM has been criticized for being notoriously inaccurate. Industry experts warn that AVM numbers should be taken "with a grain of salt." Teresa Mears, *Why Home Value Estimate Tools Aren't as Accurate as You Think*, U.S. News & World Rep. (Feb. 11, 2016), https://realestate.usnews.com/real-estate/articles/why-home-value-estimate-tools-arent-as-accurate-as-you-think.
106. Cordell et al., *supra* note 12.
107. *Id.*
108. *Id.*
109. *Id.*
110. Bair, *supra* note 19, at 132–33.
111. Thompson, *supra* note 12, at 771.
112. *Id.* at 780.
113. Cordell et al., *supra* note 12, at 21. The Obama administration's HAMP program attempted to provide such an incentive, although it was not very effective. David Dayen, *The Government Program That Failed Homeowners*, Guardian (Mar. 30, 2014), www.theguardian.com/money/2014/mar/30/government-program-save-homes-mortgages-failure-banks; *see also* SIGTARP: Office of the Special Inspector General for the Troubled Asset Relief Program, Quarterly Report to Congress 111 (Apr. 29, 2015) ("TARP's signature foreclosure prevention program, the Home Affordable Modification Program ["HAMP"], has struggled to reach the expected number of homeowners Treasury envisioned for the program.").
114. Cordell et al., *supra* note 12, at 17.
115. John Patrick Hunt, *Loan Modification Restrictions in Subprime Securitization Pooling and Servicing Agreements from 2006: Final Results* (UC Davis Sch. of Law, Research Paper Series 6, 2010).
116. Thompson, *supra* note 12, at 774–75.
117. Cordell et al., *supra* note 12, at 25; Patrick A. Randolph Jr., *Mortgage Modification and Alteration of Priorities between Junior and Senior Lienholders*, DIRT Blog, http://dirt.umkc.edu/alterationofpriorities.htm (accessed Mar. 2, 2018).
118. Cordell et al., *supra* note 12, at 25.

119. Donghoon Lee, Christopher Mayer, & Joseph Tracy, Fed. Reserve Bank of N.Y., Staff Report No. 569, A New Look at Second Liens 6 (Aug. 2012) ("At the height of the housing market in 2006, as many as 40 to 45 percent of home purchases involved a piggyback second lien in coastal markets and bubble locations [Phoenix, Las Vegas, Miami].").
120. Terry Savage, *Your Home Is Not Your Piggy Bank!*, Huffington Post (Apr. 3, 2016), www.huffingtonpost.com/terry-savage/your-home-is-not-your-pig_b_9603938.html; Akin Oyedele, *People in California Are Starting to Use Their Homes as Piggy Banks*, Bus. Insider (Oct. 6, 2016), www.businessinsider.com/california-home-equity-2016-10.
121. Cordell et al., *supra* note 12, at 26–27.
122. *Id.*
123. *Id.*
124. Bradley T. Borden & David J. Reiss, *Dirt Lawyers and Dirty REMICs*, Prob. & Prop., May/June 2013, at 13.
125. S. Rep. No. 99-313, 99th Cong., 2d Sess. 791-92, *reprinted in* 1986-3 C.B. 791-92 (vol. 3).
126. Rev. Proc. 08-28, 2008-23 I.R.B. 6.
127. Thompson, *supra* note 12, at 782.
128. *Id.* at 775.
129. Cordell et al., *supra* note 12, at 24; *see also* Fin. Accounting Standards Bd., Statement of Financial Accounting Standards No. 140, 9 (Sept. 2000) ("A transfer of financial assets . . . in which the transferor surrenders control over those financial assets shall be accounted for as a sale to the extent that consideration other than beneficial interests in the transferred assets is received in exchange.").
130. Kenneth Ayotte & Stav Gaon, *Asset-Backed Securities: Costs and Benefits of "Bankruptcy Remoteness*," 24 Rev. of Fin. Studies 1299 (2011); *Summary of Statement 140*, Fin. Acct. Servs. Bd. (Sept. 2000), www.fasb.org/summary/stsum140.shtml ("The transferred assets have been isolated from the transferor – put presumptively beyond the reach of the transferor and its creditors, even in bankruptcy or other receivership.").
131. Cordell et al., *supra* note 12, at 24–25.
132. Thompson, *supra* note 12, at 787.
133. Letter from Christopher Cox, Chairman, U.S. Sec. & Exch. Comm'n, to Barney Frank, Chairman, Comm. on Fin. Servs., U.S. House of Representatives (July 24, 2007), https://dart.deloitte.com/USDART/resource/89d56978-3f35-11e6-95db-0529929089ca.

4 The Most Important Document You've Never Read

1. Megan Dorsey & David Rockwell, Financing Residential Real Estate 29 (13th ed. 2005).
2. *See* David Reiss, *Underwriting Sustainable Homeownership: The Federal Housing Administration and the Low Down Payment Loan*, 50 Ga. L. Rev.

1019 (2016). I am indebted to David Reiss for his excellent work on the FHA and government-related housing finance. His work was immensely helpful in the writing of this chapter.
3. See id.
4. Charles Nelson Glaab & Andrew Theodore Brown, A History of Urban America 299 (3d ed. 1983).
5. Bureau of the Census, U.S. Dep't of Commerce, Historical Statistics of the United States: Colonial Times to 1970 Part 2, at 646 (1976).
6. See Reiss, supra note 2, at 1023.
7. See id. at 1022.
8. See id. at 17.
9. See id. ("To advance [mortgage credit] further, the federal government created Fannie Mae in 1938 to create a secondary market for FHA mortgages. Fannie Mae spun off Ginnie Mae in 1968 to securitize FHA mortgages while Fannie securitized mortgages that were not insured by the federal government.").
10. David Reiss, Fannie Mae and Freddie Mac and the Future of Federal Housing Finance Policy: A Study of Regulatory Privilege, 61 Ala. L. Rev. 907 (2010).
11. Julia Patterson Forrester, Fannie Mae/Freddie Mac Uniform Mortgage Instruments: The Forgotten Benefit to Homeowners, 72 Mo. L. Rev. 1077, 1082 (2007); Peter M. Carrozzo, Marketing the American Mortgage: The Emergency Home Finance Act of 1970, Standardization and the Secondary Market Revolution, 39 Real Prop., Prob. & Tr. J. 765, 766 (2005).
12. Raymond A. Jensen, Mortgage Standardization: History of Interaction of Economics, Consumerism and Governmental Pressure, 7 Real Prop., Prob. & Tr. J. 397, 398 (1972).
13. Carrozzo, supra note 11, at 777.
14. Id. at 790.
15. Pub. L. No. 91-351, 84 Stat. 450 (1970).
16. Forrester, supra note 11, at 1083.
17. Carrozzo, supra note 11, at 798–99 (citing S. Comm. on Banking, Hous. & Urban Affairs, Federal National Mortgage Association Public Meeting on Conventional Mortgage Forms, S. Doc. No. 92-21, at 103 [1971]).
18. Forrester, supra note 11, at 1085.
19. See id. at 1085–86.
20. See id.
21. See id.
22. Id.
23. See Carrozzo, supra note 11, at 802–3.
24. Forrester, supra note 11, at 1085.
25. See id. at 1087 ("Because of their widespread use and their exceptionally fair terms, Fannie Mae/Freddie Mac uniform instruments provide a significant benefit to homeowners.").
26. See id. at 1093–94.
27. See id. (citing Lucian A. Bebchuk & Richard A. Posner, One-Sided Contracts in Competitive Consumer Markets, 104 Mich. L. Rev. 827, 828–29 (2006)).

28. *See id.* at 1093.
29. *Id.* at 1095–96.
30. *See id.*
31. New York–Single Family–Fannie Mae/Freddie Mac Uniform Instrument (Form 3033) § 7(b), at 9 (Jan. 2001) (hereinafter N.Y. Mortgage). For similar provisions, *see* Florida–Single Family–Fannie Mae/Freddie Mac Uniform Instrument (Form 3010) § 7, at 8 (Jan. 2001), and California–Single Family–Fannie Mae/Freddie Mac Uniform Instrument (Form 3005) § 7(b), at 8 (Jan. 2001). Security instruments for all 50 states may be found at *Security Instruments*, Fannie Mae, www.fanniemae.com/singlefamily/security-instruments (accessed Apr. 11, 2018).
32. *See generally* Jonathan L. Hafetz, "A Man's Home Is His Castle?": *Reflections on the Home, the Family, and Privacy during the Late Nineteenth and Early Twentieth Centuries*, 8 Wm. & Mary J. Women & L. 175 (2002); *see also* Linda C. McClain, *Inviolability and Privacy: The Castle, the Sanctuary, and the Body*, 7 Yale J.L. & Human. 195 (1995); Mechele Dickerson, Homeownership and America's Financial Underclass: Flawed Premises, Broken Promises, New Prescriptions (2014).
33. *See* N.Y. Mortgage, *supra* note 31, § 9, at 10. A nearly identical provision is contained in virtual every different state version of the Fannie Mae/Freddie Mac uniform mortgage.
34. Arrington v. Liscom, 34 Cal. 365 (1868); 1 J.J. Powell, A Treatise on the Law of Mortgages 1–4 (Boston, Wells & Lilly, 1828).
35. George E. Osborne, Mortgages §§ 1–7 (2d ed. 1970).
36. 2 Baxter Dunaway, Law of Distressed Real Estate § 16:20 (2017).
37. *See, e.g.,* Eaton v. Fed. Nat'l Mortgage Ass'n, 969 N.E.2d 1118 (Mass. 2012); Mazine v. M & I Bank, 67 So. 3d 1129, 1132 (Fla. Dist. Ct. App. 2011); *see also* Douglas J. Whaley, *Mortgage Foreclosures, Promissory Notes, and the Uniform Commercial Code*, 39 W. St. U. L. Rev. 313 (2012).
38. *See* Dunaway, *supra* note 36, § 16:22.
39. *Id.* § 16:24.
40. *See, e.g.,* Tex. Prop. Code § 51.0025 (2015); Mich. Comp. Laws § 445.1595 (2017); Wash. Rev. Code § 61.24.045 (2017); N.C. Gen. Stat. § 45-21.16 (2016); Md. Code, Real Prop. § 7-102 (2017).
41. Dunaway, *supra* note 36, § 17:1.
42. *See* Grant S. Nelson, Dale A. Whitman, Ann M. Burkhart, & R. Wilson Freyermuth, Real Estate Finance Law § 1.5, at 11–12 (6th ed. 2014).
43. 1 Dunaway, *supra* note 36, § 11.25 (2016) ("Hybrid theory states include: Georgia, Maryland, Mississippi, New Jersey, North Carolina, and Vermont.").
44. *See id.*
45. *See* Nelson et al., *supra* note 42, § 4.24, at 316 (citing Stouffer v. Harlan, 74 P. 610 [Kan. 1903], but also reaching back to Phyfe v. Riley, 15 Wend. 248 [N.Y. Sup. Ct. 1836]).
46. *See id.* § 4:24; *see also* HRPT Advisors, Inc. vs. MacDonald, Levine, Jenkins & Co., P.C., 686 N.E.2d 203 (Mass. App. Ct. 1997) (involving a tenant in an

income-producing property owing rental obligation to the mortgagee-in-possession). *See generally* COMMERCIAL PROPERTY 2017 (Anne Rodell ed., 2017) (CLP Legal Practice Guide). Similarly, various state laws allow for the lender to have a person appointed to take over the property of the owner during the period between a default and the eventual foreclosure. This is called putting the property into receivership. The receiver operates and manages all aspects of the property until the foreclosure is concluded. However, as with the mortgagee-in-possession rule, receiverships are generally only used in the context of commercial real estate – not homeownership. *See* NELSON ET AL., *supra* note 42, §§ 4:33–4:43; *see also* UNIF. COMMERCIAL REAL ESTATE RECEIVERSHIP ACT (UNIF. LAW COMM'N 2015).

5 Lost and Sign on the Dotted Line

1. Sometimes if there is no more room on the note for another signature then the parties will attach another document – called an *allonge* – to the note and place the signature there. However, the allonge must be "affixed" to the promissory note for it to be effective for negotiation purposes. *See* U.C.C. § 3-204 (AM. LAW INST. & UNIF. LAW COMM'N 2002); *see also In re* Shapoval, 441 B.R. 392, 394 (Bankr. D. Mass. 2010).
2. New Orleans Canal & Banking Co. v. Montgomery, 95 U.S. 16 (1877); Batesville Inst. v. Kauffman, 85 U.S. (18 Wall.) 151 (1873); *see also* First Nat'l Bank of Quincy v. Guyton, 72 So. 460 (Fla. 1916); FV-I, Inc. for Morgan Stanley Mortg. Capital Holdings, LLC v. Kallevig, 392 P.3d 1248 (Kan. 2017); Armour Fertilizer Works v. Zills, 177 So. 136 (Ala. 1937). There have been some assorted exceptions to this rule where some states have deviated from the "mortgage follows the note" concept. *See, e.g.*, ALS-RVC, LLC v. Garvin, 201 So. 3d 687, 690 (Fla. Dist. Ct. App. 2016); U.S. Bank Nat'l Ass'n v. Ibanez, 941 N.E.2d 40, 53 (Mass. 2011). However, even those states that have taken this approach do not always do so clearly. *See* Martins v. BAC Home Loans Servicing, L.P., 722 F.3d 249, 254 (5th Cir. 2013) ("[F]oreclosure does not require possession of the note [under Texas law]."); *cf.* Preston v. Seterus, Inc., 931 F. Supp. 2d 743, 759 (N.D. Tex. 2013) ("This is because Texas follows the rule that a mortgage on real estate follows the promissory note it secures.").
3. Adam J. Levitin, *The Paper Chase: Securitization, Foreclosure, and the Uncertainty of Mortgage Title*, 63 DUKE L.J. 637, 671–74 (2013).
4. The only argument for the execution of an assignment of mortgage (although this is not necessarily an argument for requiring that the document be recorded) is that in the 30 or so states that allow for nonjudicial foreclosure processes, sometimes state statutes would require a clear chain of title to the deed of trust. This however, is in and of itself a theoretically unsound – and illogical – requirement because the theory of the security following the debt is foundational to mortgage law in those jurisdictions as well. *See* Dale A. Whitman, *What We Have Learned from the Mortgage Crisis About Transferring Mortgage Loans*, 49 REAL PROP., TR. & EST. L.J. 1, 52–53 (2014).

5. Christopher L. Peterson, *Foreclosure, Subprime Mortgage Lending, and the Mortgage Electronic Registration System*, 78 U. CIN. L. REV. 1359, 1370 (2010).
6. *See id.* at 1370 (citing Howard Schneider, *MERS Aids Electronic Mortgage Program*, MORTGAGE BANKING, Jan. 1, 1997, at 20).
7. R. K. Arnold, *Yes, There Is Life on MERS*, PROB. & PROP., July/Aug. 1997, at 32, 34.
8. *See* Peterson, *supra* note 5, at 1370.
9. Landmark Nat'l Bank v. Kesler, 216 P.3d 158, 165–66 (Kan. 2009) ("What meaning is this court to attach to MERS's designation as nominee for Millennia? The parties appear to have defined the word in much the same way that the blind men of Indian legend described an elephant – their description depended on which part they were touching at any given time.").
10. *See id.*
11. Arnold, *supra* note 7, at 34.
12. *See* RESTATEMENT (THIRD) OF PROPERTY: MORTGAGES § 5.4(a)-(b) (1997). This "split-the-note" rule has been, as mentioned earlier in this chapter, deviated from in some states. *See* Routh v. Bank of Am., N.A., No. SA-12-CV-244-XR, 2013 WL 427393, at *6 (W.D. Tex. Feb. 4, 2013) (discussing various conflicting positions among federal district courts).
13. *See* Arnold, *supra* note 7, at 34.
14. *Id.*
15. Mortg. Elec. Registration Sys., Inc. v. Saunders, 2010 ME 79, ¶ 15, 2 A.3d 289, 297.
16. *See* Whitman, *supra* note 4, at 9; Elston/Leetsdale, LLC v. CWCapital Asset Mgmt. LLC, 87 So. 3d 14, 17 (Fla. Dist. Ct. App. 2012) ("In securitization cases, a servicer may be considered a party in interest to commence legal action as long as the trustee joins or ratifies its action.").
17. *See id.*
18. *See* Whitman, *supra* note 4, at 32 n. 113. This is true even though noted commercial law scholars have commented on how this, upon closer inspection, is likely not the case. *See* Ronald J. Mann, *Searching for Negotiability in Payment and Credit Systems*, 44 UCLA L. REV. 951, 970–72 nn. 67–70 (1997).
19. U.C.C. § 3-301 (AM. LAW INST. & UNIF. LAW COMM'N 2002).
20. Many courts have held that the person entitled to enforce the promissory note under UCC article 3 (i.e., the holder) is the person who can enforce the mortgage. This result is drawn from an interpretation of the combination of UCC section 3-301 (governing enforcement of negotiable instruments) and UCC section 9-203 (governing transfer of ownership of promissory notes). There is, however, no direct authority on point and courts have been left to arrive at this result through interpretative methods.
21. Alan M. White, *Losing the Paper – Mortgage Assignments, Note Transfers and Consumer Protection*, 24 LOY. CONSUMER L. REV. 468, 475 (2012).
22. DOUGLAS J. WHALEY & STEPHEN M. MCJOHN, Problems and Materials on Payment Law 237 (10th ed. 2016).

23. Kemp v. Countrywide Home Loans, Inc. (*In re* Kemp), 440 B.R. 624 (Bankr. D. N.J. 2010).
24. White, *supra* note 21, at 475–76.
25. Alison Fitzgerald, *Losing Your House When the Bank Already Lost Your Paperwork*, Newsweek (Sept. 10, 2014), www.newsweek.com/floridas-foreclosure-nightmare-269526?amp=1.
26. White, *supra* note 21, at 475.
27. *See* Comments of the Florida Bankers Association at 4, *In re*: Amendments to Rules of Civil Procedure and Forms for Use with Rules of Civil Procedure, No. 09-1460 (Fla. Feb. 11, 2010), www.floridasupremecourt.org/clerk/comments/2009/09-1460_093009_Comments%20%28FBA%29.pdf.
28. U.C.C. § 3-604(a) (Am. Law Inst. & Unif. Law Comm'n 2002).
29. Bob Ivry, *Banks Lose to Deadbeat Homeowners as Loans Sold in Bonds Vanish*, Bloomberg, Feb. 22, 2008, https://web.archive.org/web/20120420013642/ and www.bloomberg.com/apps/news?pid=newsarchive&sid=aejJZdqodTCM&refer=home.
30. U.C.C. 3-301; *see also* Veal v. Am. Home Mortg. Servicing, Inc. (*In re* Veal), 450 B.R. 897, 911–12 (B.A.P. 9th Cir. 2011); Aum Shree of Tampa v. HSBC Bank USA, Nat'l Ass'n (*In re* Aum Shree of Tampa, LLC), 449 B.R. 584, 593–94 (Bankr. M.D. Fla. 2011).
31. Whaley & McJohn, *supra* note 22, at 237.
32. *Id.*
33. U.C.C. 3-309.
34. Whitman, *supra* note 4, at 23.
35. Am. Securitization Forum, Transfer and Assignment of Residential Mortgage Loans in the Secondary Mortgage Market 2 (ASF White Paper Series, Nov. 16, 2010).
36. Sheila Bair, Bull by the Horns: Fighting to Save Main Street from Wall Street and Wall Street from Itself 243 (2012).
37. *See* Best Fertilizers of Ariz., Inc. v. Burns, 571 P.2d 675, 676 (Ariz. Ct. App. 1977) ("The note is the cow and the mortgage the tail. The cow can survive without a tail, but the tail cannot survive without the cow."); *see also* McTevia v. Adamo (*In re* Atlantic Mortg. Corp.), 69 B.R. 321 (Bankr. E.D. Mich. 1987).
38. Peterson, *supra* note 5.
39. *Id.* at 1390.
40. *Id.* at 1391.
41. *Id.* MERS has since ceased this policy as a result of a 2011 consent decree entered into with the Office of the Comptroller of the Currency. Consent Order, *In re* MERSCorp, Inc. OCC No. AA-EC-11-20 (Apr. 13, 2011), www.occ.gov/news-issuances/news-releases/2011/nr-occ-2011-47h.pdf (interagency review).
42. Landmark Nat'l Bank v. Kesler, 216 P.3d 158, 169 (Kan. 2009).
43. Bellistri v. Ocwen Loan Servicing, LLC, 284 S.W.3d 619 (Mo. Ct. App. 2009); Federal Nat'l Mortg. Ass'n v. Conover, 428 S.W.3d 661, 669 (Mo. Ct. App. 2014) ("Under Missouri law, because the note and deed of trust are inseparable, the holder of a note is entitled to enforce the deed of trust securing that note."); Lackey v. Wells Fargo Bank, N.A., 747 F.3d 1033 (8th Cir. 2014); Rockford Tr.

Co. v. Purtell, 39 S.W.2d 733 (Ark. 1931); U.S. Bank Nat'l Ass'n v. George, 50 N. E.3d 1049, 1054 (Ohio Ct. App. 2015) ("Thus, a determination of liability under the note is a prerequisite to enforcement of the mortgage itself because a mortgage is but an incident to the debt it secures."); Johnson v. Prosperity Mortg. Corp., No. 11–cv–02532–AW, 2011 WL 5513231, at *3 (Bankr. S.D. Md. Nov. 3, 2011).

44. See Christopher L. Peterson, *Two Faces: Demystifying the Mortgage Electronic Registration System's Land Title Theory*, 53 WM. & MARY L. REV. 126 (2011).

45. Rinegard-Guirma v. Bank of Am., Nat'l Ass'n, Civil No. 10–1065–PK, 2010 WL 3945476, at *4 (D. Or. Oct. 6, 2010); *In re* Hawkins, No. BK–S–07–13593–LBR, 2009 WL 901766, at *3 (Bankr. D. Nev. Mar. 31, 2009).

46. *In re* Mortg. Elec. Registration Sys., Inc. (MERS) Litig., MDL Docket No. 09–2119–JAT, 2010 WL 4038788, at *8 (D. Ariz. Sept. 30, 2010); *see also* Commonwealth Prop. Advocates, LLC v. Mortg. Elec. Registration Sys., Inc., No. 2:10–CV–340 TS, 2010 WL 3743643, at *3 (D. Utah Sept. 20, 2010); Silvas v. GMAC Mortg., LLC, No. CV–09–265–PHX–GMS, 2009 WL 4573234, at *8 (D. Ariz. Jan. 5, 2010); Reynoso v. Fin., LLC, No. 09–3225 SC, 2009 WL 3833298, at *2 (N.D. Cal. Nov. 16, 2009); Smith v. Bank of N.Y. (*In re* Smith), 366 B.R. 149 (Bankr. D. Colo. 2007).

47. White, *supra* note 21, at 476.

48. Morgan v. HSBC Bank USA, NA, No. 2009–CA–000597–MR, 2011 WL 3207776 (Ky. App. July 29, 2011).

49. *In re* Carrsow-Franklin, 524 B.R. 33 (Bankr. S.D.N.Y. 2015).

50. *See, e.g.*, Emergency Motion to Reopen and for Leave to Propound Supplemental Discovery to Defendant for Additional Evidence Withheld Prior to Trial, *Carrsow-Franklin*, 524 B.R. 33 (Case No. 10–20010 [RDD]), http://mattweidnerlaw.com/wp-content/uploads/2014/03/Franklin-Motion-to-Reopen-1.pdf.

51. *See* AM. SECURITIZATION FORUM, *supra* note 35, at 2 ("A mortgage note and mortgage may be sold, assigned and transferred several times between the time the mortgage loan is originated and the time the mortgage loan ends up with the trust.").

52. Richard E. Gottlieb, James M. Golden, & Brett J. Natarelli, *The Foreclosure Firestorm: "Robo-Signing" Allegations Have More Bark Than Bite*, 67 BUS. LAW. 649 (2012); Matthew B. Banks, *Prima Facie Validity of Proofs of Claim in the Age of "Robo-Signers,"* AM. BANKR. INST. J., Dec./Jan. 2011, at 54; Olga Kogan, *Infinite Loop: Robo-Signers and Ethics in Bankruptcy Mortgage Cases*, 25 GEO. J. LEGAL ETHICS 645 (2012); Raymond H. Brescia, *Leverage: State Enforcement Actions in the Wake of the Robo-Sign Scandal*, 64 ME. L. REV. 17 (2011); DAVID DAYEN, CHAIN OF TITLE: HOW THREE ORDINARY AMERICANS UNCOVERED WALL STREET'S GREAT FORECLOSURE FRAUD (2016).

53. *See* Ariana Eunjung Cha, *Ally Financial Legal Issue with Foreclosures May Affect Other Mortgage Companies*, WASH. POST (Sept. 22, 2010), www.washingtonpost.com/wp-dyn/content/article/2010/09/21/AR2010092105872.html.

54. Matthew J. Petrozziello, Note, *Who Can Enforce? The Murky World of Robo-Signed Mortgages*, 67 RUTGERS U. L. REV. 1061, 1071 (2015).
55. Whitman, *supra* note 4, at 21; Silicon Valley Bank v. Miracle Faith World Outreach, Inc., 60 A. 3d 343 (Conn. App. Ct. 2013); Correa v. U.S. Bank Nat'l Ass'n, 118 So. 3d 952 (Fla. Dist. Ct. App. 2013).
56. *See* David Streitfeld, *From a Maine House, a National Foreclosure Freeze*, N.Y. TIMES (Oct. 14, 2010), www.nytimes.com/2010/10/15/business/15maine.html?pagewanted=all.
57. The discovery and continued efforts by Thomas Cox resulted in a U.S.-wide freeze on foreclosures and spurred congressional hearings.
58. *See* Gloria J. Liddell & Pearson Liddell, Jr., *Robo Signers: The Legal Quagmire of Invalid Residential Foreclosure Proceedings and the Resultant Potential Impact upon Stakeholders*, 16 CHAP. L. REV. 367, 381 (2013)(citing Adolfo Pesquera, *Key Robo-Signing Case Ends with Settlement*, FLA. BUS. REV., July 29, 2011, LEXIS, Doc. No. 1202508929895).
59. Adams v. Madison Realty & Dev., Inc., 835 F. 2d 163 (3rd Cir. 1988).
60. Whitman, *supra* note 4, at 66.
61. Tara-Nicholle Nelson, *Homeowner Forecloses on Bank of America*, TIME (June 6, 2011), http://business.time.com/2011/06/06/homeowner-forecloses-on-bank-of-america-yes-you-heard-that-right/.
62. ALEX M. JOHNSON, JR., UNDERSTANDING MODERN REAL ESTATE TRANSACTIONS 241–42 (3d ed. 2012).
63. White, *supra* note 21, at 496.
64. *Id.* at 495.
65. *Id.* at 496; *see also* R. Wilson Freyermuth, *Why Mortgagors Can't Get No Satisfaction*, 72 MO. L. REV. 1159, 1192–93 (2007) (explaining that MERS is only a tracking system and would often not have the necessary information to give the homeowner either a payoff amount or the necessary cancellation documentation).
66. Jessica Ziehler, *The 2012 Mortgage Settlement with Large Banks*, 32 REV. BANKING & FIN. L. 286 (2013).
67. Press Release, Conn. Attorney Gen. George Jepsen, Consent Judgments Filed in Mortgage Foreclosure Settlement; Include Comprehensive New Servicing Standards for Mortgage Loans (Mar. 12, 2012).
68. Chris Isidore & Jennifer Liberto, *Mortgage Deal Could Bring Billions in Relief*, CNN MONEY (Feb. 15, 2012), http://money.cnn.com/2012/02/09/news/economy/mortgage_settlement/index.htm.

6 Break-In Foreclosures

1. Ben Hallman, *Bank Contractors Break into Occupied Homes, Terrify Residents, Lawsuits Say*, HUFFINGTON POST (July 19, 2012), www.huffingtonpost.com/2012/07/18/bank-contractors-break-ins_n_1682672.html.
2. Much of the substance of this chapter is drawn from my prior work on the foreclosure abuses of mortgage servicing firms and the so-called mortgage field

services industry firms that servicers contract with to manage properties in distress. *See* Christopher K. Odinet, *Banks, Break-ins and Bad Actors in Mortgage Foreclosure*, 83 U. CIN. L. REV. 1155 (2015).
3. Chris Arnold, *Major Banks Still Grappling with Foreclosures*, NPR (Sept. 9, 2009), www.npr.org/templates/story/story.php?storyId=112660935; Les Christie, *Foreclosures Up a Record 81% in 2008*, CNN MONEY (Jan. 15, 2009), http://money.cnn.com/2009/01/15/real_estate/millions_in_foreclosure/.
4. David Streitfeld, *The Pain of Selling a Home for Less Than the Loan*, N.Y. TIMES (Sept. 18, 2008), www.nytimes.com/2008/09/19/business/19short.html.
5. Ben Hallman, *To Clean Up Foreclosure Mess, Banks Rely on Little-Known Industry Plagued by Fraud, Abuse*, HUFFINGTON POST (Apr. 3, 2013), www.huffingtonpost.com/2013/04/03/foreclosure-bank-fraud-abuse_n_2999790.html.
6. Brady Dennis, *Good Business for Bad Times: Mortgage Field Services*, WASH. POST (Oct. 29, 2011), www.washingtonpost.com/business/good-business-for-bad-times-mortgage-field-services/2011/10/24/gIQA2FT1PM_story.html?utm_term=.388c4a175273.
7. Hallman, *Occupied Homes*, *supra* note 1.
8. Safeguard Properties is one the most wellknown and most infamous of the property preservation companies. Unsurprisingly, the former president and now chairman of the company, Robert Klein, has been described as an aggressive and powerful advocate for the mortgage servicing industry – indeed, it is his source of business. *See* Dennis, *supra* note 6.
9. Hallman, *To Clean Up Foreclosure Mess*, *supra* note 5.
10. Jessica Silver-Greenberg, *Invasive Tactic in Foreclosures Draws Scrutiny*, N.Y. TIMES: DEALBOOK (Sept. 9, 2013, 8:23 PM), https://dealbook.nytimes.com/2013/09/09/invasive-tactic-in-foreclosures-draws-scrutiny/; *Bank Contractors Illegally Break into Homes across the US*, RT NEWS (July 19, 2012), www.rt.com/usa/us-bank-home-safeguard-617/; Jeff Rossen & Avni Patel, *Home Break-ins: Bank Contractors Accused of Cleaning Out Wrong Homes*, CNBC (Oct. 2, 2013), www.cnbc.com/2013/10/02/home-break-ins-bank-contractors-accused-of-cleaning-out-wrong-homes.html; Chris Morran, *Homeowners Win Lawsuit over Fraudulent Foreclosure but May Still Lose House*, CONSUMERIST (Nov. 1, 2012), https://consumerist.com/2012/11/01/homeowners-win-lawsuit-over-fraudulent-foreclosure-but-may-still-lose-house/; Melissa Yeager, *Safeguard Properties Faces Lawsuits in Five States*, 7NEWSDENVER (Apr. 30, 2013), https://web.archive.org/web/20130504083402/ and www.thedenverchannel.com/news/local-news/safeguard-properties-faces-lawsuits-in-five-states; Ben Hallman, *Banks Keep Breaking into Houses, and Homeowners Are Fighting Back*, HUFFINGTON POST (Oct. 2, 2013), www.huffingtonpost.com/2013/10/02/bank-contractor-lawsuits-safeguard_n_3975574.html.
11. Silver-Greenberg, *supra* note 10.
12. Dennis, *supra* note 6.
13. Hallman, *Banks Keep Breaking into Houses*, *supra* note 10 ("It's also unclear how much legal liability the banks that hire companies like Safeguard have for such

alleged abuses. In the past, banks have tried to shunt liability onto the contracting companies. But the $25 billion settlement struck with state attorney generals last year requires that five of the largest banks 'perform appropriate due diligence' in examining any third-party contractors' 'expertise, complaints and qualifications.' Failure to do so could hypothetically lead to fines or other penalties. No public actions have been taken yet.").

14. Complaint, State v. Safeguard Properties, LLC, No. 2013-CH-20175, 2013 WL 5290237 (Ill. Cir. Ct. Sept. 9, 2013).
15. Yuki Noguchi, *Morning Edition: The Dilemma of Walking Away from a Mortgage* (National Public Radio broadcast, Oct. 28, 2010).
16. CORINNE BANNON & ERICA WILT, WICHITA STATE UNIV., EFFECTS OF ABANDONED HOUSING ON COMMUNITIES: RESEARCH REPORT FOR THE CITY OF TOPEKA (June 2016).
17. OFFICE OF INSPECTOR GEN., FED. HOUS. FIN. AGENCY, NO. AUD-2014-012, AUDIT REPORT: FHFA OVERSIGHT ENTERPRISE CONTROLS OVER PRE-FORECLOSURE PROPERTY INSPECTIONS 14 (2014) (hereinafter FHFA AUDIT); *see also* Seller's Purchase, Warranties and Servicing Agreement between Goldman Sachs Mortgage Company and Bank One, N.A. § 4.01 (Dec. 1, 2001), www.sec.gov/Archives/edgar/data/807641/000095017202000467/s575865.txt ("The Servicer to Act as Servicer"); *id.* § 3.04 ("Repurchase").
18. Conversations with consumer lawyers that were conducted as part of the writing of this book indicated that the threat of repurchase was mostly theoretical in the private-label market. Trustees in this area are said to do very little if any servicer supervision and few lawyers reported being aware of any actual repurchase cases.
19. Complaint, *supra* note 14, 34; *see also* Odinet, *supra* note 2.
20. Complaint, *supra* note 14, 34.
21. The remaining approximate 5 percent are comprised of second mortgage loans, like home equity lines of credit. See URBAN INST., HOUSING FINANCE AT A GLANCE: A MONTHLY CHARTBOOK 6 (Dec. 2017), www.urban.org/sites/default/files/publication/95436/housing-finance-at-a-glance-a-monthly-chartbook-december-2017_0.pdf. Importantly, Fannie and Freddie can deal with loans in two ways: by managing their securitization through a trust or by holding them in their own books.
22. FHFA AUDIT, *supra* note 17, at 15.
23. Fannie Mae, Property Maintenance and Management: Property Preservation Matrix and Reference Guide (Nov. 12, 2014), www.mmmortgage.com/Download/FNMA%20Guidelines.pdf.
24. FANNIE MAE, SERVICING GUIDE: FANNIE MAE SINGLE FAMILY 733 (2014), www.fanniemae.com/content/guide/svc111214.pdf.
25. *Servicing Guide: F-1-05: Expense Reimbursement* (12/13/2017), FANNIE MAE (Apr. 11, 2018), www.fanniemae.com/content/guide/servicing/f/1/05.html.
26. Hallman, *To Clean Up Foreclosure Mess*, *supra* note 5.
27. Hallman, *To Clean Up Foreclosure Mess*, *supra* note 5; Paul Muschick, *Homeowner Suing Wells Fargo after His House Was Ransacked and Locks Were Changed*, MORNING CALL (Allentown, Pa.) (Mar. 20, 2017), www.mcall

.com/news/local/watchdog/mc-wells-fargo-foreclosure-theft-watchdog-20170318-column.html; NAT'L FAIR HOUS. ALLIANCE, THE BANKS ARE BACK – OUR NEIGHBORHOODS ARE NOT: DISCRIMINATION IN THE MAINTENANCE AND MARKETING OF REO PROPERTIES (2012); NAT'L FAIR HOUS. ALLIANCE, ZIP CODE INEQUALITY: DISCRIMINATION BY BANKS IN THE MAINTENANCE OF HOMES IN NEIGHBORHOODS OF COLOR (2014).

28. Hallman, *Occupied Homes*, supra note 1; Sarah Buduson, *Investigation: Homeowners Complain Safeguard Properties Damaged Their Homes, Trashed the Belongings*, NEW5 CLEVELAND (Dec. 11, 2013), www.news5cleveland.com/news/local-news/investigations/investigation-homeowners-complain-safeguard-properties-damaged-their-homes-trashed-the-belongings; Ben Lane, *Field Services Provider Cityside Management Pays $4.3M to Settle False Claims Act Allegations*, HOUSINGWIRE (July 27, 2017), www.housingwire.com/articles/40803-field-services-provider-cityside-management-pays-43m-to-settle-false-claims-act-allegations.

29. Hallman, *To Clean Up Foreclosure Mess*, supra note 5.

30. Hallman, *Banks Keep Breaking into Houses*, supra note 10.

31. The term *Chinese drywall* is used in connection with a massive amount of drywall material, manufactured in China and used in the United States between 2004 and 2007, that was seriously defective and caused respiratory issues and headaches in homeowners who were exposed to it. See Greg Allen, *Morning Edition: Toxic Chinese Drywall Creates a Housing Disaster* (National Public Radio broadcast, Oct. 27, 2009).

32. Hallman, *To Clean Up Foreclosure Mess*, supra note 5.

33. *Id.*; *Mitzi Osborne Sues to Recover Stolen Property*, ARK. BUS. (Mar. 11, 2013), www.arkansasbusiness.com/article/91275/mitzi-osbourne-sues-to-recover-stolen-property (using subscription) ("Widow of philanthropist Jennings Osborne seeks to recover silver, crystal and other valuables taken from a foreclosed property.").

34. Ash v. Bank of Am., No. 2:10–cv–02821–KJM–KJN, 2014 WL 301027 (E.D. Cal. Jan. 28, 2014).

35. The court indicated that it was unlikely that Mrs. Ashe knew that the foreclosure was final or had any intention of voluntarily relinquishing her rights in the personal property found within the house. In fact, it appeared that Ashe was waiting to find out the final disposition of her situation with the bank before moving any of her property out of the home.

36. Hallman, *Banks Keep Breaking into Houses*, supra note 10.

37. Napolitano v. Green Tree Servicing, No. 2:15-cv-00160-JAW, 2016 WL 447451 (D. Me. Feb. 4, 2016).

38. The homeowners alleged that Green Tree's contractor not only changed the locks, damaged personal property, and winterized the property but also took apart a sump pump and allowed the basement to flood.

39. Hallman, *Banks Keep Breaking into Houses*, supra note 10.

40. Yeager, supra note 10.

41. Obi v. Chase Home Fin., Civil Action No. 10 C 3154, 2010 WL 4810609 (N.D. Ill. Nov. 19, 2010).

42. Not that it ever seems to make a difference, despite what courts might say, but Illinois is a lien theory mortgage state. See 735 Ill. Comp. Stat. 5/15-1301 (2017). Illinois also requires judicial foreclosure. Illinois Mortgage Foreclosure Law, 735 Ill. Comp. Stat. 5/15-1101 to -1705 (2017).
43. Hallman, *To Clean Up Foreclosure Mess*, supra note 5.
44. *Id.*
45. Ben Hallman, *Safeguard Properties Internal Documents Reveal Rampant Complaints of Thefts, Break-Ins*, Huffington Post (Apr. 29, 2013), www.huffingtonpost.com/2013/04/29/safeguard-properties-complaints_n_3165191.html.
46. Hallman, *Banks Keep Breaking into Houses*, supra note 10.
47. FHFA Audit, supra note 17, at 3.
48. *Id.* at 20.
49. *Arrest Made in Illegal Lehigh Dumping*, ABC-7 (WZVN-TV, Fort Myers, Fla.) (Feb. 24, 2012), www.abc-7.com/story/17010344/arrest-made-in-illegal-lehigh-dumping; see also Hallman, *To Clean Up Foreclosure Mess*, supra note 5.
50. Included in the pile of trash was a payment document indicating that Zilen was hired by a subcontractor, REP Proz, which was engaged by the property contractor Cyprexx Services, which was in turn engaged by Fannie Mae. See Hallman, *To Clean Up Foreclosure Mess*, supra note 5.
51. *Id.*
52. Aspen Grove Solutions, Whitepaper: How Lenders Manage Third-Party Vendor Compliance for Field Services 4 (Nov. 2014).
53. Hallman, *To Clean Up Foreclosure Mess*, supra note 5.
54. Hallman, *Occupied Homes*, supra note 1.
55. Hallman, *To Clean Up Foreclosure Mess*, supra note 5.
56. See generally Complaint, supra note 14.
57. *Safeguard Client Communication in Response to Illinois Attorney General's Lawsuit*, Today (Oct. 1, 2013), www.today.com/news/safeguard-client-communication-response-illinois-attorney-generals-lawsuit-8C11311715.
58. Mary Ellen Podmolik, *Safeguard Properties' $1 Million Settlement Will Take Time to Disperse*, Chi. Trib. (June 9, 2015), www.chicagotribune.com/business/ct-safeguard-properties-0610-biz-20150609-story.html.
59. Carrie Wells, *Maryland Attorney General Settles with Safeguard Properties*, Balt. Sun (Aug. 28, 2015), www.baltimoresun.com/business/bs-bz-safeguard-settlement-20150828-story.html.
60. See, e.g., Stavitski v. Safeguard Properties Mgmt., LLC, Civ. No. 17–2033, 2018 WL 501646, at *1 (D.N.J. Jan. 22, 2018); Bund v. Safeguard Properties LLC, Case No. C16-920 MJP, 2018 WL 400235, at *1 (W.D. Wash. Jan. 12, 2018); Hunte v. Safeguard Properties Mgmt., LLC, No. 16 C 11198, 2017 WL 5891060, at *1 (N.D. Ill. Nov. 27, 2017); Nielson v. Safeguard Properties, LLC, No. 333244, 2017 WL 5196011, at *1 (Mich. Ct. App. Nov. 9, 2017).
61. John Woodrow Cox, *Federal Agents Raid Hernando Home Service Company*, Tampa Bay Times (Jan. 28, 2018), www.tampabay.com/news/publicsafety/federal-agents-raid-hernando-home-service-company/1219854.
62. Hallman, *To Clean Up Foreclosure Mess*, supra note 5.

63. FHFA AUDIT, *supra* note 17, at 17.
64. OFFICE OF INSPECTOR GEN., U.S. DEP'T OF HOUS. & URBAN DEV., AUDIT REPORT NO. 2012-LA-1010, INNOTION ENTERPRISES, INC., LAS VEGAS, NV: SINGLE FAMILY REO CONTRACT ADMINISTRATION 3–4 (2012).
65. *Id.* at 5.
66. *Id.* at 6.
67. Perhaps it is not surprising that contractors like Innotion do such shoddy work. As noted in the preceding text, the margins are slim. HUD paid Innotion Enterprises $11,210 per month for taking care of 38 homes – that amounts to about $295 per property. *See id.*
68. FHFA AUDIT, *supra* note 17.
69. *Id.* at 18.
70. Ben Hallman, *Housing Watchdog Slams Massive Property Inspection Industry*, HUFFINGTON POST (Mar. 25, 2014), www.huffingtonpost.com/2014/03/25/property-inspection-industry_n_5029000.html; *see also* Press Release, Nat'l Ass'n of Mortgage Field Servs., Inc., NAMFS Offers an Alternate Perspective on Performance of Pre-Foreclosure Inspections (Apr. 12, 2014).

7 Regulating Mortgage Servicing

1. *Democracy Now!* (WestLink syndicated television broadcast, Sept. 24, 2007) (interview with Alan Greenspan at 47:42), https://archive.org/details/dn2007-0924_vid.
2. RICHARD SCOTT CARNELL, JONATHAN R. MACEY, & GEOFFREY P. MILLER, THE LAW OF FINANCIAL INSTITUTIONS 92 (6th ed. 2017).
3. JOHN F. BOVENZI, INSIDE THE FDIC: THIRTY YEARS OF BANK FAILURES, BAILOUTS, AND REGULATORY BATTLES (2015).
4. CARNELL ET AL., *supra* note 2, at 94. Bank holding companies are companies that own one or more banks but do not engage in banking activities. These companies enjoy greater flexibility to raise capital but are also subject to more oversight than a private company normally would be.
5. Brena Swanson, *FHFA-OIG: GSE Mortgage Servicing Needs Oversight*, HOUSINGWIRE (Feb. 13, 2014), www.housingwire.com/articles/28951-fhfa-oig-gse-mortgage-servicing-needs-oversight.
6. Pub. L. No. 93-533, 88 Stat. 1724 (1974) (codified as amended at 12 U.S.C. §§ 2601–2617 [2012]).
7. Federally related mortgage loans are loans that meet two requirements. First, the loan must be secured by a mortgage on residential real estate (easy enough to meet for our purposes). Second, the loan must be made by any number of certain eligible lenders. These include financial institutions that hold federally insured deposits (like your run-of-the-mill bank or credit union), that the loan is insured by any kind of federal program (like FHA, USDA, or VA), loans that are going to be sold to Fannie or Freddie or backed by Ginnie Mae, and any kind of creditor that invests in residential real estate of at least $1,000,000 per year (a rather all-encompassing category). *See* 12 U.S.C. § 2602; 12 C.F.R. § 1024.2.

8. Pub. L. No. 101-625, 104 Stat. 4079 (1990) (codified as amended in scattered sections of 42 U.S.C.).
9. Congress would again amend RESPA in 1992 to bring junior mortgage loans under the regulatory umbrella.
10. Pub. L. No. 104-208, tit. II, 110 Stat. 3009-394 (codified in scattered sections of 12 U.S.C.). Dan Roberts, *Wall Street Deregulation Pushed by Clinton Advisers, Documents Reveal*, GUARDIAN (Sept. 19, 2014), www.theguardian.com/world/2014/apr/19/wall-street-deregulation-clinton-advisers-obama. Bill Clinton was president from 1993 to 2001.
11. 73 Fed. Reg. 68,204 (Nov. 7, 2008).
12. PHILLIP L. SHULMAN & HOLLY M. SPENCER, K&L GATES, RESPA REFORM: DÉJÀ VU ALL OVER AGAIN (Mortgage Banking & Consumer Credit Alert, Mar. 2008), www.klgates.com/files/tempFiles/db28413c-a697-48d8-b2aa-b6553d52a7a2/MBA_032408.pdf.
13. OMRI BEN-SHAHAR & CARL E. SCHNEIDER, MORE THAN YOU WANTED TO KNOW: THE FAILURE OF MANDATED DISCLOSURE (2014)(discussing the failures of consumer disclosure requirements to achieve their stated goals of addressing information asymmetry).
14. *2008 RESPA Reform Regulation*, AM. BANKERS ASS'N, www.aba.com/Advocacy/Issues/Pages/Issues_RESPAReform.aspx (accessed Jan. 27, 2018) ("Banks are very concerned, however, with the 2008 changes to Regulation X, as these final regulations impose far-reaching revisions to existing law and generate significant compliance burdens for all entities involved in mortgage lending. In addition, the rules remain ambiguous, and subject to constant revisions and change, which creates enormous compliance difficulties for banks.").
15. Pub. L. No. 90-321, §§ 101–145, 82 Stat. 146, 146-59 (1968). The Consumer Credit Protection Act also includes the Equal Credit Opportunity Act, which prohibits discrimination in a number of areas when it comes to the provision of credit. Today, TILA can be found at 15 U.S.C. §§1601-1666j.
16. 12 C.F.R. 1026 (1969).
17. Pub. L. No. 103-325, tit. I, subtit. B, 108 Stat. 2160, 2190-98 (codified as amended in scattered sections of 15 U.S.C.).
18. Pub. L. No. 110-289, tit. V, §§ 2501-2503, 122 Stat. 2654, 2855 (codified as amended at 15 U.S.C. § 1638(b)(2)). The act was only a part of the larger HERA of 2008.
19. Pub. L. No. 111-22, 123 Stat. 1632 (codified as amended in scattered sections of 12 U.S.C. and 15 U.S.C.).
20. A year later, in 2010, the Federal Reserve Board amended Regulation Z to now prohibit certain types of kickbacks between parties that originated the loan and others who participated in the mortgage lending process. In essence, the regulation made it illegal for mortgage loan originators and brokers, including loan officers at banks, to receive money in connection with a mortgage loan that is based on anything but the actual amount of credit being extended. Therefore, a party may receive a commission for originating or helping to make a loan, but that amount can only be based on the amount of the loan – not, for instance, whether it contains certain terms and features that might make the borrower

more likely to default and need to come back and refinance in the future (a hallmark of pre-2008 mortgage lending). The goal of this regulatory endeavor tried to fundamentally change the mortgage industry's insidious compensation design to prohibit the steering of prospective homeowners toward more expensive and dangerous financial products. But again, many of these changes were too little, too late. The predatory loans had already been made to weak borrowers and the promises of endless refinancing were accepted as gospel. While these front-end changes might have a mitigating effect on future subprime lending, the carnage from the lending of the past was in full swing – and servicers were at the center.

21. Adam J. Levitin & Tara Twomey, *Mortgage Servicing*, 28 YALE J. ON REG. 1, 68 (2011). The state of Pennsylvania, for instance, only started regulating nonbank mortgage servicers in early 2018. See Ben Lane, *Pennsylvania Now Requires Nonbank Servicers to Be Licensed to Operate in State*, HOUSINGWIRE (June 30, 2018), www.housingwire.com/articles/42361-pennsylvania-now-requires-non bank-servicers-to-be-licensed-to-operate-in-state.
22. See, e.g., LA. STAT. ANN. § 6:1086 (2014); HAW. REV. STAT. ANN. § 454M-2 (West 2016); CONN. GEN. STAT. ANN. § 36a-719 (West 2017); N.Y. BANKING LAW § 590 (McKinney 2012); MISS. CODE. ANN. § 81-18-7 (West 2016); KAN. STAT. ANN. § 9-2203 (West 2017).
23. See, e.g., LA. STAT. ANN. § 6:1088; HAW. REV. STAT. ANN. § 454M-4; CONN. GEN. STAT. ANN. § 36a-719.
24. It is unknown whether any state has ever seen a bond under these circumstances called upon. At a meeting of state banking regulators attended by the author where the issue was raised, no one seemed to remember such an event happening.
25. See, e.g., HAW. REV. STAT. ANN. § 454M-2 ("No person shall engage in the business of mortgage servicing in this State unless the person providing services has a physical presence in the State.").
26. See, e.g., LA. STAT. ANN. § 6:1087; CONN. GEN. STAT. ANN. § 36a-719; HAW. REV. STAT. ANN. § 454M-4; VT. STAT. ANN. tit. 8, § 2907 (West 2011); MISS. CODE. ANN. § 81-18-11; KAN. STAT. ANN. § 9-2211.
27. Levitin & Twomey, *supra* note 21, at 68.
28. Id. at 69; *see also* N.Y. C.P.L.R. 3408 (McKinney 2017); CONN. GEN. STAT. ANN. § 49-31l (West 2016).
29. See, e.g., MICHAEL J. HIGHTOWER, BANKING IN OKLAHOMA, 1907–2000, at 291 (2014) (discussing insider trading of the stock of a bank owned by the state's banking supervisor); *cf.* Jessica Silver-Greenberg & Ben Protess, *Benjamin Lawsky, Sheriff of Wall Street, Is Taking Off His Badge*, N.Y. TIMES (May 20, 2015), www.nytimes.com/2015/05/21/business/dealbook/benjamin-lawsky-to-step-down-as-new-yorks-top-financial-regulator.html.
30. Kendall Baer, *Laws Combating Blight May Present Challenges to Servicers*, DSNEWS (Aug. 19, 2016), http://dsnews.com/daily-dose/08-19-2016/laws-combating-blight-may-present-challenges-servicers.

31. Madhawa Palihapitiya & Kaila Eisenkraft, Univ. of Mass. Boston, A Study for the Design and Administration of a Successful Foreclosure Mediation Program in Massachusetts 2 (Feb. 2013); Ilyce Glink, *Foreclosure Mediation Programs Aren't Working Because of Net Present Value (NPV) Calculations*, CBSNews MoneyWatch (Sept. 23, 2009), www.cbsnews.com/news/foreclosure-mediation-programs-arent-working-because-of-net-present-value-npv-calculations/.
32. Michael S. Waldron, *CFPB Sends Warning to Mortgage Servicers*, 67 Consumer Fin. L.Q. Rep. 285 (2013).
33. 78 Fed. Reg. 10,695 (Feb. 14, 2013).
34. Jeff Horwitz, *Ties to Insurers Could Land Mortgage Servicers in More Trouble*, Am. Banker (Nov. 9, 2010), www.americanbanker.com/news/ties-to-insurers-could-land-mortgage-servicers-in-more-trouble (using subscription).
35. *Force-Placed Insurance: What You Need to Know*, N.Y. State: Dep't of Fin. Servs., www.dfs.ny.gov/consumer/forced-placed.htm (last updated Oct. 1, 2015).
36. 78 Fed. Reg. 10,901 (Feb. 14, 2013).
37. 78 Fed. Reg. 44,685 (July 24, 2013).
38. 78 Fed. Reg. 60,381 (Oct. 1, 2013).
39. 79 Fed. Reg. 65,299 (Nov. 3, 2014).
40. Consumer Fin. Prot. Bureau, Bulletin 2013-12, Implementation Guidance for Certain Mortgage Servicing Rules (Oct. 15, 2013). The bureau has variously issued other bulletins and guidance to mortgage servicers over time on topics ranging from bankruptcy, debt collection, servicing transfers, management of third-party vendors, and successors in interest to the mortgaged property. *See, e.g.*, Consumer Fin. Prot. Bureau, Bulletin 2012-03, Service Providers (Apr. 13, 2012); Consumer Fin. Prot. Bureau, Bulletin 2014-01, Compliance Bulletin and Policy Guidance: Mortgage Servicing Transfers (Aug. 19, 2014).
41. 79 Fed. Reg. 65,300, 65304 (Nov. 3, 2014).
42. 79 Fed. Reg. 74,175 (Dec. 15, 2014).
43. These consisted of how to deal with the continued problem of successor in interest to mortgaged property, what constitutes a delinquency, how servicers should deal with consumer requests for information (such as with loan ownership), forced-place insurance, servicer obligations to intervene early in the process when a homeowner is in financial difficulty with respect to the loan, how to handle the all-important process of loss mitigation, payment processing and crediting to the borrower's loan, the management of the periodic mortgage statement, and exemptions for small firm servicers.
44. 81 Fed. Reg. 72,160 (Oct. 19, 2016).
45. Am. Bankers Ass'n, Mortgage Lending Rules 8 (May 2017); David Stein, *Subtitle E: Dodd-Frank Mortgage Servicing – Something Old, Something New*, Mortgage Compliance Mag., July 2015, at 42.
46. *See, e.g.*, Comments of the National Consumer Law Center (on Behalf of Its Low-Income Clients) and Americans for Financial Reform, National Association of Consumer Advocates, and National Fair Housing Alliance to

the Consumer Financial Protection Bureau Regarding the Notice of Assessment of 2013 RESPA Servicing Rule and Request for Public Comment (Docket No. CFPB-2017-0012) 1-2 (July 10, 2017), www.nclc.org/images/pdf/foreclosure_mort gage/mortgage_servicing/comments-to-cfpb-servicing-assessment-respa.pdf.
47. THOMAS P. LEMKE, GERALD T. LINS, & MARIE E. PICARD, Mortgage-Backed Securities § 3:6 (2017).
48. Laurie Goodman, *Quantifying the Tightness of Mortgage Credit and Assessing Policy Actions* 3 (Urban Inst., Hous. Fin. Pol'y Ctr., Working Paper, Mar. 2017).
49. *Id.* at 6.
50. *Id.* at 8.
51. *Id.* at 9.
52. BD. OF GOVERNORS OF THE FED. RESERVE SYS. ET AL., REPORT TO THE CONGRESS ON THE EFFECT OF CAPITAL RULES ON MORTGAGE SERVICING ASSETS 13 (2016) (hereinafter MSA FED. REPORT).
53. LAURIE GOODMAN, URBAN INST., SERVICING IS AN UNDERAPPRECIATED CONSTRAINT ON CREDIT ACCESS 2 (Hous. Fin. Pol'y Ctr. Brief, Dec. 2014) (hereinafter GOODMAN, SERVICING AND ACCESS).
54. Sarah Ludwig, *Credit Scores in America Perpetuate Racial Injustice. Here's How*, GUARDIAN (Oct. 13, 2015), www.theguardian.com/commentisfree/2015/oct/13/your-credit-score-is-racist-heres-why; *see also* Kerry Close, *Why Big Banks Are Approving Fewer Mortgages for Blacks and Hispanics*, MONEY (June 2, 2016), http://time.com/money/4354981/mortgages-blacks-hispanics-banks/ ("The trend toward jumbo loans shows how big banks are pivoting their mortgage operations toward more affluent customers who also tend to be white or Asian.").
55. *Tell Me More: Black and Latino Wealth Falls Further Behind* (National Public Radio broadcast, May 6, 2013).
56. GOODMAN, SERVICING AND ACCESS, *supra* note 53, at 2.
57. *Id.* at 1–2.
58. *Id.* at 5.
59. Goodman, *Tightness*, *supra* note 48, at 19.
60. Luke Mullins, *Obama's Loan Modification Plan: 7 Things You Need to Know*, U.S. NEWS & WORLD REP. (Mar. 4, 2009), https://money.usnews.com/money/personal-finance/real-estate/articles/2009/03/04/obamas-loan-modification-plan-7-things-you-need-to-know.
61. The CFPB supervises all mortgage servicers but only for compliance with consumer-related regulations. They do not deal with safety and soundness. *See* CONSUMER PROT. FIN. BUREAU, SUPERVISORY HIGHLIGHTS MORTGAGE SERVICING SPECIAL EDITION 2 (Issue 11, June 2016) ("Supervisory examinations of mortgage servicers now generally focus on reviewing for compliance with these servicing rules and for unfair, deceptive, and abusive acts or practices.").
62. There is one caveat to this shift: Within the larger category of "banks" there has been growth in mortgage servicing by small banks. The share of total mortgage servicing assets held by banks with less than $10 billion in assets (which typically results in a bank being classified as small) from 2009 to 2015 went from less than 2 percent to about 8 percent. For context, there are 5,258 banks in the United

States with assets of less than $10 billion. See MSA Fed. Report, *supra* note 52, at 26–28. Much of this growth, however, has been concentrated in about 1 percent of these 5,258 small banks.
63. Karan Kaul & Laurie Goodman, Urban Inst., Nonbank Servicer Regulation: New Capital and Liquidity Requirements Don't Offer Enough Loss Protection 2 fig.1 (Feb. 2016).
64. Office of Inspector Gen., Fed. Hous. Fin. Agency, Evaluation Report EVL-2012-008, Evaluation of FHFA's Oversight of Fannie Mae's Transfer of Mortgage Servicing Rights from Bank of America to High Touch Servicers 22 (Sept. 18, 2012).
65. Sheila Bair, Bull by the Horns: Fighting to Save Main Street from Wall Street and Wall Street from Itself 27 (2012). The group is named after the town of Basel, Switzerland, where it holds its meetings.
66. Darryl E. Getter, Cong. Research Serv., R42744, U.S. Implementation of the Basel Capital Regulatory Framework 3 (2014).
67. The reason for this is due to the fact that banks must hold a certain amount of assets that qualify as "Tier 1 capital" (this includes mostly common stock and retained cash). Mortgage servicing can count as Tier 1 capital but only a small amount of it (no more than 10 percent). This represented a change from prior Basel rules.
68. Faye Ricci, *The Adverse Impact of Basel III on the Retention of Mortgage Servicing Assets*, Bank L. Monitor (Jan. 5, 2015), www.banklawmonitor.com/2015/01/the-adverse-impact-of-basel-iii-on-the-retention-of-mortgage-servicing-assets/.
69. MSA Fed. Report, *supra* note 52, at 3 (noting that if bank capital requirements were applied to many nonbank servicers they would fail to meet the standards). Regulatory arbitrage is when a firm uses a so-called loophole in the law to avoid a burdensome rule or regulation. The loophole here is that nonbank servicers are doing exactly what bank servicers do (i.e., service mortgage loans), but nonbanks do not have the burden of having mandatory capital requirements.
70. U.S. Gov't Accountability Office: Nonbank Mortgage Servicers: Existing Regulatory Oversight Could Be Strengthened 9 (Mar. 2016) (hereinafter GAO, Nonbank Servicers).
71. David McLaughlin, Dakin Campbell, & Kathleen M. Howley, *Nationstar Fights Ocwen for Servicer Supremacy: Mortgages*, Bloomberg (Oct. 24, 2012), www.bloomberg.com/news/articles/2012-10-24/nationstar-fights-ocwen-for-servicer-supremacy-mortgages (using subscription).
72. Zachs Equity Research, *Ocwen to Buy Ally Bank's MSRs*, Zachs (Mar. 13, 2013), www.zacks.com/stock/news/94678/ocwen-to-buy-ally-banks-msrs; Kathleen Chaykowski, *Ocwen to Buy Rights to Service $78 Billion of Mortgages*, Bloomberg (June 13, 2013), www.bloomberg.com/news/articles/2013-06-13/ocwen-to-buy-rights-to-service-78-billion-of-mortgages (using subscription). Ocwen paid only $2.5 billion for the $78 billion bundle of mortgage loans.
73. Camilla Hall & Eric Platt, *US Mortgage Servicer Ocwen Settles Customer Mistreatment Claims*, Fin. Times (Dec. 19, 2013), www.ft.com/content/

8e51650a-68cc-11e3-996a-00144feabdco (using subscription) (describing Ocwen as a shadow bank).
74. David Dayen, *Banks Find Appalling New Way to Cheat Homeowners*, SALON (Sept. 24, 2013), www.salon.com/2013/09/24/banks_find_appalling_new_way_to_cheat_homeowners_partner/.
75. Richard J. Rosen, *Competition in Mortgage Markets: The Effect of Lender Type on Loan Characteristics*, 35 ECON. PERSP. 2, 6 (2011).
76. MORTG. BANKERS ASS'N & PwC, THE CHANGING DYNAMICS OF THE MORTGAGE SERVICING LANDSCAPE 11 (June 2015) (hereinafter CHANGING DYNAMICS).
77. GAO, NONBANK SERVICERS, *supra* note 70, at 14. Recent data suggest that the percentage remains roughly the same as of the end of 2017. *See* You Suk Kim et al., Liquidity Crisis in the Mortgage Market 4 (Brookings Papers on Economic Activity Conference Draft, Feb. 27, 2018), www.brookings.edu/wp-content/uploads/2018/03/5_kimetal.pdf (hereinafter Brookings, Mortgage).
78. CHANGING DYNAMICS, *supra* note 76, at 11.
79. When nonbank servicers lack the cash to make the required payments in the face of homeowner delinquencies, they often use a combination of borrowing the money from a bank (using a so-called warehouse line of credit) and raising the funds through a bond securitization. *See* Brookings, Mortgage, *supra* note 77, at 33–35. In today's market, however, banks are reluctant to extend warehouse lines of credit for these purposes and investors are likewise hesitant to buy these bonds when the likelihood of payment is not guaranteed. This leaves nonbank servicers with very few options for raising money in the event of a macroeconomic downturn and widespread mortgage loan defaults.
80. Brookings, Mortgage, *supra* note 77, at 28 (for a discussion of GSE vs. private-label securitization rules); *see also* Seller's Purchase, Warranties and Servicing Agreement Between Goldman Sachs Mortgage Company and Bank One, N.A. § 5.03 (Dec. 1, 2001), www.sec.gov/Archives/edgar/data/807641/000095017202000467/s575865.txt ("Monthly Advances by the Servicer") ("The Servicer's obligation to make such Monthly Advances as to any Mortgage Loan will continue ... ; provided, however, that such obligation shall cease if the Servicer determines, in its sole reasonable opinion, that advances with respect to such Mortgage Loan are non-recoverable by the Servicer from Liquidation Proceeds, Insurance Proceeds, Condemnation Proceeds, or otherwise with respect to a particular Mortgage Loan.").
81. Brookings, Mortgage, *supra* note 77, at 28; *see also* GINNIE MAE, MBS GUIDE 4-2 (A)(7) (2016) (stating that the issuer is responsible for servicing the mortgage loans); *id.* at 14-4(A) (2018) ("The Issuer is obligated ... to make timely monthly payments of principal and interest to the security holders ... without regard to whether the Issuer will be able to recover such amounts from liquidation proceeds, insurance proceeds, or otherwise.").
82. Brookings, Mortgage, *supra* note 77, at 32–33.
83. *Id.* at 32.
84. GAO, NONBANK SERVICERS, *supra* note 70, at 16.

85. Yolanda Bobeldijk, *Banks Face Spiraling Costs from 50-Year-Old IT*, Fin. News (Sept. 2, 2017), www.fnlondon.com/articles/banks-face-spiraling-costs-from-archaic-it-20170912.
86. Marcus Heidmann, *Overhauling Banks' IT Systems*, McKinsey & Co. (Mar. 2010), www.mckinsey.com/business-functions/digital-mckinsey/our-insights/overhauling-banks-it-systems.
87. Office of Inspector Gen., Fed. Hous. Fin. Agency, No. AUD-2014-014, Audit Report: FHFA Actions to Manage Enterprise Risks from Nonbank Servicers Specializing in Troubled Mortgages 4 (2014) (hereinafter FHFA, Audit Report: Nonbank Servicers).
88. Shayndi Raice, *Regulator Halts Ocwen-Wells Fargo Mortgage-Servicing Deal*, Wall. St. J. (Feb. 6, 2014), www.wsj.com/articles/ny-regulator-to-halt-ocwen-wells-fargo-mortgageservicing-deal-1391704672 (using subscription).
89. FHFA, Audit Report: Nonbank Servicers, *supra* note 87, at 5.
90. *Id.* at 23–24.
91. Steven L. Schwarcz, *Lawyers in the Shadows: The Transactional Lawyer in a World of Shadow Banking*, 63 Am. U. L. Rev. 157, 163 (2013).
92. John R. Boatright, *Fiduciary Duties and the Shareholder-Management Relation: Or, What's So Special About Shareholders?*, 4 Bus. Ethics Q. 393 (1994).
93. *U.S. Banks Give Way to Specialists in Subprime Servicing*, Fitch Ratings (June 27, 2013), www.fitchratings.com/gws/en/fitchwire/fitchwirearticle/U.S.-Banks-Give?pr_id=794879.
94. *See* Schwarcz, *supra* note, at 163–64; *see also* Lane v. Chowning, 610 F. 2d 1385 (8th Cir. 1979); Julie A. D. Manasfi, *Systemic Risk and Dodd-Frank's Volcker Rule*, 4 Wm. & Mary Bus. L. Rev. 181 (2013).
95. Mehrsa Baradaran, *Banking and the Social Contract*, 89 Notre Dame L. Rev. 1283 (2014).
96. Matthew Goldstein, *As Banks Retreat, Private Equity Rushes to Buy Troubled Home Mortgages*, N.Y. Times (Sept. 28, 2015), www.nytimes.com/2015/09/29/business/dealbook/as-banks-retreat-private-equity-rushes-to-buy-troubled-home-mortgages.html.
97. Kaul & Goodman, *supra* note 63, at 1 ("Our key findings are that . . . the newly issued capital and liquidity requirements are somewhat unsophisticated and unlikely to offer adequate protection when these [interest rate and default] risks rise.").
98. CSBS is a national organization that supports state-level banking and financial services regulators. CSBS's mission is to promote safety, soundness, and consumer protection; promote economic growth; and foster innovative and responsive supervision of regulated entities across the various states.
99. AARMR is the national organization representing residential mortgage regulators at the state level. The group's mission is to promote the exchange of information between and among the agencies of the various states that are charged with the administration and regulation of residential mortgage lending, brokering, and servicing.

100. Dodd-Frank Wall Street Reform and Consumer Protection Act of 2010, Pub. L. No. 111-203, § 1061(a)(1), 124 Stat. 1376, 2036 (codified at 12 U.S.C. § 5581 (2012)). Related, the CFPB also had authority over mortgage originators under TILA (section 1402 of Dodd-Frank). For a discussion of the power of Congress to delegate quasilegislative authority to governmental agencies, see Sean P. Sullivan, Powers, *But How Much Power? Game Theory and the Nondelegation Principle*, 104 VA. L. REV. (forthcoming 2018), https://papers.ssrn.com/sol3/papers.cfm?abstract_id=2720723.
101. In 2011, the bureau issued new Regulations G and H, which were designed to address SAFE Act legislative mandates.
102. Some state laws are stricter. For instance, some states expand what constitutes a "crime of dishonesty" when it comes to criminal background checks. *See, e.g.,* WASH. REV. CODE ANN. § 19.146.310 (West).
103. STATE REGULATORY REGISTRY, LLC, 2016 SRR ANNUAL REPORT 2 (2016).
104. CAL. FIN. CODE § 50130 (West 2009).
105. NEB. REV. STAT. ANN. §§ 45-705, 1033.01 (West 2010).
106. TENN. CODE ANN. §§ 45-13-201, -501 (West 2013).
107. VT. STAT. ANN. tit. 8, §§ 2901, 2902 (West 2011).
108. COLO. REV. STAT. ANN. §§ 12-61-902 to -903 (West 2017).
109. Angela Littwin, Why Process Complaints? Then and Now, 87 TEMP. L. REV. 895, 898–99 (2015). The CFPB has supervisory authority over certain nonbank institutions, but that mostly involves asking for information about the practices of these firms or conducting examinations. But again, these are done with an aim toward ensuring compliance with federal consumer protection laws. Supervision is not oriented toward the financial health of the firm or industry. *See* Steve Antonakes & Peggy Twohig, *Be a Part of Our Supervision Team*, CONSUMER FIN. PROT. BUREAU: CFPB BLOG (Mar. 18, 2011), www.consumerfinance.gov/about-us/blog/be-a-part-of-our-supervision-team/.
110. GAO, NONBANK SERVICERS, *supra* note 70, at 2 ("CFPB does not have a mechanism to develop a comprehensive list of nonbank servicers and, therefore, does not have a full record of entities under its purview.").
111. CPFB, SUPERVISORY HIGHLIGHTS, *supra* note 61, at 4.
112. Nat'l Consumer Law Ctr., Model State Law on Mortgage Servicing: An Outline (Jan. 2011), www.nclc.org/images/pdf/foreclosure_mortgage/mortgage_servicing/model-state-law-mortgage-servicing.pdf.
113. 2013 CFPB-State Supervisory Coordination Framework (May 7, 2013), https://files.consumerfinance.gov/f/201305_cfpb_state-supervisory-coordination-framework.pdf.

8 Reforming Mortgage Law and Practice

1. The substance of this section on revising the mortgage contract is derived chiefly from my prior work on the standard mortgage contract. *See* Christopher K. Odinet, *The Unfinished Business of Dodd-Frank: Reforming the Mortgage Contract*, 69 SMU L. REV. 653 (2016).

2. Nat'l Ass'n of Realtors, Survey of Mortgage Originators, Second Quarter 2017 (2017) (showing that 98.8 percent of new mortgage loans made by originators across the country meet the high underwriting and safe loan feature standards of Dodd-Frank's "qualified mortgage" safe harbor).
3. Restatement (Third) of Property: Mortgages § 4.6 (Am. Law. Inst. 1997) (describing appropriate remedies such as foreclosure, an injunction, and the awarding of damages).
4. Michael Collins, Millennial Hous. Comm'n, Pursuing the American Dream: Homeownership and the Role of Federal Housing Policy 5 (Jan. 2002); Thomas P. Boehm & Alan M. Schlottmann, *Housing and Wealth Accumulation: Intergenerational Impacts*, in *Low-Income Homeownership: Examining the Unexamined Goal* 407 (Nicolas P. Retsinas & Eric S. Belsky eds., 2002); Michal Grinstein-Weiss & Clinton Key, *Homeownership, the Great Recession, and Wealth: Evidence from the Survey of Consumer Finance* 2 (Jan. 2013) (Federal Reserve Bank of St. Louis symposium draft paper).
5. Restatement (Second) of Property: Landlord and Tenant § 14.1 (Am. Law. Inst. 1977).
6. *See, e.g.*, Del. Code Ann. tit. 25, §§ 5701–15 (West 1974); Ga. Code Ann. §§ 61-301-309 (West 1966 & Supp. 1975); Nev. Rev. Stat. Ann. § 40.215 (West); N.Y. Real Prop. Acts. Law §§ 701–767 (McKinney 1963). *See generally* Matthew Desmond, Evicted: Poverty and Profit in the American City (2016) (providing an ethnography of the experience of evicted tenants).
7. *See, e.g.*, State *ex rel.* Payne v. Walden, 190 S.E.2d 770, 773 (W. Va. 1972); Edwards v. C. N. Inv. Co., 272 N.E.2d 652, 655 (Ohio Shaker Heights Mun. Ct. 1971); Rivers v. Tessitore, 165 So. 2d 888 (La. Ct. App. 1964).
8. Eichhorn v. De La Cantera, 255 P.2d 70, 73 (Cal. Dist. Ct. App. 1953) ("Even in cases where a landlord's right of re-entry in case of default is expressly reserved in a lease, it has been held that he cannot re-entry by force."); Mass. Gen. Laws Ann. ch. 184, § 18 (West) ("No person shall attempt to recover possession of land or tenements in any manner other than through an action brought pursuant to chapter two hundred and thirty-nine or such other proceedings authorized by law.").
9. Alaska Stat. Ann. § 09.45.060 (West) ("A person may not enter upon any land, tenement, or other real property except in cases where entry is given by law. In those cases, the entry may not be made with force but only in a peaceable manner."); *see also* Krasner v. Gurley, 40 So. 2d 328, 329 (Ala. 1949).
10. Winn v. State, 18 S.W. 375, 376 (Ark. 1892); Mo. Ann. Stat. § 534.010 (West); Lucas Hunt Vill. Co. v. Klein, 218 S.W.2d 595 (Mo. 949). To the extent these statutes also limit self-help by mortgagees, courts have nevertheless focused more on the landlord–tenant relationship and have been more willing to uphold self-help provisions in the mortgage contracts.
11. Aldrich v. Olson, 531 P.2d 825, 827 (Wash. Ct. App. 1975); Bass v. Equity Residential Holdings, LLC, 849 N.W.2d 87, 93 (Minn. Ct. App. 2014); Robinson v. Valladares, 738 N.E.2d 278, 281 (Ind. Ct. App. 2000); Sengul v. CMS Franklin, Inc., 265 P.3d 320, 326 (Alaska 2011); 2 Richard R. Powell &

PATRICK J. ROHAN, POWELL ON REAL PROPERTY § 16B.02[2][a] (Michael Allan Wolf ed., 2010); *see also* DAVID S. HILL, LANDLORD AND TENANT LAW IN A NUTSHELL 26 (3d ed. 1995).

12. Ford Motor Credit Co. v. Ryan, 189 Ohio App. 3d 560, 2010-Ohio-4601, 939 N. E.2d 891, at ¶ 34; Butler v. Ford Motor Credit Co., 829 F.2d 568, 570 (5th Cir. 1987).
13. A credit sale is one in which the seller allows the buyer to pay the purchase price at a later date, usually in exchange for some form of interest. Sometimes car dealers will engage in this arrangement with buyers or will have a third party or an affiliate finance company make the loan to the buyer. LENDOL CALDER, FINANCING THE AMERICAN DREAM: A CULTURAL HISTORY OF CONSUMER CREDIT 18 (1999).
14. U.C.C. § 9–609 (AM. LAW INST. & UNIF. LAW COMM'N 2010) ("After default, a secured party ... may take possession of the collateral ... without judicial process, if it proceeds without breach of the peace.").
15. Deavers v. Standridge, 242 S.E.2d 331, 333–34 (Ga. Ct. App. 1978) ("[T]he appellants' combined acts of blocking-in the appellee's auto and speaking to him in offensive, insulting language were sufficiently provocative of violence to constitute a breach of the peace.").
16. Fulton v. Anchor Sav. Bank, FSB, 452 S.E.2d 208, 213 (Ga. Ct. App. 1994).
17. Freeman v. Gen. Motors Acceptance Corp., 171 S.E. 63, 63 (N.C. 1933).
18. Martin v. Dorn Equip. Co., 821 P.2d 1025, 1028 (Mont. 1991).
19. U.C.C. § 9–625.
20. Lewis v. Nicholas Fin., Inc., 686 S.E.2d 468, 470 (Ga. Ct. App. 2009).
21. Peter M. Carrozzo, *Marketing the American Mortgage: The Emergency Home Finance Act of 1970, Standardization and the Secondary Market Revolution*, 39 REAL PROP., PROB. & TR. J. 765, 799 (2005).
22. *See* Jordan v. Nationstar Mortg., LLC, 374 P.3d 1195, 1200 (Wash. 2016) ("Possession has slightly different meanings in different areas of the law."). A "possessory estate" is defined as a "physical relation to the land of a kind which gives a certain degree of physical control over the land, and an intent so to exercise such control as to exclude other members of society in general from any present occupation of the land." *Id.* at 1201 (quoting RESTATEMENT (FIRST) OF PROPERTY § 7 (AM. LAW INST. 1936)); *see* State v. Strutt, 236 A.2d 357 (Conn. Cir. Ct. 1967) (discussing the definition of possession under different areas of the law).
23. Kautsman v. Carrington Mortg. Servs., LLC, No. C16-1940-JCC, 2018 WL 513588, at *1 (W.D. Wash. Jan. 23, 2018).
24. *See, e.g.*, COLO. REV. STAT. ANN. § 38–35–117 (West); Pope v. Parker, 271 P. 1118 (Colo. 1928); IDAHO CODE ANN. § 6–104 (West); Kerr Land & Livestock, Inc. v. Glaus, 692 P.2d 1199 (Idaho Ct. App. 1984); NEV. REV. STAT. § 40.050 (West); OKLA. STAT. ANN. tit. 42, § 10 (West); Rives v. Mincks Hotel Co., 1934 OK 182, 167 Okla. 500, 30 P.2d 911; UTAH CODE ANN. § 78B–6–1310 (West).
25. 374 P.3d 1195 (Wash. 2016).
26. *Id.* at 1199.

27. *Id.* at 1201.
28. No. 308227, 2013 WL 1286020, at *5 (Mich. Ct. App. Mar. 28, 2013).
29. No. CIV.A. RDB-12-02200, 2013 WL 1316341, at *5 (D. Md. Mar. 28, 2013).
30. *Id.*
31. *See, e.g.*, Bennett v. Bank of Am., N.A., No. 3:12CV34-HEH, 2012 WL 1354546 (E.D. Va. Apr. 18, 2012).
32. Livonia Prop. Holdings, L.L.C. v. 12840–12976 Farmington Rd. Holdings, L.L.C., 717 F. Supp. 2d 724, 751 (E.D. Mich. 2010) ("Under Michigan law, a mortgage is not an estate in land, it is a lien on real property intended to secure performance or payment of an obligation.") (quoting Prime Fin. Servs. v. Vinton, 761 N.W.2d 694, 703 (Mich. App. 2008)).
33. Riley v. Wells Fargo Bank, N.A., No. 16-CV-157-JMH, 2017 WL 2240570, at *7 (E.D. Ky. May 22, 2017).
34. Grafton v. Shields Mini Markets, Inc., 346 S.W.3d 306, 310 (Ky. Ct. App. 2011) ("Kentucky law has long subscribed to the 'lien theory' of mortgages.").
35. Courts and scholars have been critical of the difference between the two theories. *See* Maglione v. BancBoston Mortg. Corp., 557 N.E.2d 756, 757 (Mass. App. Ct. 1990); Andrea Clark, Comment, *Amidst the Walking Dead: Judicial and Nonjudicial Approaches for Eradicating Zombie Mortgages*, 65 EMORY L.J. 795, 806 (2016).
36. Pettingil v. Turo, 193 A.2d 367, 373 (Maine 1963). The court notes that section 9 of the mortgage, despite what it says, does not give servicers the "unrestricted right" to enter the property without more facts.
37. *See* Timothy H. Harris, *You Can't Lock the Doors! Are Lenders Powerless to Stop Zombie Properties in Lien Theory States?*, 52 REAL PROP., TR. & ESTATE L.J. 195, 212–14 (2018) (citing municipal code provisions in Boston, Chicago, and Spokane).
38. RESTATEMENT (THIRD) OF PROPERTY: MORTGAGES § 4.1 (AM. LAW. INST. 1997).
39. 24 C.F.R. § 203.377 (1997).
40. David H. Stevens, Assistant Sec'y for Hous. – Fed. Hous. Comm'r, U.S. Dep't of Hous, & Urban Dev., Mortgage Letter 2010–18: Update of Property and Preservation (P&P) Requirements and Cost Reimbursement Procedures 5 (May 13, 2010), www.hud.gov/sites/documents/DOC_14634.PDF.
41. It is worth noting that the FHFA challenged the Washington Supreme Court's decision in *Jordan v. Nationstar Mortgage* in federal district court on the theory that federal law with respect to property preservation of federally related mortgage loans preempted any state law limitations on preforeclosure activities. *See* Jordan v. Nationstar Mortgage, LLC, 240 F. Supp. 3d 1114 (E.D. Wash. 2017). However, the federal court said that "[s]tates have traditionally regulated state foreclosure laws," *id.* at 1123, and that federal rules dealing with mortgage servicing must "comply with state law," *id.* at 1124.
42. National Mortgage Settlement: Servicing Standards Highlights 1 (2013), https://d9klfgibkcquc.cloudfront.net/Servicing%20Standards%20Highlights.pdf (subtitle I, "Return Integrity & Accuracy to Foreclosure and Bankruptcy Proceedings") (emphasis added).

43. *See, e.g.,* Exhibit A: Settlement Term Sheet at A-12, United States v. Bank of Am., No. 1:12-cv-00361-RMC (D.D.C. Feb. 12, 2013), www.jasmithmonitoring.com/omso/wp-content/uploads/sites/4/2014/05/Servicing-Standards.pdf.
44. Under the terms of the settlement, the rules reached their sunset. Kate Berry, *Oversight of the National Mortgage Settlement Is Done, Monitor Says,* Am. Banker (Mar. 3, 2016), www.americanbanker.com/news/oversight-of-the-national-mortgage-settlement-is-done-monitor-says.
45. Joint State-Federal National Mortgage Servicing Settlements, www.nationalmortgagesettlement.com (accessed Feb. 11, 2018).
46. The CFPB has authority over "service providers" for certain types of financial institutions, including consumer financial service providers generally (non-banks) and insured-depositary institutions (i.e., banks and credit unions) and their affiliates with assets in excess of $10 billion. *See* 12 U.S.C. §§ 5514–5515 (2012). The CFPB can also reach service providers of smaller banks and credit unions if the firm provides services to a "substantial number" of such banks and credit unions. *See* 12 U.S.C. § 5516.
47. Consumer Fin. Prot. Bureau, Bulletin 2012–03, Service Providers (Apr. 13, 2012) (hereinafter CFPB Bulletin 2012–03).
48. 12 U.S.C. § 5481(26)(A) (2012) ("The term 'service provider' means any person that provides a material service to a covered person in connection with the offering or provision by such covered person of a consumer financial product or service, including a person that – (i) participates in designing, operating, or maintaining the consumer financial product or service.").
49. CFPB Bulletin 2012–03, *supra* note 47.
50. Consumer Fin. Prot. Bureau, Supervisory Highlights: Issue 13, Fall 2016, at 4 (Oct. 2016).
51. Consumer Fin. Prot. Bureau, Supervisory Highlights: Issue 12, Summer 2016, at 7 (June 2016).
52. Consumer Fin. Prot. Bureau, Compliance Bulletin and Policy Guidance; 2016-02, Service Providers 1–4 (Oct. 31, 2016).
53. Robert Schmidt, *CFPB Chief Mulvaney Says Days of "Pushing the Envelope" Are Over,* Bloomberg (Jan. 23, 2018), www.bloomberg.com/news/articles/2018-01-23/cfpb-chief-mulvaney-says-days-of-pushing-the-envelope-are-over; Renae Merle, *Trump Administration Strips Consumer Watchdog Office of Enforcement Powers in Lending Discrimination Cases,* Wash. Post (Feb. 1, 2018), www.washingtonpost.com/news/business/wp/2018/02/01/trump-administration-strips-consumer-watchdog-office-of-enforcement-powers-against-financial-firms-in-lending-discrimination-cases/?noredirect=on&utm_term=.bed7123c51c4.
54. Joseph F. Yenouskas & John C. Raffetto, *Class Actions Challenging Property Preservation Activities,* 72 Bus. Law. 595 (2017) (surveying the results of class action litigation in these cases).
55. Christopher K. Odinet, *Banks, Break-ins, and Bad Actors in Mortgage Foreclosure,* 83 U. Cin. L. Rev. 1155, 1186 (2015).

56. *See, e.g.*, Lougee Conservancy v. CitiMortgage, Inc., 2012 ME 103, ¶ 23, 48 A.3d 774, 783.
57. *Id.* ¶ 26, 48 A.3d at 784; *see also* Jackson v. Bank of N.Y., No. 11-CV-6410, 2012 WL 2503956, at *4 (N.D. Ill. June 28, 2012) (holding that the lack of physical interaction between the homeowner and the contractor precluded the conduct from being outrageous enough); *cf.* Gordon v. Bank of N.Y. Mellon Corp., 964 F. Supp. 2d 937, 940 (N.D. Ind. 2013). In *Gordon*, an individual returned home and found that "all of the doors in the house were damaged, and the inside of the house was trashed. Most of plaintiffs' personal property was gone, and there were signs that the house had been winterized by a contractor." *Id.* (citation omitted).
58. Arndt v. Wells Fargo Bank, N.A., No. CIV.A. 14-5586, 2015 WL 2395484, at *5 (E.D. Pa. May 20, 2015).
59. *Id.* at *6.
60. *Lougee* ¶ 30, 48 A.3d at 785; *see also* Fed. Nat'l Mortg. Ass'n v. Obradovich, No. 14-CV-04664, 2016 WL 1213920, at *5 (N.D. Ill. Mar. 29, 2016); Bly v. Field Asset Servs., No. C14-0254JLR, 2014 WL 2452755, at *7 (W.D. Wash. June 2, 2014) ("Mr. Bly pleads sufficient facts to show that Defendants breached that duty by entering his home when it was occupied, removing his belongings, and then denying responsibility."); Jackson v. Bank of N.Y., 62 F. Supp. 3d 802 (N.D. Ill. 2014); Azzam v. Rightway Dev. Inc., 789 F. Supp. 2d 110, 118 (D.D.C. 2011).
61. Warren v. Bank of Am., N.A., No. 3:16-CV-1373-M-BN, 2016 WL 8346565, at *9 (N.D. Tex. Aug. 19, 2016), *report and recommendation adopted in part*, No. 3:16-CV-1373-M-BN, 2017 WL 728260 (N.D. Tex. Feb. 23, 2017).
62. Openiano v. Bank of Am. Corp., No. D060901, 2012 WL 6721005, at *9 (Cal. Ct. App. Dec. 28, 2012) (quoting Perlas v. GMAC Mortg., LLC, 113 Cal. Rptr. 3d 790, 796 [Cal. Ct. App. 2010]) (quoting in turn Oaks Mgmt. Corp. v. Superior Court, 51 Cal. Rptr. 3d 561 [Cal Ct. App. 2006]); *see also* Kautsman v. Carrington Mortg. Servs., LLC, No. C16-1940-JCC, 2018 WL 513588, at *4 (W.D. Wash. Jan. 23, 2018) (rejecting any duty owed through a contractual relationship between the servicer, Carrington Mortgage Services, LLC, and the homeowners on the theory that privity only existed between the homeowners and their originating lender, Countrywide Financial).
63. Wells Fargo Bank, N.A. v. Sinnott, No. 2:07 CV 169, 2009 WL 3157380, at *10 (D. Vt. Sept. 25, 2009).
64. Deerman v. Fed. Home Loan Mortg. Corp., 955 F. Supp. 1393 (N.D. Ala. 1997), *aff'd*, 140 F.3d 1043 (11th Cir. 1998); Roberts v. Cameron–Brown Co., 556 F.2d 356, 362 (5th Cir. 1977); Thorien v. Baro Enters., LLC (*In re* Thorien), No. 06-00081-TLM, 2008 WL 5683488, at *8 (Bankr. D. Idaho Nov. 6, 2008); Blair v. Source One Mortg. Servs. Corp., No. CIV.A. 96–2497, 1997 WL 732407, at *2 (E.D. La. Nov. 20, 1997).
65. *See* Ruling on Motions to Dismiss at 9, Bittinger v. Wells Fargo, No. 3:14cv1255 (D. Conn. July 21, 2016) (on file with author).
66. Sw. Bell Tel. Co. v. DeLanney, 809 S.W.2d 493, 494 (Tex. 1991).

67. Warren v. Bank of Am., N.A., No. 3:16-CV-1373-M-BN, 2016 WL 8346565, at *9 (N.D. Tex. Aug. 19, 2016), *report and recommendation adopted in part*, No. 3:16-CV-1373-M-BN, 2017 WL 728260 (N.D. Tex. Feb. 23, 2017).
68. No. 11-20896-TPA, 2013 WL 1953275, at *15 (Bankr. W.D. Pa. May 7, 2013).
69. Tennant v. Chase Home Fin., LLC, 187 So. 3d 1172, 1181-82 (Ala. Civ. App. 2015).
70. PNC Bank, N.A. v. Van Hoornaar, 44 F. Supp. 3d 846, 857 (E.D. Wis. 2014); *see also* Vinal v. Fed. Nat'l Mortg. Ass'n, 131 F. Supp. 3d 529, 540 (E.D.N.C. 2015) ("In agreeing to the provisions in the deeds of trust, Vinal contractually limited his equitable interests in the property . . . . Thus, Safeguard's entries were not trespasses. Rather, because they were authorized entries onto Vinal's properties. Accordingly, Vinal's trespass claim fails.").
71. Gray v. Safeguard Real Estate Properties, 953 N.E.2d 1280 (Ind. Ct. App. 2011); *see also* Nielson v. Safeguard Properties, LLC, No. 333244, 2017 WL 5196011, at *11 (Mich. Ct. App. Nov. 9, 2017) (discussing the difficulty in determining whether subcontractors used by Safeguard Properties are indeed independent contractors or whether there is enough control to impose master-servant liability); Halkiotis v. WMC Mortg. Corp., 144 F. Supp. 3d 341, 362 (D. Conn. 2015); Pinkney-Price v. PNC Mortg., No. 3:17-CV-00189, 2017 WL 6892913, at *3 (M.D. Pa. Nov. 17, 2017), *report and recommendation adopted*, No. 3:17-CV-0189, 2018 WL 386163 (M.D. Pa. Jan. 11, 2018) ("[T]he allegations, at best, allege an independent contractor agreement.").
72. Machado v. City of Hartford, 972 A.2d 724 (Conn. 2009).
73. Ruling on Motions to Dismiss at 10, Bittinger v. Wells Fargo, No. 3:14cv1255 (D. Conn. July 21, 2016) (on file with author).
74. *Id.*
75. Hesling v. Wells Fargo Bank, NA, No. 1:12-CV-1249, 2013 WL 12109432, at *5 (W.D. Mich. Dec. 12, 2013); Nieporte v. CitiMortgage, Inc., No. 11-10940, 2011 WL 3032331 (E.D. Mich. July 25, 2011); Jackson v. Bank of N.Y., No. 11-CV-6410, 2012 WL 2503956 (N.D. Ill. June 28, 2012).
76. *See, e.g.*, Coble v. SunTrust Mortg. Inc., No. C13-1878-JCC, 2014 WL 631206 (W.D. Wash. Feb. 18, 2014).
77. Memorandum of Decision at 1-2, Norboe v. Wells Fargo Bank, N.A., No. NNH-CV-13-6038377 (Conn. Super. Ct. Jan. 31, 2018) (on file with author).
78. This act would be fashioned based on principles developed by the ULC in its failed Uniform Home Foreclosure Procedures Act and as seen in various other attempts at state legislation in this area. *See* UNIF. HOME FORECLOSURE PROCEDURES ACT (UNIF. LAW COMM'N 2015); *see also* S. 243, 128th Leg., 1st Reg. Sess. (Me. 2017) (vetoed by the governor).
79. U.C.C. § 9-609 cmt. 3 (AM. LAW INST. & UNIF. LAW COMM'N 2010).
80. Gretchen Morgenson, *If Lenders Say "The Dog Ate Your Mortgage*,*"* N.Y. TIMES (Oct. 24, 2009), www.nytimes.com/2009/10/25/business/economy/25gret.html.
81. Tanya Marsh, *Foreclosures and the Failure of the American Land Title Recording System*, 111 COLUM. L. REV. SIDEBAR 19, 25 (2011), https://columbialawreview.org/content/foreclosures-and-the-failure-of-the-american-land-title-recording-system/.

82. Dale A. Whitman, *A Proposal for a National Mortgage Registry: MERS Done Right*, 78 Mo. L. Rev. 1 (2013).
83. *See generally* Fed. Hous. Fin. Agency, A Strategic Plan for Enterprise Conservatorships: The Next Chapter in a Story That Needs an Ending 13 (2012); Bd. of Governors of the Fed. Reserve Sys., The U.S. Housing Market: Current Conditions And Policy Considerations 24-25 (2012).
84. In July 2015, the ULC charged a drafting committee with developing a framework for a uniform electronic registry for residential mortgage notes. *See* Drafting Comm. on Elec. Registry for Residential Mortg. Notes, Agenda for March 17–18 (Mar. 6, 2017), www.uniformlaws.org/shared/docs/Electronic%20Registry%20for%20Residential%20Mortgage%20Notes%20Act/1_2017mar_ERRMNA_Agenda.pdf. However, in April 2017 the committee subsequently decided not to move forward with drafting legislation and to instead follow the work in this area being done by the Federal Reserve Bank of New York. *See Update from the Drafting Committee on an Electronic Registry for Residential Mortgage Notes*, Uniform Law Commission: ULC Updates (Apr. 17, 2017), https://uniformlaws.wordpress.com/2017/04/17/update-from-the-drafting-committee-on-an-electronic-registry-for-residential-mortgage-notes/.
85. National Mortgage Note Repository Act of 2016 (Mar. 11, 2015 draft), www.uniformlaws.org/shared/docs/UCC%201,%203,%209/2016mar_ERRMNA_Nat'l%20Mortgage%20Repository%20Act_Draft.pdf.
86. 12 U.S.C. § 2605(b)(1) (2012) ("Each servicer of any federally related mortgage loan shall notify the borrower in writing of any assignment, sale, or transfer of the servicing of the loan to any other person."). TILA also requires the identity of the owner of the loan be disclosed as well. *See* 15 U.S.C. 1641(g)(1) (2012) ("[N]ot later than 30 days after the date on which a mortgage loan is sold or otherwise transferred or assigned to a third party, the creditor that is the new owner or assignee of the debt shall notify the borrower in writing of such transfer.").
87. Hous. Fin. Pol'y Ctr., Urban Inst., Housing Finance at a Glance: A Monthly Chartbook 6 (Dec. 2017), www.urban.org/sites/default/files/publication/95436/housing-finance-at-a-glance-a-monthly-chartbook-december-2017_0.pdf. These portfolio loans are held on the books of commercial banks, savings institutions, Fannie Mae, Freddie Mac, and credit unions.
88. 16 C.F.R. 433 (1977), *amended by* 42 Fed. Reg. 46,510 (Sept. 16, 1977). The rule was originally called "The Trade Regulation Rule Concerning Preservation of Consumers' Claims and Defenses" but is now known as the "The Preservation of Consumers' Claims and Defenses [Holder in Due Course Rule]." The rule was promulgated under the FTC's rulemaking authority in connection with section 5 of the Federal Trade Commission Act, which deals with an unfair or deceptive act or practice in connection with the sale or lease of goods or services to consumers in or affecting commerce.
89. Dale E. Whitman, *How Negotiability Has Fouled Up the Secondary Mortgage Market, and What to Do About It*, 37 Pepp. L. Rev. 737 (2010); Mark B. Greenlee & Thomas J. Fitzpatrick IV, Reconsidering the Application of the Holder in Due Course Rule to Home Mortgage Notes (Fed. Reserve Bank of Cleveland,

Working Paper No. 08-08, Nov. 2008); DOUGLAS J. WHALEY & STEPHEN M. MCJOHN, PROBLEMS AND MATERIALS ON PAYMENT LAW ch. 6 (10th ed. 2016).

90. Consent Order, *In re* MERSCORP, Inc. OCC No. AA-EC-11-20 (Apr. 13, 2011), www.occ.gov/news-issuances/news-releases/2011/nr-occ-2011-47h.pdf (interagency review).

91. Order Terminating the April 13, 2011 Consent Order, *In re* MERSCorp, Inc. OCC No. AA-EC-11-20 (Jan. 12 2018), www.federalreserve.gov/newsevents/press releases/files/enf20180112a3.pdf (interagency review).

92. Letter from Bill Beckmann, President & CEO, MERSCORP Holdings, Inc., to Stephanie Heller, Deputy General Counsel & Senior Vice President, Fed. Reserve Bank of N.Y. at 1 (Nov. 7, 2017), www.uniformlaws.org/shared/docs/UCC%201,%203,%209/2017nov7_UCC139_Comment%20letter_MERS.pdf ("Based on 20 years of operating mortgage loan registries, we believe without a quantifiable value proposition, the fiscal sustainability of the proposed repository remains questionable.").

Conclusion

1. MICHELLE PARK LAZETTE, FED. RESERVE BANK OF CLEVELAND, THE CRISIS, THE FALLOUT, THE CHANGE: THE GREAT RECESSION IN RETROSPECT 4 (2017).
2. Danny Yagan, *Employment Hysteresis from the Great Recession* 1 (Nat'l Bureau of Econ. Research, Working Paper No. 23844, 2017).
3. Annie Lowrey, *The Great Recession Is Still with Us*, ATLANTIC (Dec. 1, 2017), www.theatlantic.com/business/archive/2017/12/great-recession-still-with-us/547268/.
4. *America's Shrinking Middle Class: A Close Look at Changes within Metropolitan Areas*, PEW RES. CTR. (May 11, 2016), www.pewsocialtrends.org/2016/05/11/americas-shrinking-middle-class-a-close-look-at-changes-within-metropolitan-areas/.
5. *The American Middle Class Is Losing Ground*, PEW RES. CTR. (Dec. 9, 2015), www.pewsocialtrends.org/2015/12/09/the-american-middle-class-is-losing-ground/.
6. Lowrey, *supra* note 3; *see also* SARAH BURD-SHARPS & REBECCA RASCH, SOC. SCI. RESEARCH COUNCIL, IMPACT OF THE US HOUSING CRISIS ON THE RACIAL WEALTH GAP ACROSS GENERATIONS 13 (June 2015).
7. Lowrey, *supra* note 3; Matt Egan, *America's 7-Year Bull Market: Can It Last?*, CNN MONEY (Mar. 9, 2016), http://money.cnn.com/2016/03/09/investing/stocks-bull-market-turns-seven/index.html.
8. US Census Bureau, Quarterly Residential Vacancies and Homeownership, Fourth Quarter 2017 (Release No. CD18-08, Jan. 30, 2018), https://web.archive.org/web/20180226041356/ and www.census.gov/housing/hvs/files/currenthvspress.pdf.
9. *Id.* at 9.

10. Gillian B. White, *Why Blacks and Hispanics Have Such Expensive Mortgages*, ATLANTIC (Feb. 25, 2016), www.theatlantic.com/business/archive/2016/02/blacks-hispanics-mortgages/471024/.
11. Rachel Louise Ensign, Paul Overberg & AnnaMaria Andriotis, *Banks' Embrace of Jumbo Mortgages Means Fewer Loans for Blacks, Hispanics*, WALL ST. J. (June 1, 2016), www.wsj.com/articles/banks-embrace-of-jumbo-mortgages-means-fewer-loans-for-blacks-hispanics-1464789752 (using subscription).
12. CHI CHI WU, NAT'L CONSUMER LAW CTR., SOLVING THE CREDIT CONUNDRUM: HELPING CONSUMERS' CREDIT RECORDS IMPAIRED BY THE FORECLOSURE CRISIS AND GREAT RECESSION 3 (Dec. 2013).
13. Andrew Ross Sorkin, *President Obama Weighs His Economic Legacy*, N.Y. TIMES MAG. (Apr. 28, 2016)
14. Listen And Read Along, *President Obama – June 4th, 2016 – Video Caption – Building on America's Economic Recovery*, YOUTUBE at 1:31 (June 4, 2016), www.youtube.com/watch?v=BWMVL49jkZY.
15. NBC News, *President Donald Trump's Speech at the 2018 World Economic Forum (Full)*, YOUTUBE at 1:04 (Jan. 26, 2018), www.youtube.com/watch?v=3UgKxAfN4o4.
16. *Id.* at 1:12.
17. *Derivatives*, US SEC. & EXCHANGE COMMISSION, www.sec.gov/spotlight/dodd-frank/derivatives.shtml (accessed Apr. 12, 2018). Prior to Dodd-Frank, federal law passed in 2000 prohibited either the SEC or the Commodities Futures Trading Commission from regulating over-the-counter swap contracts. Dodd-Frank filled this gap.
18. Matt Scully, *Can JPMorgan Save the Private-Label MBS Market?*, NAT'L MORTGAGE NEWS (Sept. 19, 2014), www.nationalmortgagenews.com/news/can-jpmorgan-save-the-private-label-mbs-market.
19. "Make America Great Again" was Donald Trump's 2016 campaign slogan.
20. David Dayen, *$5M Jury Award for One Foreclosure Fraud Makes U.S. Punishment Look Trivial*, INTERCEPT (Nov. 13, 2015), https://theintercept.com/2015/11/13/5m-jury-award-for-one-foreclosure-fraud-makes-u-s-punishment-look-trivial/.
21. David Dayen, *Leaked Seattle Audit Concludes Many Mortgage Documents Are Void*, INTERCEPT (Sept. 18, 2015), https://theintercept.com/2015/09/18/leaked-seattle-audit-concludes-many-mortgage-documents-void/.
22. *Id.*
23. Kevin McCoy & Roger Yu, *Lawsuits Allege Mortgage Servicer Ocwen's Mistakes Cost Some Borrowers Their Homes*, USA TODAY (Apr. 20, 2017), https://web.archive.org/web/20170528200812/amp.usatoday.com/story/100701104/.
24. Paul Muschick, *Homeowner Suing Wells Fargo after His House Was Ransacked and Locks Were Changed*, MORNING CALL (Allentown, Pa.) (Mar. 20, 2017), www.mcall.com/news/local/watchdog/mc-wells-fargo-foreclosure-theft-watchdog-20170318-column.html.
25. *Id.*

26. Matt Egan, *Wells Fargo Uncovers Up to 1.4 Million More Fake Accounts*, CNN Money (Aug. 31, 2017), http://money.cnn.com/2017/08/31/investing/wells-fargo-fake-accounts/index.html.
27. Kevin McCoy, *Wells Fargo Revamps Pay Plan After Fake-Accounts Scandal*, USA Today (Jan. 11, 2017), www.usatoday.com/story/money/2017/01/11/wells-fargo-revamps-pay-plan-after-fake-accounts-scandal/96441730/.
28. Gretchen Morgenson, *Wells Fargo Forced Unwanted Auto Insurance on Borrowers*, N.Y. Times (July 27, 2017), www.nytimes.com/2017/07/27/business/wells-fargo-unwanted-auto-insurance.html.
29. Id.
30. Id.
31. Gretchen Morgenson, *Wells Fargo Borrower Got Unneeded Insurance, and Ruined Credit*, N.Y. Times (Aug. 18, 2017), www.nytimes.com/2017/08/18/business/wells-fargo-loan-auto-insurance.html.
32. Stacy Cowley & Matthew Goldstein, *Accusations of Fraud at Wells Fargo Spread to Sham Insurance Policies*, N.Y. Times (Dec. 9, 2016), www.nytimes.com/2016/12/09/business/dealbook/wells-fargo-accusations-sham-insurance-policies.html.
33. Id.
34. Pete Schroeder, *Banks Spent Record Amounts on Lobbying in Recent Election*, Reuters (Mar. 8, 2017), www.reuters.com/article/usa-banks-lobbying-idUSL2N1GL1ZC.
35. Id.
36. Id.
37. John Carney & Anupreeta Das, *Hedge Fund Money Has Vastly Favored Clinton over Trump*, Wall St. J. (July 29, 2016), www.wsj.com/articles/hedge-fund-money-has-vastly-favored-clinton-over-trump-1469784601 (using subscription).
38. Emily Kaiser, *Wall Street Puts Its Money Behind Obama*, Reuters (June 5, 2008), https://uk.reuters.com/article/analysis-shares-obama/wall-street-puts-its-money-behind-obama-idUKNOA53525520080605.
39. Brian Wingfield, *Wall Street's Favorite Congressmen*, Forbes (June 1, 2010), www.forbes.com/2010/05/28/schumer-gillibrand-scott-brown-business-washington-wall-street-contribution.html#4b3c71ed4587.
40. Glenn R. Simpson, *Lender Lobbying Blitz Abetted Mortgage Mess*, Wall St. J. (Dec. 31, 2007), www.wsj.com/articles/SB119906606162358773 (using subscription).
41. *Presidential Executive Order on Reducing Regulation and Controlling Regulatory Costs*, White House (Jan. 30, 2017), www.whitehouse.gov/presidential-actions/presidential-executive-order-reducing-regulation-controlling-regulatory-costs/.
42. Brena Swanson, *[Video] Trump Wants to Cut All Regulation by 75%*, HousingWire (Jan. 23, 2017), www.housingwire.com/articles/39014-video-trump-wants-to-cut-all-regulation-by-75.
43. *Presidential Executive Order on Core Principles for Regulating the United States Financial System*, White House (Feb. 3, 2017), www.whitehouse.gov/presiden

tial-actions/presidential-executive-order-core-principles-regulating-united-states-financial-system/.
44. Lalita Clozel, *Federal Reserve's Quarles Calls for Tailored Approach to Supervision*, WALL ST. J. (Jan. 19, 2018), www.wsj.com/articles/federal-reserves-quarles-calls-for-tailored-approach-to-supervision-1516387102 (using subscription).
45. Press Release, Fed. Trade Comm'n, FTC Launches New Website Dedicated to Economic Liberty (Mar. 16, 2017).
46. Dave Michaels, *Trump's Man for the SEC: Time to Ease Regulation*, WALL ST. J. (Feb. 19, 2017), www.wsj.com/articles/trumps-man-for-the-sec-time-to-ease-regulation-1487505602 (using subscription).
47. Ben Lane, *Comptroller of the Currency Otting Expresses Support for Mulvaney's CFPB*, HOUSINGWIRE (Feb. 6, 2018), www.housingwire.com/articles/42465-comptroller-of-the-currency-otting-expresses-support-for-mulvaneys-actions-at-cfpb.
48. Ben S. Carson, *Experimenting with Failed Socialism Again*, WASH. TIMES (July 23, 2015), www.washingtontimes.com/news/2015/jul/23/ben-carson-obamas-housing-rules-try-to-accomplish-/.
49. Jim Puzzanghera & James Rufus Koren, *Mnuchin Calls for Major Rollbacks of Dodd-Frank Financial Reforms*, L.A. TIMES (June 12, 2017), www.latimes.com/business/la-fi-treasury-dodd-frank-20170612-story.html.
50. President Trump was able to name an acting director because Richard Cordray, Obama's appointee to the job, resigned early from the position before his term has expired. Renae Merle, *Richard Cordray Is Stepping Down as Head of Consumer Financial Protection Bureau*, WASH. POST (Nov. 15, 2017), www.washingtonpost.com/news/business/wp/2017/11/15/richard-cordray-is-stepping-down-as-head-of-consumer-financial-protection-bureau/?utm_term=.bf58f1ad8b6c.
51. *OMB Chief Mulvaney Could Be Temporary CFPB Boss*, AM. BANKER (Nov. 16, 2017), www.americanbanker.com/articles/omb-chief-mulvaney-could-be-temporary-cfpb-boss.
52. Mick Mulvaney, *The CFPB Has Pushed Its Last Envelope*, WALL ST. J. (Jan. 23, 2018), www.wsj.com/articles/the-cfpb-has-pushed-its-last-envelope-1516743561 (using subscription).
53. E-mail from Mick Mulvaney to CFPB Staff (Jan. 23, 2018, 12:59:57 PM CST), www.covfinancialservices.com/wp-content/uploads/sites/19/2018/01/Mulvaney-Memo.pdf.
54. Steve Vockrodt, *CFPB Drops Kansas Payday Lending Case, Stoking Fears Trump Is Backing Off the Industry*, KAN. CITY STAR (Jan. 19, 2018), www.kansascity.com/news/politics-government/article195623824.html#storylink=cpy.
55. Kate Berry, *CFPB's Mulvaney Shows Lighter Touch with Tribal Lenders*, AM. BANKER (Mar. 16, 2018), www.americanbanker.com/news/cfpbs-mulvaney-shows-lighter-touch-with-tribal-lenders.
56. Steve Vockrodt, *Federal Regulator Sues Four Payday Lending Companies Operating in Kansas*, KAN. CITY STAR (Apr. 27, 2017), www.kansascity.com/news/local/article147218324.html.
57. Vockrodt, *CFPB Drops Kansas Payday Lending Case*, supra note 54.

58. Chris Arnold, *All Things Considered: Under Trump Appointee, Consumer Protection Agency Seen Helping Payday Lenders* (National Public Radio broadcast, Jan. 24, 2018).
59. Kate Berry, *Not So Fast: CFPB Effort to Reopen Payday Rule Faces Hurdles*, AM. BANKER (Jan. 17, 2018), www.americanbanker.com/news/not-so-fast-cfpb-effort-to-reopen-payday-rule-faces-hurdles.
60. *Id.* (citing information provided by the Center for Responsive Politics).
61. *See* L. FRANK BAUM, THE WONDERFUL WIZARD OF OZ 45 (Hill Co. 1900); John Howard Payne & Henry R. Bishop, *Home! Sweet Home!, from Clari, or The Maid of Milan* (1823) (opera).
62. CHASING THE AMERICAN DREAM: NEW PERSPECTIVES ON AFFORDABLE HOMEOWNERSHIP (William M. Rohe & Harry L. Watson eds., 2007); Johan Norberg, FINANCIAL FIASCO: HOW AMERICA'S INFATUATION WITH HOMEOWNERSHIP AND EASY MONEY CREATED THE FINANCIAL CRISIS (2009).
63. *See* ERIC S. BELSKY, JOINT CTR. FOR HOUS. STUDIES, HARVARD UNIV., THE DREAM LIVES ON: THE FUTURE OF HOMEOWNERSHIP IN AMERICA (Jan. 2013).
64. *See* ALEX F. SCHWARTZ, HOUSING POLICY IN THE UNITED STATES (3d ed. 2014); *see also* The FUTURE OF HOUSING FINANCE: RESTRUCTURING THE U.S. RESIDENTIAL MORTGAGE MARKET (Martin Neil Baily ed., 2011).
65. Eduardo M. Peñalver, *Property Metaphors and Kelo v. New London: Two Views of the Castle*, 74 FORDHAM L. REV. 2971, 2973 (2006).
66. JOHN R. NOLON & PATRICIA E. SALKIN, LAND USE AND SUSTAINABLE DEVELOPMENT LAW: CASES AND MATERIALS (8th ed. 2012); Matthew L. McGinnis, Note, *Sex, but Not the City, Adult-Entertainment Zoning, the First Amendment, and Residential and Rural Municipalities*, 46 B.C. L. REV. 625 (2005).
67. Nathan A. Hertzog, *Regulatory Future of Fannie Mae and Freddie Mac*, 31 REV. BANKING & FIN. L. 62 (2011); Kate Pickert, *A Brief History of Fannie Mae and Freddie Mac*, TIME (July 14, 2008), http://content.time.com/time/business/article/0,8599,1822766,00.html.
68. *See, e.g.*, William P. Quigley, *Obstacle to Opportunity: Housing that Working and Poor People Can Afford in New Orleans Since Katrina*, 42 WAKE FOREST L. REV. 393 (2007).
69. Anne B. Shlay, *Low-Income Homeownership: American Dream or Delusion?*, 43 URB. STUD. 511, 512 (2006).
70. MICHAEL COLLINS, MILLENNIAL HOUS. COMM'N, PURSUING THE AMERICAN DREAM: HOMEOWNERSHIP AND THE ROLE OF FEDERAL HOUSING POLICY 5 (Jan. 2002).
71. *See* Shlay, *supra* note 69, at 511 (citing Thomas P. Boehm & Alan M. Schlottmann, *Housing and Wealth Accumulation: Intergenerational Impacts*, in LOW-INCOME HOMEOWNERSHIP: EXAMINING THE UNEXAMINED GOAL 407 (Nicolas P. Retsinas & Eric S. Belsky eds., 2002).
72. *See* Michal Grinstein-Weiss & Clinton Key, Homeownership, the Great Recession, and Wealth: Evidence from the Survey of Consumer Finance 5 (Jan. 2013)(Federal Reserve Bank of St. Louis symposium draft paper) ("Generations of American households and financial advisers have shared the

long-standing belief that homeownership was a safe, efficient way to build wealth.").
73. *Id.* at 2.
74. Christopher Hitchens, *A Man's Home Is His Constitutional Castle*, Slate (July 29, 2009), www.slate.com/articles/news_and_politics/fighting_words/2009/07/a_mans_home_is_his_constitutional_castle.html; 4 William Blackstone, Commentaries *223 ("And the law of England has so particular and tender a regard to the immunity of a man's house, that it stiles it his castle, and will never suffer it to be violated with immunity.").

Index

AARMR (American Association of Residential Mortgage Regulators), 127, 128, 130
AIG, 8, 31
    bailout, 36,
    bonuses to executives, 37
allonges, 86
Ally Financial
    lawsuits against, 91
American Mortgage Field Services
    abuses, 103
Ameriquest, 8, 21, 28, 156
Associates First, 21

bailouts, 34–37
Bair, Sheila, 24, 31, 56
Bank of America, 3, 23, 41, 50
    lawsuits against, 91
    loan modification and foreclosure, 49
    property contractors, use of, 99
Basel III
    bank capital requirements, 121
Bear Stearns, 21, 35
    acquisition by JPMorgan Chase, 34
Berkshire Hathaway, 122
Bernanke, Ben, 32
Bittinger v. *Wells Fargo*, 144
bond insurance, 30
breach the peace standard, 135, 137

Caliber Home Loans, 126
Carrington Mortgage, 42
Carson, Ben, 157
CDOs (collateralized debt obligations), 29
    ratings, 30
CFPB (Consumer Financial Protection Bureau), 7, 130
    amendments to RESPA/TILA, 115–117
    authority over mortgage servicers, 110
    under Mick Mulvaney, 157
    primary consumer regulatory agency after Dodd-Frank, 115
    rules for mortgage servicers, 127
    SAFE Act and, 128
    servicing guidelines, 116
    vendor oversight and, 141–142
Chase Home Finance, 100
Citigroup, 21, 23, 34
    bailout, 36
    lawsuits against, 91
    private-label securitizations, 29–30
CitiMortgage, 4, 41, 50
Comptroller of the Currency, 23, 24
Conference of State Bank Supervisors, 49
Consumer Financial Protection Bureau. *See* CFPB
Countrywide Financial, 8, 18, 21, 28
    borrowers overcharged by, 52
Cox, Thomas
    robo-signing litigation, 88
credit default swap, 31, 36
credit rating agencies
    rating of CDOs, 30
    rating of mortgage-backed securities, 30
    rating of mortgage servicers, 47
CSBS (Conference of State Banking Supervisors), 127, 128, 130

deregulation
    under Donald Trump, 156
Dimon, Jamie, 9
Dodd-Frank Act, 7, 128
    attempt to change mortgage servicing industry, 115
    criticism of, 9
    mortgage servicing regulation after, 114–117
    mortgage servicing regulation before, 111–114

double liability, 89
dual-tracking, 47, 50

Economic Growth and Regulatory Paperwork Reduction Act, 111
Emergency Home Finance Act, 68
equity of redemption, 73

Fannie Mae and Freddie Mac, 16
  bailout, 34
  compensation of property contractors, 96
  development of uniform mortgage contract, 69
  foreclosures and, 47
  High Touch Mortgage Servicing Program, 121
  incentives for loan modifications, 54–55
  mortgage credit, mandated to expand, 67
  securitization and, 28
  servicing guidelines, 48, 96, 110, 143
FAS 140 (Financial Accounting Statement 140), 59, 60
FASB (Financial Accounting Standards Board), 60,
FDIC (Federal Deposit Insurance Corporation), 23
  authority over state-chartered banks, 110
Federal Reserve, 110
  changes to TILA, 112
  failure to act on predatory loan practices, 24
  interest rates lowered in 2000s, 17
  recommendations for mortgage reform, 23
FHA (Federal Housing Administration), 65
  reform of housing finance and, 66
FHA loans, 66
  shadow banks, serviced by, 8
FHFA (Federal Housing Finance Agency), 35
  actions against property contractors, 103
  conservatorship of Fannie Mae and Freddie Mac, 35
  report on property contractors, 105
Financial Crisis Inquiry Commission, 29
financial services industry
  bailout, 35–37
  promoting rollback of regulations, 155
force-placed insurance, 2, 115
foreclosure
  nonjudicial, 75
foreclosures
  abuses, 93
  break-in, 94, 102, 133, 135, 142, 143
  cost to investors, 43, 44
  housing crash and, 33, 38–39
  judicial, 74–75
  missing notes and, 86
  process of, 74
  property contractors and, 93
  protections for borrowers, 74, 75
foreclosure statutes
  amendments
Frank, Barney, 61

Ginnie Mae, 67
  guarantee for mortgage-backed securities, 28
GMAC
  robo-signing, 88
Goldman Sachs, 8, 21, 37
Goodman, Laurie, 118
Greenspan, Alan, 24
Green Tree Servicing, 99
GSEs (government-sponsored enterprises), 67
  creation of standard mortgage form, 69
  rating of mortgage servicers, 55
  securitization of loans, 123
GSE securities, 28

HAMP (Home Affordable Mortgage Program), 39
  largely unsuccessful, 39
Helping Families Save Their Homes Act
  amended TILA, 113
holder in due course, 89, 148, 150,
homeowners
  lawsuits against servicers/contractors, 142–145
  proposed cause of action for wrongful acts of servicers, 145
homeownership
  all-time high in 2005, 17
  impact of mortgage servicers on, 2, 6
  push to expand, 16
  rate in early twentieth century, 66
  rates lower for blacks and Latinos, 153
  value of, 158
Home Ownership and Equity Protection Act of 1994, 112
House Committee on Financial Services, 61
household wealth
  loss following financial crisis, 37
housing bubble, 15–16
  bursting of, 32
Housing and Economic Recovery Act (HERA), 35, 127
HUD (Department of Housing and Urban Development)
  licensing of mortgage loan originators and, 128
  rules for servicers need to be changed, 140
Hunt, John Patrick
  report on subprime loan modifications, 57

IndyMac, 50,
Innotion Enterprises

Index

failure to maintain properties, 104
In re Carpenter, 144

Jordan v. Nationstar Mortgage, LCC, 138
JPMorgan Chase, 9, 23, 41, 50
  lawsuits against, 91

Kautsman v. Carrington Mortgage Services, LLC, 137
Kheder v. Seterus, Inc., 138

landlord tenant law
  contrasted with mortgage law, 135
Lehman Brothers, 8, 21
  bankruptcy, 35
Litton Loan Servicing, 5
loan modifications, 44, 46
  diminished returns for investors and, 45
loan workouts, 44
loss mitigation, 43, 44, 117, 125
  lengthy process, 50
  liquidation, 44
  repeat offender rate for defaults and, 56
lost note affidavits, 84, 87–88

McCray v. Specialized Loan Servicing, 138
Merrill Lynch, 21, 28
  purchase by Bank of America, 36
MERS (Mortgage Electronic Registration Systems), 79–81, 149, 150
  breakdown of system, 81, 92
  caused serious losses for homeowners, 89
  difficulty tracking promissory notes, 83, 90
  foreclosure and, 82
  inaccurate records, 91
  mortgage cancellation errors, 91
  mortgagee of record, 81, 85
  mortgage servicers and, 81
  mortgage servicers as certifying officers of, 85
  nominee of lender, 80, 86
  problems with clear title, 90
MERSCORP, 150, 151
Mnuchin, Steven, 157
Morgan Stanley, 8, 21, 37
mortgage
  assignment of, 79, 82, 87
mortgage-backed securities (MBSs), 26, 40, 42
  financial crisis and, 33
  intra-investor conflict and, 45
  payment of investors in the event of default, 53
  ratings, 30
Mortgage Bankers Association of America, 80
mortgage contract, uniform, 69
  abandonment of property, 136–137, 139, 140
  contributions by consumer groups to development of, 70
  drafting, 69
  favorable to lenders, 70
  lender allowed to inspect property, 71
  lender's rights upon default, 72
  material threat to value as proposed trigger for servicer's exercise of rights, 136
  need to balance interests of servicer and homeowner, 134
  need for review and reform, 132–137
  property preservation clause, 138
  role in housing finance market, 70
  section 7, 71–72, 76, 98, 133–134
  section 9, 72–73, 76, 98, 134–135
mortgage credit
  availability, 119
  debt-to-income, 118
  denied to communities of color, 119
  FICO scores and, 118
  loan-to-value ratio and, 118
mortgage credit crisis (1960s), 68
mortgage defaults, 32, 33, 49
mortgaged property
  inheritance of, 117
Mortgage Disclosure Improvement Act of 2008
  added provisions to TILA, 112
mortgagee-in-possession doctrine, 76
Mortgage Electronic Registration Systems. *See* MERS
mortgage field services industry, 93, 142
mortgage finance industry
  importance of understanding for homeowners, 9–10
  lack of uniformity of documents, 68
mortgage insurance, 66
mortgage law, 132
  changes needed, 138–139
  intermediate theory, 75
  lien theory, 75, 138
  proposed model state law, 145–146
  title theory, 75
mortgage loan originators
  licensing, 127
mortgage loans
  before Great Depression, 65
  transfer of, 78
  underwater, 32
mortgage market, secondary, 67, 68, 79
mortgage recordkeeping
  need for better system, 147
  proposed nationwide electronic registry, 147–149
mortgage servicers, 26
  borrowers in default and, 43–47

mortgage servicers (cont.)
  compensation, 50–52
  failure to help distressed homeowners, 49, 50
  failure to vet and supervise property contractors, 100–101, 144
  fees charged by, 52
  foreclosures and faulty paperwork, 85
  illegal and fraudulent practices, 91
  ill-equipped following financial crisis, 61
  ill-equipped for role, 4
  incentives to foreclose, 54
  lack of trained staff, 50, 53
  lawsuits against, 91
  liability for damages by contractors not allowed, 144
  licensing and prudential standards, 129–131
  loss mitigation and, 47, 49
  lost note affidavits, use of, 87
  obligation to oversee contractors, 140–146
  outsourcing and offshoring, 53
  power over homeowners, 2–3
  property contractors, use of, 93, 95, 96
  right to inspection of property at will, 133
  robo-signing and, 88
  role in housing finance system, 1, 40, 41
  specialization, 42
  varieties of, 41
mortgage servicing
  access to credit and, 119
  banks and legacy technology costs, 124
  costs passed to black and Latino borrowers, 120
  incentives for servicing high-risk borrowers, 120
  market failures, 114
  proposed state-federal regulatory partnership, 129–131
  prudential standards for, 129
  regulation, 6
  regulation, federal, 111–113, 114–117
  regulation, state, 113–114
  regulations not effective, 114
  shift to shadow banks, 121
  system broken during financial crisis, 109
  transfer of loan servicing rights, 3
  transfer of servicing rights, 125
  transparency mandated, 117
Mulvaney, Mick, 157

Nader, Ralph, 69, 136
National Affordable Housing Act, 111
National Homeownership Strategy, 16
National Mortgage Settlement, 91, 141
  rules regarding third-party vendors, 95
National Mortgage Settlement Monitor, 141
Nationstar Mortgage, 3, 42
  acquisition of Bank of America and Aurora Bank Servicing rights, 122
NeighborWorks America, 50
New Century Financial, 8, 21, 29
NMLS (Nationwide Multistate Licensing System), 127, 128, 129
nonbank servicers. *See* shadow banks
Norboe v. Wells Fargo, 145
NPV (net present value) calculations, 48
  guidance from Fannie Mae and Freddie Mac, 48, 55
  reliant on servicer's discretion in private-label market, 48

Ocwen Financial, 52, 54
  acquisition of Residential Capital and Ally Bank servicing rights, 122
  acquisition of Wells Fargo servicing rights prevented, 125
  payment obligations as share of total assets, 123
  wrongdoing, sued for, 154
Ocwen Loan Servicing, 42
Office of Thrift Supervision, 23, 24, 36
Openiano v. Bank of America, 143
Otting, Joseph, 157
Ownership Society, 16

Paulson, Henry, 34, 35
PNC Bank v. Van Hoornaar, 144
pooling and servicing agreements, 42, 45
  limits on loan modifications, 46
  servicer's duty to ensure property is maintained, 95
private-label market
  lack of incentive for loan modifications, 55, 57
promissory note, 78, 79, 147
  double enforcement, 89
  holders and, 82
  negotiable instrument as, 82
  physical possession of, 83
  separation from mortgage, 85
property contractors
  abuses, 96, 98–100, 140
  authority to preserve property, 97, 98
  compensation, 96
  lack of background checks, 101
  lawsuits against, 95
Proposed Regulatory Prudential Standards for Non-Bank Mortgage Servicers, 129

regulators slow to act on mortgage lending, 23
REMIC (Real Estate Mortgage Investment Conduit), 59

servicers reluctant to modify loans in the pool, 59
tax advantages for investors and, 59
REO Proz, 101, 102
Residential Capital, 50
Resolution Trust Corporation, 40
RESPA (Real Estate Settlement Procedures Act), 111–112, 150
  amendments, 115–117
  Reform Rule, 111
  Regulation X, 111, 121
Riley v. Wells Fargo, 138
robo-signing, 85, 88, 89, 147
robo-signing litigation, 88
Ross, Wilbur, 122

SAFE Act (Secure and Fair Enforcement for Mortgage Licensing Act), 127–128
Safeguard Properties, 3, 94
  abuses, 99, 102
  background checks for property contractors, 102
  lawsuit against, 102–103, 144
  settlement, 103
Salomon Brothers, 28
savings and loan crisis, 40
Saxon Mortgage, 5
securitization, 25–31
  definition, 1
  drop following housing crash, 34
  incentives for aggressive policing of properties, 95
  subprime loans and, 27–28
  third-party servicing and, 40
shadow banks, 7
  Basel III, not subject to, 121
  buying mortgage servicing rights from banks, 8
  expanding market share in mortgage servicing, 123, 124
  imposition of capital requirements by GSEs, 126
  lack of capital reserve requirements, 125
  less consumer-oriented than banks, 126
  outside regulatory system, 8
  private equity ownership, 125
  proposed regulation of, 24
  servicing Ginnie Mae, Freddie Mac, and Fannie Mae loans, 123
  state-federal mortgage settlement system and, 141
structured finance. *See* securitization
subprime lenders
  predatory practices, 22, 23
subprime loans, 17–22
  black borrowers and, 21–22
  defaults after housing crash, 33
  fees, high, 18
  interest rates, high, 19
  junior mortgages and, 57–58
  lack of regulation, 22–25
  loss mitigation, 56
  pay-option terms, 18
  role of rating agencies in modifications, 57
  underwriting fraud, 20

TARP (Troubled Asset Relief Program), 36
  most funds not used to directly help homeowners, 39
TILA (Truth in Lending Act), 23, 111
  amendments, 112, 117
  Regulation Z, 112, 121
toxic assets, 34,
tranches, 29, 30, 44, 55

Uniform Commercial Code, 82
Urban Institute, 118, 119, 120
U.S. Bank, 98

Wachovia, 34
  purchased by Wells Fargo, 36
Warren v. Bank of America, 144
Washington Mutual, 28, 34,
  failure and purchase by JPMorgan Chase, 36
Wells Fargo, 23, 41, 50
  fraudulent practices, 154
  lawsuits against, 91, 154
  robo-signing, 88

Printed in the United States
By Bookmasters